An Introduction
to Macroeconomic Policy

Also by Howard R. Vane and John L. Thompson,
Monetarism: Theory, Evidence and Policy (Martin Robertson, 1979)

An Introduction to Macroeconomic Policy

Second Edition

Howard R. Vane
Senior Lecturer in Economics, Liverpool Polytechnic
and
John L. Thompson
Senior Lecturer in Economics, Liverpool Polytechnic

Wheatsheaf Books

DISTRIBUTED BY HARVESTER PRESS

This second edition published in Great Britain in 1985 by
WHEATSHEAF BOOKS LTD
A MEMBER OF THE HARVESTER PRESS GROUP
Publisher: John Spiers
Director of Publications: Edward Elgar
16 Ship Street, Brighton, Sussex

© Howard R. Vane and John L. Thompson, 1982, 1985

First published by Wheatsheaf Books Ltd in 1982

British Library Cataloguing in Publication Data

Vane, Howard R.
An introduction to macroeconomic policy
— 2nd ed.
1. Macroeconomics
I. Title II. Thompson, John L.
339   HB1725

ISBN 0-7450-0003-7
ISBN 0-7450-0004-5 Pbk

Printed in Great Britain by
Whitstable Litho Ltd, Millstrood Road, Whitstable, Kent

THE HARVESTER PRESS PUBLISHING GROUP
The Harvester Press Publishing Group comprises Harvester Press
Limited (chiefly publishing literature, fiction, philosophy,
psychology, and science and trade books), Harvester Press
Microform Publications Limited (publishing in microform
unpublished archives, scarce printed sources, and indexes to
these collections) and Wheatsheaf Books Limited (a wholly
independent company chiefly publishing in economics,
international politics, sociology and related social sciences),
whose books are distributed by The Harvester Press Limited and
its agencies throughout the world.

To Dad, Christine and Linus, and Margaret, Nicola and Guy

Contents

Preface

Macroeconomics is concerned with the behaviour and performance of the economy as a whole. Our primary aim in writing this book is to introduce the reader to the *theory* of macroeconomic policy. To this end we have split the book into three main parts. Part I discusses the theoretical and institutional framework of how the economy works. Part II examines the main instruments of macroeconomic policy available to the authorities. Finally, Part III deals with international monetary relations.

Constraints of time and space preclude all but the briefest of references to recent economic history. For those interested we have provided, at the end of the book, a list of texts recommended for further reading. At appropriate places throughout our book, however, we have related key macroeconomic concepts to the way in which they are measured in the UK economy. In this respect reference is made to a number of important official statistical publications (see list of official sources recommended for further reading). Given the time lags between (a) the collection and publication of official data and (b) the writing and publication of this book, the data cited in the text will necessarily be somewhat out of date. The reader is strongly recommended to turn to the various sources quoted to update the data provided in the various tables and graphs.

We would like to thank Mr S.R. Maycraft (Midland Bank Limited) who read the draft chapters and made many helpful suggestions and comments. Any remaining errors are our responsibility.

October, 1981 Howard R. Vane (Department of Social Studies)
John L. Thompson (Department of Business Studies)

Preface to the Second Edition

In writing this second edition we have made three main changes to the original text. First, all time-series data has been extensively revised and updated. In contrast most of the data cited at a point in time has been left unchanged as our main purpose in including it is to illustrate how key concepts are measured. Second, certain material has been deleted (notably the appendix to Chapter 2 on the Financial System of the USA) or restructured (notably the latter half of Chapter 3). Finally, this new edition contains a fuller discussion of certain areas of analysis and also includes new material. One example of the former is the amplified discussion of the rational expectational hypothesis (Chapter 7, section 7.6) Examples of new material added to the text include a discussion of: the financial futures market in London (Chapter 2, section 2.9); inflation rates in Western economies since 1960 (Chapter 5, section 5.5.3); and macroeconomic models of the UK economy (Chapter 15, section 15.4).

October, 1983 Howard R. Vane (Department of Social Studies)
John L. Thompson (Department of Business Studies)

Introduction

Macroeconomics is concerned with the behaviour and performance of the economy as a whole. The main areas of study are (i) the level of output and employment, (ii) inflation and (iii) the balance of payments. By examining the various factors which lead to fluctuations in these variables, economists are able to advise policy makers on ways to improve the overall performance of the economy or interpret the effects of policies to those who are affected. These issues are of vital importance at the present time and are the subject of much discussion in newspapers and political circles. This text aims to provide the reader with a greater insight into these matters so that he will be in a better position to make up his own mind on some of these controversies.

Our book is concerned with both economic theory and economic policy. In any advanced industrial economy consisting of thousands of firms and millions of workers and consumers and producing a wide variety of goods, some simplification is necessary to reduce the mass of detail into a comprehensible summary of how the economy operates. Clearly such a simplification entails a compromise between (i) comprehensiveness and (ii) manageability, and leaves economic theorists open to the criticism that they are out of touch with the 'real' world. Nevertheless this argument misses the point that unless discussion of macroeconomic policy is linked to some theory of how the economy operates it is likely to be futile. The criticism also overlooks the fact that the modern tendency is to 'confront' economic theory with the facts. In other words the tendency is to examine the statistical evidence to see whether it supports the body of theory in question. It must be admitted, however, that in many instances neither economic theory nor the relevant statistical evidence provides clear, unambiguous answers to these problems. Consequently there are many important controversies in macroeconomics at the present time and we shall discuss these at appropriate places in the text.

For the reasons outlined above we start our discussion with a statement of the relevant economic theory in Chapters 1 to 5. This section provides the necessary platform for the consideration of macroeconomic policies in Chapter 6 to 13. Finally, given that no economy operates in isolation but is part of the larger world economy, we examine in Chapter 14 the international framework within which a single economy operates.

As a prelude to our discussion of macroeconomic theory and the potential for government policy to improve the overall performance of the economy, it is worthwhile looking at the performance of the UK economy over recent years. Table 1 contains statistics for the period 1950-82 for (i) the relationship between actual and capacity output, (ii) the growth of output and (iii) the rate of inflation. Figure 1 shows the relationship between actual and capacity output over the period 1950-82.

Before commenting on the performance of the UK economy in the light of the statistics contained in Table 1, it is necessary to explain

TABLE 1. Performance of the UK economy, 1950−82

Year	A Gross Domestic Product (1975 = 100)	B Capacity Output	C Growth of Output per annum (percentages)	D Inflation per annum
1950	53.4	59.6	3.1	2.9
1951	55.0	61.0	3.0	9.0
1952	54.8	62.5	−0.4	9.4
1953	57.0	64.0	4.0	3.1
1954	59.3	65.5	4.0	1.7
1955	61.6	67.1	3.9	4.6
1956	62.4	68.7	1.3	5.0
1957	63.4	70.3	1.6	3.6
1958	63.2	72.0	−0.3	3.2
1959	65.7	73.7	4.0	0.6
1960	69.3	75.5	5.5	1.1
1961	71.1	77.4	2.6	3.3
1962	71.9	79.2	1.1	4.2
1963	74.7	81.1	3.9	2.0
1964	78.9	83.0	5.6	3.2
1965	81.2	85.0	2.9	4.8
1966	82.7	87.0	1.8	3.9
1967	84.4	89.2	2.1	2.4
1968	88.1	91.3	4.4	4.8
1969	90.3	93.5	2.5	5.4

Table 1. *Cont'd.*

Year	A Gross Domestic Product (1975 = 100)	B Capacity Output	C Growth of Output per annum (percentages)	D Inflation per annum
1970	92.1	95.7	2.0	6.3
1971	93.5	98.0	1.5	9.4
1972	96.0	100.4	2.7	7.3
1973	102.8	102.8	7.1	9.1
1974	101.1	105.3	−1.7	16.0
1975	100.0	107.8	−1.1	24.2
1976	102.6	110.4	2.6	16.5
1977	105.3	113.1	2.6	15.9
1978	108.7	115.8	3.2	8.3
1979	110.7	118.5	1.8	13.4
1980	108.0	121.4	−2.4	18.0
1981	105.4	124.3	−2.4	11.9
1982	106.7	127.3	1.2	8.6

Source: Central Statistical Office (1983), *Economic Trends: Annual Supplement & August 1983* (London: HMSO).

briefly their derivation. Detailed discussion of the measurement of output and national income is contained in Chapter 1 so at this stage it is only necessary to note that we are using gross domestic product at factor cost (valued at constant 1975 prices) as a measure of output. On its own a summary of actual output of an economy is not particularly interesting as no details are provided of what level of output that economy could produce if all the various factors of production (i.e. land, labour and capital) were fully utilised. This concept of the maximum possible output of an economy is called capacity output. The question immediately arises of how to calculate capacity output over a period of years? One way would be to select a 'peak' year or a series of peak years and treat the trend growth between these peaks as the growth of capacity output. Alternatively it is possible to estimate the growth of actual output from the data and assume that capacity output grows at the same rate. This growth rate could then be applied to a peak year on the assumption that all economic resources were being utilised in that year, i.e. that output equalled capacity output. This is in fact the method we adopt in Table 1. The year 1973 is generally assumed to be one in which actual output was at least equal to capacity output. The average growth rate within the period 1950-82 was 2.2 per cent per annum. Alternatively, fitting a statistical trend to the data produces a growth

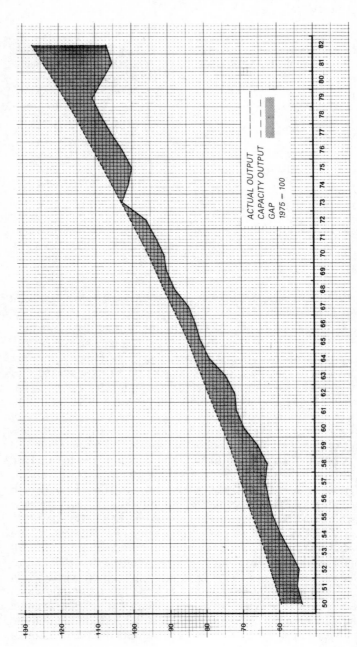

Figure 1. Actual and capacity output of the UK economy, 1950–82
Source: Central Statistical Office (1983), *Economic Trends: Annual Supplement & August 1983* (London: HMSO).

rate of 2.4 per cent per annum. We use this latter figure for the calculations necessary to derive the series of capacity output shown in Table 1. To demonstrate this methodology further, capacity output in any one year (Y^c_t) is obtained by using the following formula:

$$Y^c_t = A(1+r)^t$$

where (i) A = real gross domestic product (GDP) for year 1973,
   (ii) r = growth rate, 0.024 (i.e. 2.4 per cent expressed as a decimal).
   (iii) t = units of time measured from 1973.

Thus, for example, capacity output for 1975 is obtained in the following manner.

$$Y^c_{1975} = 102.8 (1+0.024)^2$$
$$= 107.8$$

The gap between actual and capacity output is a measure of output lost because the economy operated at less than full capacity. It therefore provides a measure of the gain if policy makers were able to stabilise output at the capacity level of the economy. The figures contained in Table 1 should be interpreted with caution. First of all the rate of growth used (i.e. 2.4 per cent per annum) is indicative only. Adoption of a different growth rate would alter both capacity output and the gap between capacity and actual output. For example, use of a growth rate of 3 per cent per annum would lower capacity output prior to 1973 but increase it afterwards. This would have the effect of decreasing the gap prior to 1973 but widening it afterwards. Our figure of 2.7 per cent is, however, unlikely to be wildly inaccurate. Second, we have assumed a constant rate of growth in our calculations. Again this should not be too far from the truth because growth of output depends on the growth rates of (i) supply of all factors of production and (ii) productivity i.e. the efficiency with which the factors are combined. As these influences are slow to change the approximation of capacity output should be close enough to reality for our purposes. Third, our series of capacity output depends critically on the assumption that actual output in 1973 was equal to capacity output. It is sometimes argued that this year was in fact a period of excess demand so that actual output exceeded capacity ouptut in the sense that it could only be produced at the cost of rising prices.

The remaining sets of figures used in Table 1 require little explanation. Growth of output is calculated as the percentage change in output from one year to another. For example the growth rate of 3.9 per cent for 1955 is calculated as

$$\frac{61.6 - 59.3}{59.3} \times 100$$

The percentage rate of inflation is calculated as the percentage change in the index of retail prices from the end of the previous year to the end of the year in question (see Chapter 5, section 5.2).

Figure 1 and Table 1 show the rather poor peformance of the UK economy after 1973. The figures confirm that 1973 was the last good year as far as utilisation of capacity output is concerned. After 1973 the gap between capacity and actual output widened considerably and this is of course reflected in the growth of unemployment discussed in Chapter 6, section 6.2. The average rate of growth of output fell below that achieved by other European countries and declined after 1973. In fact 1974, 1975, 1980 and 1981 were particularly bad years with absolute decreases in the levels of output (hence the negative rates of growth for these years). The situation with regard to inflation deteriorated rather earlier. From the late 1960s the rate of inflation started to accelerate but the increases after 1973 were, to say the least, dramatic. In order to highlight the deterioration of the UK economy since 1973 we show in Table 2 the average values taken by these variables over the whole period and two sub-periods, (i) 1950 to 1973 and (ii) 1974 to 1982. In relation to the objectives of government macroeconomic policy discussed in Chapter 6, these results must have been disappointing for the policy makers.

TABLE 2. Indicators of the decline of the UK economy, 1950−82

	Average Rate of Growth per annum	Average Rate of Inflation per annum
1950 to 1982	2.2	7.4
1950 to 1973	2.9	4.6
1974 to 1982	0.4	14.8

Source: Central Statistical Office (1983), *Economic Trends: Annual Supplement & August 1983* (London: HMSO).

Part I
THEORETICAL AND INSTITUTIONAL FRAMEWORK

1 National Income Determination

1.1 The circular flow of income

We begin our discussion of macroeconomic theory by examining the related concepts of the circular flow of income and national income.

In any economy people are employed in a wide and varied range of activities producing an equally diverse number of different goods and services which are sold both at home and abroad. For ease of exposition we will start by discussing a highly simplified economy and gradually introduce complications to bring the framework closer to the complexity of the real world. At this stage we will therefore assume that there is no government sector in the economy or international trade undertaken (i.e. it is a closed economy) thus avoiding consideration of factors such as government spending and taxation, and exports and imports. In this economy there are two main sectors which contribute to the flow of goods and services, domestic firms (producers) and domestic households (consumers). Domestic households consume the goods and services produced by domestic firms. In order to make these goods firms hire the services of factors of production (e.g. labour and land) from households to whom they pay an income. Two flows occur: (i) a flow of factors services from households to firms; and (ii) a flow of income from firms to households in payment for these factor services. In addition two further flows arise: (i) a flow of final goods and services from firms to households; and (ii) a flow of payments for these finished goods and services from households to firms. Thus a real flow of factor services and goods will circulate between households and firms, and this will be matched by corresponding money flows of income and expenditure (Figure 1.1).

As long as (i) households spend all their income on firms' final output and (ii) firms pay back to households all the money they receive from such sales, income will circulate at an unchanged level.

If we now drop out initial simplifying assumptions (i.e. no government sector or international trade) and broaden the discussion we find that there are three main additions or injections to this

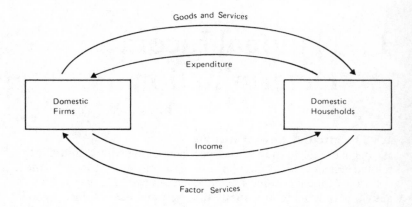

Figure 1.1. The circular flow of income

circular flow of income. These injections are additional to the expenditure made by domestic households on firms' output and the income paid to households by domestic firms for factor services. First, firms may sell some of their output abroad. This means they receive income from a source outside the circular flow (i.e. from foreign households and foreign firms rather than from domestic households). The receipts from export sales *(X)* increase the level of income circulating between firms and households. Second, government expenditure *(G)* on goods and services represents an injection of income into the circular flow. Both government capital expenditure (e.g. on school and hospital building) and current expenditure on goods and services (e.g. payment of income to public employees like teachers and nurses) create income for firms and households. Third, in addition to selling output abroad to foreigners, and at home to households and the government, firms also produce and sell various types of plant and machinery to domestic firms wishing to invest *(I)* in capital equipment. This again is an addition to the circular flow since it is not financed by current income receipts via the circular flow. Total injections *(J)* therefore consist of government expenditure *(G)*, investment *(I)* and exports *(X)*.

$$J = G + I + X \tag{1.1}$$

Just as there are three main injections to the circular flow so too are there three main leakages or withdrawals. Leakages occur when households and firms do not spend all the income they receive via the circular flow. First, households and firms may decide to buy foreign instead of domestically produced goods. Imports *(Im)* are equivalent to a negative item of domestic expenditure as they result in payments to foreign rather than domestic firms. Second, households and firms are unable to spend all their income on domestic output and services since they have to pay taxes *(T)* to the government. Third, households and firms may consciously decide to save *(S)* some part of their income rather than spending it on domestically produced goods and services. This cause a further leakage from the circular flow of income. Total leakages *(L)* therefore consist of savings *(S)*, taxes *(T)* and imports *(Im)*.

$$L = S + T + Im \qquad (1.2)$$

Clearly these leakages will result in a fall in the level of the circular flow of income passing between domestic households and domestic firms.

With the introduction of these additional complications it should be apparent that the level of income will only remain unchanged when injections $(G + I + X)$ are exactly matched by leakages $(T + S + Im)$. If injections are greater than leakages income will increase and vice versa. We will discuss the importance of this condition in section 1.3 after a discussion of national income accounting in the UK.

1.2 National income accounting
1.2.2 *The concept of national income*
In the conceptual framework we have been using the circular flow of income forms the basis of national income accounting. National income itself is the money value of finished goods and services produced in a country within a given time period. It is impossible to add up in any direct or meaningful way the vast range of goods and services produced in an economy (e.g. tons of coal, bottles of milk, number of haircuts) other than by using a common denominator or unit of account i.e. their money value. The main measure of total output is known as the Gross National Product (GNP).

GNP can be valued in two different ways. First, in current prices, i.e. in the prices ruling at the time of measurement. GNP valued at current prices is known as nominal GNP. On the other hand if we wish to obtain an indication of the volume of output of goods and services produced it is necessary to distinguish between changes in nominal GNP due to changes in the real quality of goods produced, and those due to changes in their prices. One method is to revalue GNP in terms of fixed prices (known technically as GNP at constant prices) thus obtaining a comparison of the volume of goods available in different time periods. This is termed real GNP as opposed to nominal GNP. The current UK practice is to use 1980 prices as the constant price level.

1.2.2 *Measurement of national income*

Conceptually national income can be measured in three ways. First, by summing the expenditure made on final goods and services. Second, by adding together the incomes paid to the factors of production used to produce the national product. Third, by aggregating the final output of goods and services produced within an economy. When national income is measured by estimating the net output of all industries in the economy the method involves calculating the value added by each industry to final output. Industries buy raw materials and goods and services from other industries (i.e. inputs) to produce output which they sell to other industries and to final buyers (e.g. final sales to consumers). Value added can be defined as the gross value of an industy's output minus the value of its inputs from other industries. For example, the car industry which sells its output to final buyers makes intermediate purchases of iron and steel, glass, tyres, etc. from other industries in producing the finished output. Value added for the car industry is therefore the value of its sales minus the cost of three intermediate products. It is the net output of each industry that is of prime interest and only by estimating the value added by each industry can the problem of double counting both intermediate and final output be avoided. In consequence the sum total of the value added by all industries in the economy is equal to the total expenditure made on final goods and services and the total of all factor incomes. It makes no difference whether the circular flow is measured from the income, expenditure[1] or output sides as all three are merely different methods of measuring the same circular flow.

---

1. It is important to realise that expenditure in this context refers to expenditure on the output of the economy (i.e. consumption, investment, government expenditure and net exports) not expenditure by residents which (i) includes payments made by residents to non-residents for imports and (ii) excludes receipts from non-residents in respect of exports.

1.2.3 *The UK national income accounts*

To illustrate UK practice we will now examine the expenditure and income methods in a little more detail, mentioning some of the main complications that arise in preparing the accounts. In order to give some idea of the magnitude and importance of the various components of national income Table 1.1 shows the breakdown of nominal Gross National Product for the UK in 1982 for all three methods. The figures presented in Table 1.1 are taken from summary tables 1.1, 1.2 and 1.9 of the Central Statistical Office's annual 'Blue Book' on National Income and Expenditure.

Expenditure on domestic production can be divided into the major categories of household spending, government expenditure, investment and exports. Households' or consumers' expenditure (item a in Table 1.1) includes purchases of such goods and services as food, clothing and entertainment and spending on consumer durables (e.g. washing machines) but excludes spending on new owner occupied property (i.e. houses). General government final consumption (item b) consists of all current expenditure of the

TABLE 1.1 UK Gross National Product, 1982 (current prices)

I	Expenditure Method	£ million
a	Consumers' expenditure	167,128
b	General government final consumption	60,082
c	Gross domestic fixed capital formation	42,172
d	Value of physical increase in stocks and work in progress	−1,162
	Total domestic expenditure	268,220
e	Exports of goods and services	73,128
	Total final expenditure	341,348
f	*less* Imports of goods and services	−67,165
	Gross domestic product at market prices	274,183
g	*less* Taxes on expenditure	−47,082
h	*plus* Subsidies	5,452
	Gross domestic product at factor cost	232,553
	Net property income from abroad	1,577
	Gross national product at factor cost	234,130

TABLE 1.1 (cont.)

II Income Method	£ million
a Income from employment	155,133
b Income from self-employment	20,068
c Gross trading profits of companies	33,344
d Gross trading surplus of public corporations	9,068
e Gross trading surplus of general government enterprises	124
f Rent	16,166
g Imputed charge for consumption of non-trading capital	2,507
Total domestic income	236,410
h *less* Stock appreciation	− 3,907
Gross domestic product	232,503
i Residual Error	50
Gross domestic product (factor cost): expenditure method	232,553
Net property income from abroad	1,577
Gross national product	234,130

III Output Method	£ million
a Agriculture, forestry and fishing	5,752
b Energy and water supply	26,037
c Manufacturing	56,492
d Construction	13,480
e Distribution, hotels and catering; repairs	29,971
f Transport	10,311
g Communication	6,853
h Insurance, banking, finance and business services and leasing	29,040
i Ownership of dwellings	14,690
j Public administration, national defence and compulsory social security	16,724
k Education and health services	20,868
l Other services	14,543
Total	244,761
*Adjustment for financial services	− 12,258
Residual error	50
Gross domestic product at factor cost	232,553

*Represents net interest receipts

Source: Central Statistical Office (1983), National Income and Expenditure (Blue Book) (London: HMSO), Tables 1.1, 1.2 and 1.9.

central government and local authorities. Spending by government trading bodies (e.g. nationalised industries) is excluded and is treated like that of private firms for accounting purposes. General government final consumption covers expenditure on a wide range of goods and services including, for example, the provision of the National Health Service, education, law and passenger transport. It should be noted that only current expenditure (as opposed to capital or investment expediture) is included. Excluded from government expenditure and therefore total GNP are transfer payments which are transfers from one section of the community to another (e.g. unemployment benefits, social security and welfare payments, and interest payments on government debt). Unlike other forms of income they are not paid out in return for the production of goods and services but are merely transfers between different sections of the community. Both private companies and the public authorities invest in plant, buildings, vehicles, machinery, equipment, etc., which increases the country's capacity to produce goods and services. Expenditure on such fixed or long-lived assets includes not only new investment (i.e. adding to the existing stock of fixed assets) but also expenditure to replace the existing capital stock due to wear and tear and obsolescence. Houses can also be regarded as productive assets and purchases of new houses by households are also included as part of fixed capital formation. In the official UK accounting framework the total of the various forms of investment spending referred to above is known as Gross Domestic Fixed Capital Formation (item c). Producers may also invest by increasing their stocks of raw materials or unsold semi-finished and finished goods (item d). The problem with such items is to distinguish between increases in the quantity of stocks and work in progress and changes in value due to increases in the prices at which stocks and work in progress are valued (known as stock appreciation). As interest is centred on the output of the economy only the value of the physical increase in stocks is estimated (valued at average annual prices) when measuring national income. The four categories of expenditure mentioned so far together provide a figure for total domestic expenditure by UK residents on consumption and investment. Reference to Table 1.1 will show that as percentages of total domestic expenditure in 1982 consumption was approximately 62.5 per cent

$$\left(\text{i.e. } \frac{167,128}{268,220} \times 100\right),$$

government expenditure was 22.5 per cent and investment in fixed assets and stocks was 15.5 per cent and -0.5 per cent respectively. Adding the value of exported goods and services (item e) to this total provides an estimate of total final expenditure. Subtracting purchases of imported goods and services from abroad by UK residents (item f) from total final expenditure provides an estimate of the value of goods and services produced by UK residents known as Gross Domestic Product (GDP) at market prices.

The figure from GDP at market prices is different from the value that would be obtained from measuring GDP by the aggregation of incomes received. This is because there is a difference between the price paid by the consumer and the price received by the producer. This gap is due to the government which both raises taxes on goods (e.g. VAT) and grants subsides on other goods. Thus if expenditure is measured according to the price paid by the purchaser it is said to be valued at 'market prices'. On the other hand if it is valued according to the price received by the producer it is said to be valued at 'factor cost'. Therefore by subtracting taxes on expenditure (item g) and adding subsidies (item h) to GDP at market prices an estimate of the total value, at factor cost, of goods and services produced by UK residents (i.e. GDP at factor cost) is obtained which accords to the aggregation of incomes received.

An alternative method of measuring the circular flow is to add together the incomes paid to the factors of production in contributing to the current production of goods and services. The main factor incomes which form total domestic income are presented in Table 1.1. Although the categories listed are largely self explanatory it would be useful to make some comments about the divisions made. Income from employment (item a) includes not only wages and salaries but also certain supplements made by employers to their employee's income (e.g. national insurance contributions) and an imputed value for certain forms of income paid in kind (e.g. food for HM forces). For self-employed persons (item b) it is impossible to distinguish between income from employment and profits. Income from unincorporated businesses (e.g. farmers, shopkeepers) is measured after deducting all business operating expenses. The next category of factor income presented is profits. Profits accrue when the operating receipts of an enterprise (private or public) exceed its operating expenses. In the UK accounts the gross profits/surpluses (i.e. before providing for depreciation and stock appreciation) are listed separately for private companies (item c), public corporations e.g. nationalised industries (item d), and general government enterprises e.g. local authorities providing passenger transport (item e). Rent (item f) consists of the gross receipts from the ownership of buildings and land and is presented after deducting certain expenditures by the owners (e.g. repairs, maintenance and insurance). One interesting facet of income from rent is the inclusion of an imputed, that is to say estimated, rent for owner-occupied dwellings. Lastly an imputed income (item g) is estimated for owner occupied non-trading property of the general government and private non-profit making bodies. Similar imputed figures are also included in the other methods of measuring national income so that equality among the three methods is preserved. The seven categories of income mentioned above together comprise total domestic income. Reference to Table 1.1 will show that the most important forms of income as percentages of total domestic income in 1982 were: income from employment 65.5 per cent

$$(\text{i.e.} \frac{155,133}{236,410} \times 100),$$

income from self-employment 8.5 per cent, gross trading profits of companies 14.0 per cent, gross trading surplus of public corporations 4 per cent, and rent 7.0 per cent. These figures indicate approximate percentages only.

Two further adjustments need to be made to the figure of total domestic income before it is possible to obtain an estimate of GDP at factor cost which corresponds to the figure derived by the expenditure method. First, it is necessary to deduct stock appreciation (item h) since what is being estimated is the value of changes in the physical volume of stocks at factor cost not the price stocks will fetch when eventually sold on the market. Second, the statistics collected to calculate national income by the expenditure and income methods come largely from independent sources and are subject to a margin of error. In theory, but not in practice, the expenditure and income methods should provide precisely the same valuation of GDP. The convention in the UK is to adjust the statistics to the expenditure method. A residual error (item i) which may be positive or negative is applied to factor incomes to ensure equality of GDP at factor cost from both methods.

UK residents will also earn income from assets and property owned and held abroad. This is known as property income received from abroad. Net property income (i.e. receipts from abroad minus corresponding payments made to overseas residents) is added to GDP to provide a measure known as Gross National Product (GNP) which as noted earlier is the main official measure of national income in Britain. GNP at factor cost measures the total income of UK residents and is equal to the value of goods and services produced (at factor cost) by UK residents plus net property income from abroad.

GDP at factor cost can also be estimated by the output method. The contribution of each industry to GDP in 1982 for the UK (after providing for stock appreciation) is shown in Table 1.1. It is possible to divide economic activity roughly between: (i) a primary sector of industries such as farming, fishing and energy which directly extract natural resources (item a-b); (ii) a secondary sector, including manufacturing and construction industry, which purchases inputs from the primary sector for industrial production (items c-d); and (iii) a tertiary sector which provides services such as transport, banking, central and local government and education and health (items e-l). Following this classification the primary sector accounted for approximately 13.0 per cent.

$$(\text{i.e.} \frac{31,789}{244,761} \times 100)$$

of total UK output in 1982, the secondary sector 28 per cent and the tertiary sector 58.5 per cent. Table 1.2 shows: (i) consumption, government expenditure, investment and stocks as percentages of total domestic expenditure: (ii) the most important forms of income as percentages of total domestic income; and (iii) the percentage of total UK output accounted for by the primary, secondary, and tertiary sectors respectively, over the period 1972-82 in the UK economy.

Finally it is worth pointing out that while the UK, along with most other countries, uses the United Nations standardised system of national accounting certain countries do not follow this pattern. For example, in the USSR calculations of GNP do not in general include such services as those of the government, teachers and passenger transport. This makes comparisons of national income between certain countries rather difficult.

Having discussed the concept of a circular flow of income and seen how national income is measured we are now in a position to examine how national income is determined.

1.3 The determination of national income

Our discussion of what determines the level of real GNP follows what is sometimes called the Keynesian cross model.[1] First of all it is worth

1. After the famous British economist, John Maynard Keynes (1883 - 1946)

TABLE 1.2 Domestic expenditure, income and output in the UK, 1972–82

Percentage of total domestic expenditure	1972	1973	1974	1975	1976	1977	1978	1979	1980	1981	1982
Consumers' expenditure	63	61	60	61	60	60	61	61	62	63	62
General government final consumption	18	18	19	21	21	20	20	20	22	22	22
GDFCF	18	19	19	19	19	18	18	18	18	16	16
Value of physical increase in stocks and work in progress	0	2	1	−1	1	1	1	1	−1	−1	0

Percentage of total domestic income	1972	1973	1974	1975	1976	1977	1978	1979	1980	1981	1982
Income from employment	66	64	65	69	67	65	65	64	66	66	66
Income from self-employment	10	11	10	9	9	9	9	9	8	8	8
Gross trading profits of companies	14	15	14	12	13	15	15	17	15	14	14
Gross trading surplus of public corporations	3	3	3	3	4	4	4	3	3	3	4
Rent	6	6	7	6	6	6	6	6	7	7	7

Percentage of total UK output	1972	1973	1974	1975	1976	1977	1978	1979	1980	1981	1982
Primary sector	7	7	7	8	8	9	9	10	11	12	13
Secondary sector	38	38	36	35	34	35	35	33	32	30	29
Tertiary sector	55	55	57	58	58	56	56	57	57	58	58

Source: Central Statistical Office (1983), National Income and Expenditure (Blue Book) (London: HMSO), Tables 1.1, 1.2 and 1.9

Note: Due to rounding percentage figures may not exactly sum to 100 noting the following assumption underlying the analysis. Unemployment is held to exist so that prices are taken as constant. This means that all variables specified in the model are in real terms. The level of output and employment is determined by the total or aggregate volume of spending. Again with unemployed resources and constant prices, any increase in demand can and will be met by an increase in output (supply). Supply constraints are therefore ignored and the level of national income/output is entirely determined by aggregate demand/expenditure. It is important to stress that the assumption that prices are constant when unemployment exists is made only for analytical convenience and is dropped later in the book.

1.3.1. *Aggregate demand*

Aggregate demand (AD) can be defined as the total demand for the output of an economy. It is the sum of the following individual components: consumption *(C)*, investment *(I)* (both fixed domestic capital formation and increases in stock levels), government expenditure *(G)*, and net exports i.e. export minus imports *(X-Im)*. It is necessary to deduct imports from domestic expenditure and exports because each of these components includes an import content.

More formally:

$$AD = C + I + G + (X - Im) \qquad (1.3)$$

The next consideration is what determines each of those components of aggregate demand. The determinants of the level of exports and imports are discussed in Chapter 4. Government expenditure is treated as a policy variable i.e. determined by government policy. This leaves the determinants of consumption and investment which are examined in the following two sections.

Consumption. In the simple Keynesian model consumption depends positively on disposable income (i.e. income including transfer incomes left over after paying direct taxes such as income tax). The higher the level of disposable income the higher the level of consumption. This relationship (known technically as the consumption function) is shown graphically in Figure 1.2.

The 45° line is a geometric device which shows points of equality between the two axes. Thus in figure 1.2 point *a* shows the level of disposable income at which consumption *(OC₁)* equals disposable income (OY_{D1}) i.e. there is no saving. To the left of this point annual household expenditure is greater than annual income and households must finance this excess spending from past savings or by borrowing. The intercept (α) shows the amount households would spend in the extreme hypothetical case where their annual income was zero. To the right of point a annual household expenditure is less than annual income. Algebraically this function can be described by the following formula:

$$C = \alpha + \text{ß } Y_D \qquad (1.4)$$

Where (1) C = aggregate household expenditure
     (2) Y_D = disposable income
and (3) α (intercept) and ß (slope of line) are known as coefficients

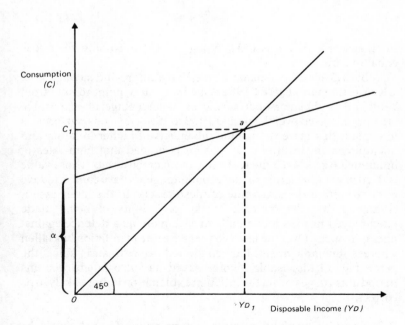

Figure 1.2. Consumption function
Note: We have assumed a linear relationship for convenience.

The slope (ß) of the relationship between household spending and disposable income indicates the degree to which consumption changes when income changes. Economists use the term marginal propensity to consume (MPC) to describe how much of any extra income people desire to spend. By presenting the consumption function as a straight line it should be apparent that the MPC (ß) is constant. The other interesting coefficient with respect to the consumption function is the average propensity to consume (APC) which shows how much, on average, a society is spending on consumption. This is obtained by dividing total consumption by total disposable income. In terms of Figure 1.2 APC is greater than 1 for all income levels less than OY_{D1} (i.e. the public is spending on consumption more than it earns as disposable income); APC is equal to 1 at OY_{D1} and is less than 1 for all the points to the right of OY_{D1}. The average propensity to consume will only equal the marginal propensity to consume when the consumption factor: (i) is linear and (ii) passes through the origin. This can easily be seen by dividing equation (1.4) throughout by Y_D to obtain:

$$\frac{C}{Y_D} = \frac{\alpha}{Y_D} + ß \qquad (1.4a)$$

In other words APC (i.e. C/Y_D) equals MPC (i.e. ß) only when α is equal to zero.

Table 1.3 shows personal income, expenditure and saving in the UK over the period 1972-1982. One interesting point to note from Table 1.3 is that personal saving as a percentage of disposable income increased over the period 1972 to 1980. Reasons put forward to explain this increase include the effects of higher inflation and unemployment. In the former case it is argued that high rates of inflation have reduced the real value of financial assets whose value is fixed in nominal terms so that economic agents have chosen to save more to restore the real value of these assets. In the latter case it is argued that the increase in the probability of being made unemployed has led individuals to save more as a defence against unemployment. Over the last two years the rate of inflation has fallen whereas unemployment has continued to rise and, since the percentage of disposable income saved has also fallen over this period, this suggests that the inflation explanation is more likely to be correct.

Investment.   One of the important determinants of investment is the cost of borrowing funds to finance investment expenditure i.e. the rate of interest. Even if funds necessary to finance investment are obtained from within a firm, the rate of interest represents the return a firm could have obtained by lending those funds. In other words the rate of interest represents the opportunity cost of using funds for investment. The return on investment comes from future expected profits directly attributable to the investment. The profits a firm expects to receive in the future depend on the revenue obtained from selling the output produced by the machinery minus the various costs involved (e.g. maintenance, labour and material costs) in producing the output. The difference between revenue and costs is called net revenue and determines net additions to profit over the life of the capital equipment. However, even assuming a constant price level money received in the future is not worth as much as money today. For example, at a 10 per cent rate of interest (i.e. $r=0.10$) an individual with £100 today could lend it out and receive £110 in one year's time i.e. £100 $(1 + r)$. The present value of £110 received in a year's time is £100

$$\text{(i.e. } \frac{£100}{(1 + r)} = £100).$$

After two years the individual would receive £121 i.e. £100 $(1 + r)^2$, so that the present value of £121 received in two year's time is £100

$$\text{(i.e. } \frac{£121}{(1 + r)^2}).$$

This procedure, known as discounting, involves calculating the present value of future receipts.

The expected rate of return on investment, technically called the marginal efficiency of capital (MEC) is the rate of discount (p) which causes the future expected stream of profits to equal the present cost of the investment project. More formally we can solve the following equation for p (MEC) to obtain the return on an investment project.

$$C = \frac{A_1}{(1 + p)} + \frac{A_2}{(1 + p)^2} + \frac{A_3}{(1 + p)^3} \cdots \frac{An}{(1 + p)^n} + \frac{SV}{(1 + p)^n} \qquad (1.5)$$

TABLE 1.3 Personal income, expenditure and saving in the UK, 1972–82

	1972	1973	1974	1975	1976	1977	1978	1979	1980	1981	1982
					(£ million)						
(1) Total personal income (before tax)	54,830	63,721	75,859	96,659	111,634	124,576	143,001	169,334	200,671	219,309	237,943
(2) Total personal disposable income	44,830	51,980	60,343	74,659	85,814	96,919	113,319	135,928	160,620	173,973	187,302
Consumers' expenditure	40,500	46,150	53,087	65,339	75,792	86,712	99,596	118,383	136,890	152,239	167,128
(3) Personal saving	4,330	5,830	7,256	9,320	10,022	10,207	13,723	17,545	23,730	21,734	20,174
(4) Personal saving as a percentage of personal disposable income	9.7	11.2	12.0	12.5	11.7	10.5	12.1	12.9	14.8	12.5	10.8

Source: Central Statistical Office (1983), National Income and Expenditure (Blue Book) (London: HMSO), Table 1.3.

Notes (1) Income from employment and self-employment *plus* rent, dividends and net interest paid to persons, *plus* other forms of personal income (e.g. current grants from general government).

    (2) Total personal income (before tax) *minus* taxes on income, national insurance, etc. contributions and transfers abroad (net).

    (3) Total personal disposable income *minus* consumers' expenditure.

    (4) Correct to one decimal place.

Where (1) A_i = net additions to profit for each year over the life of
the capital equipment
(2) n = life of the capital equipment
(3) SV = scrap value of the equipment
(4) C = cost of the equipment
(5) p = return on investment (i.e. MEC).

If the market rate of interest (r) is less than the MEC (i.e. return is greater than cost) the investment project is worth carrying out. Conversely if the market rate of interest is greater than the MEC then the project will not be worthwhile. Thus investment will be carried out by a firm up to the point where the MEC equals the rate of interest. Aggregation over all firms produces an aggregate MEC schedule and total investment will be carried out up to the point where the aggregate MEC is equated with the rate of interest. This is demonstrated in Figure 1.3.

If the rate of interest is r_o then investment will be I_o. Note as the rate of interest falls (e.g. from r_o to r_1) investment increases (e.g. from I_o to I_1). Conversely, if the rate of interest rises investment falls. The slope of the schedule indicates the degree to which investment responds to a change in the rate of interest. Economists use the term elasticity to describe the degree of response. Investment is said to be: (i) interest-

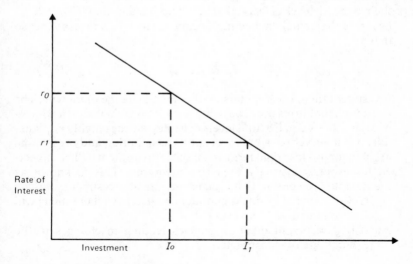

Figure 1.3. MEC schedule

inelastic (unresponsive) when the proportional change in investment is less than the proportional change in the rate of interest and; (ii) interest-elastic (responsive) when the proportional change in investment is greater than the proportional change in the rate of interest. This inverse relationship between the rate of interest and investment will be important in the discussion in Chapter 3 of how money affects economic activity.

A second important determinant of investment is a change in national income (or equivalently output). The basic idea is that the desired capital stock (K^*) is some function of output (Y)

$$K^*_t = v\, Y_t \tag{1.6}$$

If we lag this relationship by one period we obtain:

$$K^*_{t-1} = v\, Y_{t-1} \tag{1.7}$$

Subtracting (1.7) from (1.6) gives:

$$K^*_t - K^*_{t-1} = vY_t - vY_{t-1} = v(\Delta\, Y_t) \tag{1.8}$$

where the Greek capital letter, delta (Δ), is used to symbolise a change in a variable. The next stage in the analysis is to make the critical assumption that firms' actual level of capital stock equals their desired level of capital stock. This means that $K^*_t - K^*_{t-1}$ becomes the actual change in the capital stock (i.e. investment) so that

$$I_t = v\,(\Delta\, Y_t) \tag{1.9}$$

Investment therefore depends on the rate of change of income. The restriction that firms are always in the situation where desired levels of capital stock equal actual levels of capital stock is highly implausible. It is however possible to relax this assumption and present the accelerator in a less rigid form. In this case investment will be expected to respond positively to a rise in output. This is known as the flexible accelerator. Other determinants of investment are:

   (i) variations in business confidence e.g. renewed optimism will
      lead to increases in investment;
and (ii) government taxation policies leading to changes in the
      profitability of investment.

1.3.2 *The equilibrium level of national income*
In order to simplify the analysis the value of certain key variables is

assumed to be determined within the model while the value of other variables is assumed to be fixed. Variables whose value are determined within the model are referred to as dependent, induced, or endogenous variables. The variables whose value is fixed are referred to as independent, autonomous, or exogenous variables. They affect the determination of endogenous variables in a model but are themselves assumed to be unaffected by any changes of income occurring in the model (i.e. they remain unchanged).

For example, the three main injections of government expenditure, investment and gross exports (not including imports) are all taken as being exogenously determined (i.e. constant). This does not mean they cannot change but that changes in them will induce changes in income. For example, as we have just seen a reduction in the rate of interest will increase investment.

On the other hand consumption expenditure and the three leakages (i.e. savings, taxes and imports) all depend on income (i.e. they are endogenous). As we discussed earlier the marginal propensity to consume shows how consumption responds to changes in disposable income. Similarly the marginal tax rate shows the fraction of extra income paid to the government in taxes and the marginal propensity to import the fraction of extra income spent on imports.

It is now possible to discuss what determines the level of GNP. In section 1.1 we stated that it was apparent that income would remain unchanged if injections equalled leakages. The same condition can be stated in an alternative way. If aggregate demand equals output firms will be selling all the goods they produce. On the other hand if firms are selling in total less than they produce (i.e. aggregate demand is less than total output) stock levels will be increasing and firms will cut back production. Conversely, if firms are selling more than they produce (i.e. aggregate demand is more than total output) stock levels will be decreasing and firms will increase production. In both cases we are assuming that the firms in question do not expect the decreases/increases in demand to be temporary. This situation is illustrated in Figure 1.4.

The aggregate demand schedule shows how aggregate demand varies as national income varies. The aggregate demand schedule slopes upward to the right because, although injections are assumed to be unaffected by changes in national income, household expenditure increases as income increases. Y_1 is the level of income at which output equals aggregate demand. This is called the equilibrium level of income i.e. it is a point of balance since there is no tendency for income to change. If aggregate demand and output are not equal there is a tendency for income to move towards Y_1 for the reasons discussed above.

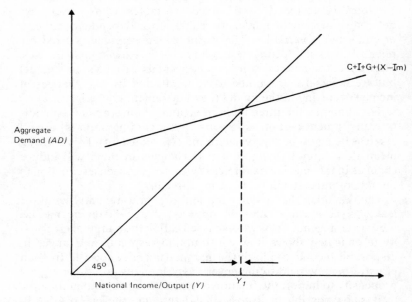

Figure 1.4. The determination of the equilibrium level of national income

An increase in aggregate expenditure will lead, ceteris paribus, to an increase in the level of output and employment. This is the first time we have used the term 'ceteris paribus' which simply means that everything else remains unchanged. Thus here we are assuming that only one component of aggregate demand changes while all other factors remain constant. The effect of an increase in aggregate demand is demonstrated in Figure 1.5. The aggregate demand curve shifts upwards from AD_1 to AD_2. National income increased from Y_1 to Y_2 (i.e. ΔY) whereas the increase in aggregate demand is ΔAD (i.e. $AD_1 - AD_2$). The increase in income is more than the increase in aggregate demand and this phenomenon is called the multiplier.

1.3.3 *The multiplier*
In order to simplify the analysis we will consider a highly simplified economy with no government (expenditure or taxation) or international trade (exports and imports). The output (Y) of such a hypothetical economy would be distributed between the production of consumption (C) and investment (I) goods.

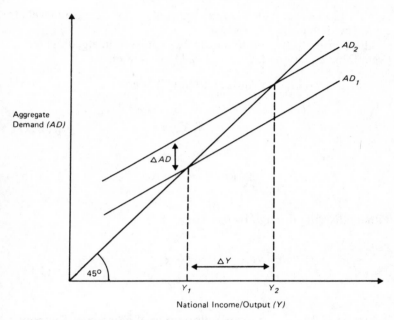

Figure 1.5. An increase in aggregate demand

$$Y = C + I \qquad (1.10)$$

Investment expenditure (I) is assumed to be exogenous while household spending (C) depends positively upon income (Y). The form of the consumption function will be represented by a simple linear equation:

$$C = \alpha + \beta Y \qquad (1.11)$$

Starting from an equilibrium position suppose there occurs a rise in the amount of investment expenditure undertaken in the economy (e.g. due to a fall in the rate of interest). This rise in spending will result in new jobs being created in firms producing capital goods. Newly employed workers will spend some of their income on consumption goods (e.g. clothing, consumer durables) and save the rest. The rise in demand for consumer goods will in turn lead to increased employment in these industries and cause further rounds of expenditure. Income will rise via the multiplier process to a new equilibrium level at which output equals the new increased level of aggregate demand.

More formally the mulitplier can be expressed in algebraic form. Combining equations (1.10) and (1.11) we obtain:

Rearranging and factorising equation (1.12) gives:

$$Y = \alpha + \beta Y + I \qquad (1.12)$$

$$Y(1 - \beta) = I + \alpha \qquad (1.13)$$

Finally dividing through by $(1 - \beta)$:

$$Y = \frac{1}{1-\beta} [I + \alpha] \qquad (1.14)$$

Equation (1.14) shows the equilibrium level of income. The multiplier showing how income changes when investment changes is given by

$$\frac{1}{1-\beta}$$

and is equal to the reciprocal of one minus the marginal propensity to consume (β). Alternatively the multiplier can be defined with reference to the marginal propensity to save and in fact is equal to the reciprocal of the marginal propensity to save. For example, if $\beta = 0.8$ (MPS = 1 − MPC = 0.2) the multplier would be equal to 5

$$\text{i.e. } \frac{1}{1-0.8} = \frac{1}{0.2} = 5$$

The change in income (ΔY) will be some multiple of the original change in investment expenditure (ΔI). For example, if investment expenditure increased by £3m ($\Delta I = 3$) income would increase by £15m (i.e. $\Delta Y = \Delta I \times 5$). In other words the multiplier process will continue until a new and higher level of income is established (£15m) where the higher level of investment expenditure (£3m) is matched by a higher level of savings (i.e. 0.2 × £15m = £3m). The value of the multiplier itself will of course be larger the higher is the marginal propensity to consume and vice versa.

Although we have presented the multipler in its simplest form possible the analysis can be easily extended to an open economy (i.e. one that engages in international trade) with a government sector. For example, the government might decide to increase its expenditure on new schools. The initial effect would be felt in the construction industry where extra employment, income and spending would generate further induced rounds of expenditure. The main difference would be that as consumption expenditure increased leakages from the circular flow would occur via taxes and import spending, as well as savings. The multiplier would in consequence depend on all leakages from the circular flow, i.e. savings, taxes, and imports. In fact as we show in Appendix A the general formula is:

$$\frac{1}{1-\beta(1-t)+m} \qquad (1.15)$$

where (1) t = marginal tax rate (i.e. the fraction of extra income paid to the government in taxes)

(2) m = Marginal propensity to import (i.e. fraction of extra income spent on imports)

and (3) β = marginal propensity to consume.

It can be seen from this formula that the multiplier will be larger: (i) the greater the marginal propensity to consume; (ii) the smaller the marginal propensity to import; and (iii) the smaller the marginal tax rate. In terms of Figure 1.5 the multiplier will be larger the steeper the aggregate demand schedule. The reader should verify this for himself.

Before we illustrate the nature of economic disturbances using this particular model it is worth highlighting the importance of the assumption that the volume of injections (i.e. G, I, and X which are exogenously determined) and leakages (i.e. T, S, and Im which depend upon income) are not closely related. For example, the model predicts that, ceteris paribus, if people decide to save more the level of income will fall via the multiplier process which in this case will work in reverse. As long as decisions regarding saving and investment are made independently there may be no guarantee that increased savings will be chanelled into investment expenditure. Consequently it is possible for the economy to settle in an equilibrium position where unemployment prevails. In such a situation full employment could be achieved by active government intervention to stimulate aggregate expenditure.

1.4. The capacity of the economy

So far we have assumed that the economy can produce all the goods demanded. This assumption can be relaxed by introducing the idea of a maximum capacity of the economy to produce goods. This capacity of the economy is determined by:

    (i) the stocks of capital equipment;

    (ii) labour;

and (iii) the state of technology (assumed to be constant).

The relationship between the inputs of (i) capital and (ii) labour and final output, is called the production function.

In the situations we have so far considered, increases in aggregate demand lead to increased inputs; especially of labour. Thus as aggregate demand increases so more labour will be required to produce the goods demanded. Eventually all available labour will be employed and no further increases in output will be possible. This is what we call the capacity of the economy. We represent this in Figure 1.6 by a straight line at Y_c but it should be realised that this is a convenient over-simplification. In the real world some industries will reach their capacity before others so that more correctly Y_c should be represented by a zone rather than a single unit of output.

The area to the right of Y_c in Figure 1.6 represents an area in which output cannot expand to meet aggregate demand. Excess demand will lead only to price increases without any change in output. On the other hand the area to the left of Y_c represents a region in which real output can expand and this is the region in which we have based our analysis up to now. In future analysis we shall assume that increases in aggregate demand lead to changes in real output without price changes, provided output is less than Y_c, but only to price increases if output is greater than Y_c.

1.5 The effect of changes in aggregate demand

It would be useful at this stage to summarise the effects of changes in aggregate demand on the equilibrium level of national income. For illustrative purposes we consider the case of an autonomous (i.e. independent) increase in exports and assume that the other components of aggregate demand remain unchanged. It should also

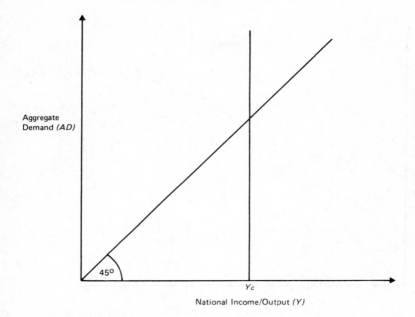

Figure 1.6. Capacity output

be noted that national income will be affected in the same manner, ceteris paribus, by an autonomous increase in consumption, investment or government expenditure or by an autonomous decrease in imports.

Assume that the initial equilibrium level of national income/output (Y_1) is less than capacity output (Y_c). In this instance an autonomous increase in exports causes the equilibrium level of national income to rise by the full extent of the multiplier, discussed in section 1.3.3. This is illustrated in Figure 1.7.

Following an increase in exports from X_1 to X_2 producers' stock levels fall as aggregate demand now exceeds output at the initial equilibrium level of output (Y_1). For the reasons discussed earlier in section 1.3.2 domestic firms will expand output until once again output is equal to the demand for their goods. For domestic firms in aggregate this occurs at Y_2 where the aggregate demand schedule intersects the 45° line i.e. where aggregate demand equals aggregate output. The increase in output from Y_1 to Y_2 (ΔY) is greater than the increase in exports from X_1 to X_2 (ΔX) due to the multiplier process.

In contrast assume that the initial equilibrium level of national income (Y_1) is already equal to capacity output (Y_c). In this instance

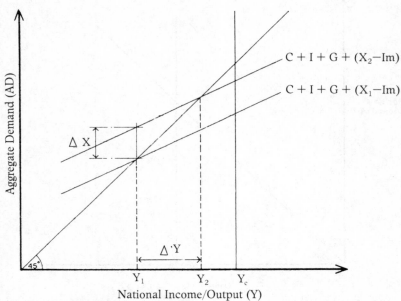

Figure 1.7. An increase in exports (excess capacity)

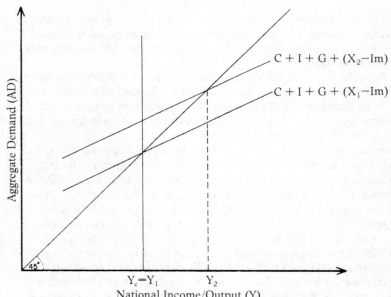

Figure 1.8. An increase in exports (zero excess capacity)

no further increase in real output is possible and the increase in exports leads to excess demand which causes prices to rise. This is illustrated in Figure 1.8.

Domestic producers are now unable to meet the increased demand for their output due to the rise in exports (i.e. there is excess demand equal to $Y_2 - Y_1$) and this leads to price increases until such time as the excess demand is choked off. Output remains at Y_c.

The converse situations arise following a decrease in aggregate demand. In the case where the initial equilibrium level of national income is equal to or less than the capacity output, a decrease in aggregate demand will cause output to fall due to the familiar multiplier process. On the other hand if the initial equilibrium level of national income exceeds capacity output (i.e. excess demand exists in the economy) a decrease in aggregate demand will reduce inflationary pressure. It is only in the situation where the equilibrium level of national income falls below capacity output that real income will fall.

1.6 The nature of economic disturbances

As we have seen in the preceding section it is possible to use the simple Keynesian model to illustrate how certain economic disturbances (i.e. changes) affect economic activity. The main economic disturbances can be defined, in very broad terms, by their source of origin. There are three principal sources, namely real, monetary and supply shocks.

In traditional Keynesian analysis most of the disturbances are held to occur from the real sector. For example, investment spending held to occur from the real sector. For example, investment spending might decrease due to an unexplained downward revision of businessmen's expectations of the future returns from investment. In his *General Theory of Employment, Interest and Money* (1936) Keynes referred to this as a change in investor's 'animal spirits'. This would cause the aggregate demand schedule in Figure 1.5 to shift downwards. For simplicity we will assume that national income is initially (i.e. before the disturbance) at Y_1 and that the government's overriding objective is to maintain output at this level. If this economic disturbance persisted, and there occurred no offsetting influence to it, output would fall below the target level. In terms of this particular model the obvious policy response would be a compensatory increase in government expenditure and/or decrease in taxes. This would cause the aggregate demand schedule to shift upwards and push output back towards its target level. The extent to which the government decided to stimulate aggregate expenditure would depend upon the size of the multiplier.

In contrast to this traditional Keynesian viewpoint monetarists argue that most of the disturbances which affect the economy are monetary in origin. We will leave the discussion of the role and importance of money to the economy to Chapter 3.

1.7 Concluding remarks

So far we have explained the determination of national income largely without reference to financial variables. This is clearly an omission and in Chapter 2 we review the financial institutions of the United Kingdom and in Chapter 3 the role of money in the determination of national income.

APPENDIX A

Algebraic Description of the Simple Keynesian Model

Consumption Function	*Equation in the Main Text*

(1) $C = \alpha + \beta Y_D$ (1.4)
where   (i) C = aggregate household expenditure
         (ii) Y_D = disposable income
         (iii) α = autonomous consumption
         (iv) β = marginal propensity to consume

Disposable income
(2) $Y_D = Y - T$
Where   (i) Y = national income
         (ii) T = amount paid in income tax

Tax function
(3) $T = To + tY$
Where   (i) To = tax payments when national income is zero
         (negative with a progressive tax system since,
         because of allowances, a positive income is
         necessary before any tax is paid)
         (ii) t = marginal rate of tax

Imports
(4) $Im = Mo + mY$
Where   (i) Im = imports
         (ii) Mo= autonomous element of imports
         (iii) m = marginal propensity to import

Exogenous variables
(5) I, G, X
Where   (i) I = investment
         (ii) G = government expenditure
         (iii) X = exports

Definition of national income
(6) $Y = C + I + G + (X - Im)$ (1.3)
Substituting (2) into (1):
(7) $C = \alpha + \beta (Y - T)$

Substituting (3) into (7):
(8) $C = \alpha + \beta\,(Y - To - tY)$
Rearranging and factorising (8):
(9) $C = \alpha - \beta To + \beta\,(1 - t)\,Y$
Therefore as stated in the main text it is possible to substitute so that
C becomes a function of Y rather than Y_D.
Substituting into (6) for C from (9) and Im from (4):
(10) $Y = \alpha - \beta To + \beta\,(1 - t)\,Y + I + G + (X - Mo - mY)$
Rearranging:
(11) $Y - \beta\,(1 - t)\,Y + mY = \alpha - \beta To - Mo + I + G + X$
*Factorising and noting that the first three terms on the right-hand side of
(11) are constant and can be denoted by Z (i.e. autonomous demand).*
(12) $Y\,[1 - \beta(1 - t) + m] = Z + I + G + X$
Dividing through by $1 - \beta(1 - t) + m$:
(13) $Y = \dfrac{1}{1 - \beta(1 - t) + m}\,[Z + I + G + X]$

Thus the term $\dfrac{1}{1 - \beta(1 - t) + m}$ (1.15)

in the main text is the multiplier showing the effect of changes in
I, G, or X on Y.

2 Financial Institutions

2.1. Introduction

In discussing the determinants of the level of income and employment within an economy in Chapter 1 we concentrated on real influences (i.e. those other than financial). In this chapter we go on to discuss the provision of finance for expenditure within an economy. Finance for expenditure is not provided in a vacuum; it is provided within a framework of financial institutions so it is necessary to examine the UK financial sytsem. For students whose studies do not require them to have a detailed knowledge of the UK financial system an outline of the various institutions will be sufficient to understand subsequent chapters.

Throughout this chapter we will mention various financial assets and it is useful at this stage to indicate the general nature of three important types of asset.

(i) *Equities.* Equities refer to the shares issued by a company. Holders of the equities are the owners of a company. They therefore undertake the risk of business failure and reap the rewards of profits earned by a company

(ii) *Bonds.* Bonds are securities issued with a fixed rate of interest based on the face or nominal value of the security. They are normally issued for a fixed term and the date of repayment is called the date of maturity. Thus a five-year, 10 per cent, £100 bond would be redeemed (i.e. the holder repaid) in five years' time. In the meantime, the holder would receive £10 interest per year on his bond. Since the rate of interest on a bond (the coupon value in American terminology) is fixed, the price people are willing to pay for a bond will alter as market interest rates change. As market interest rates fall the market value of a bond will rise. This is most easily demonstrated for a bond with no redemption date. Take for example a non-redeemable £100 bond which gives the holder 10 per cent return on the face value of the security. The holder will receive £10 per annum interest indefinitely. If the market rate of interest falls, say to 5 per cent, this bond will become more attractive. Purchases of the bond will bid up the price and equilibrium will be re-established when the price of the bond has risen to £200 so that the £10 interest per annum is exactly 5 per cent of the market price of £200. Conversely if the market rate of interest rises to 20 per cent, the fixed £10 return on the bond will be unattractive. Bond sales will lower the price of the bond. Equilibrium will be re-established when the market price of the bond falls to £50 so that £10 is 20 per cent of the market value. More formally the price individuals are willing to pay for a perpetual (i.e. non-redeemable) bond is given by:

$$P_B = \frac{r_n}{r_m} \times V \qquad (2.1)$$

where (1) P_B = market price of the bond
(2) r_n = fixed rate of interest on the bond (i.e. coupon value)
(3) r_m = market rate of interest
(4) V = nominal (or face) value of the bond.

This formula demonstrates quite clearly that the price of the bond is inversely related to the market rate of interest e.g. as r_m increases so P_B falls.

The principle of the inverse relationship between the rate of interest and the market price of bonds is important and will be referred to throughout the text.

The yield on a bond can be defined as that rate of interest which will cause equality between (i) the present market value of a bond and (ii) the future dividends on plus repayments of the principle. In other words it is the return on holding a bond to maturity. For example, suppose the five-year, 10 per cent, £100 bond referred to earlier has a market price of £85 then the yield to maturity can be calculated by solving for y (where y is the yield to maturity) in the following formula:

$$£85 = \frac{£10}{(1+y)} + \frac{£10}{(1+y)^2} + \frac{£10}{(1+y)^3} + \frac{£10}{(1+y)^4} + \frac{£10}{(1+y)^5} + \frac{£100}{(1+y)^5} \quad (2.2)$$

Note we are assuming that interest is paid once a year at the end of the year.

Bonds are mainly issued by central and local government, private and nationalised industries and financial institutions. Central government bonds are termed Gilt-Edged Securities, so-called because they are free of any risk of default.

(iii) *Bills of exchange.* A bill is best considered as a promise to pay a certain sum of money at some fixed future date i.e. it is similar to a post-dated cheque. Commercial bills are used to finance trade and reconcile the interests of buyers and sellers of goods. By promising to pay the seller of goods in the future – three months being the most common time – the buyer delays making any payments; this is a considerable advantage if the receipt of the goods is subject to transport delays. On the other hand the seller of the goods receives a 'negotiable' instrument which he can sell in a financial market i.e. he can receive money immediately. The price he receives from such a sale is less than the maturity value of the bill and hence the bill is said to be 'discounted' with the rate of discount (i.e. the gap between the maturity value and the cash actually received) being dependent on market rates of interest for loans over the same period. For example, a £20,000 bill may be sold for £19,610. This gives the buyer a profit of £390 on redemption after say three months. The rate of discount (the return to the buyer) over the three-month period is approximately 2 per cent.

$$(\frac{390}{19610} \times 100).$$

Bills are also issued by the central government, termed Treasury Bills, and local government.

Bonds and equities can be bought and sold on the Stock Exchange. The London Stock Exchange is a specialist market providing two separate functions (i) trading in existing securities (or secondary market) and (ii) new issues (or primary market). The secondary market is an essential support to raising finance because it enables holders of securities to cash them by selling them via the stock exchange. This encourages wider holdings of financial assets. The new issues market is that section of the stock market concerned with selling new shares and/or bonds so that the total level of financial securities is increased rather than their distribution. Additional funds are raised through the new issue market via new shares by firms and the public sector.

2.2 The role of financial intermediaries
In the circular flow system examined in Chapter 1, the sum of all payments is equal to the sum of all receipts so that the system as a

whole can never be in surplus or deficit. This is not true however of individual sectors within the economy e.g. the personal sector may, in total, spend less than it earns in income so that it is in surplus (i.e. it saves). The role of the financial system in this connection is twofold. It provides (i) a means of transmitting payments between individuals within an economy and (ii) a means of transferring funds from surplus (lenders) to deficit units (borrowers).

The second function is called financial intermediation. The question arises why do we need financial intermediaries? Why do surplus units not lend directly to those who need to borrow to finance their proposed expenditure (i.e. deficit units)? Financial institutions help to bridge the gap between borrowers and lenders by creating markets in two types of security, one for the lender (i.e. a deposit at the financial institution concerned) and the other for the borrower. This is shown in Figure 2.1.

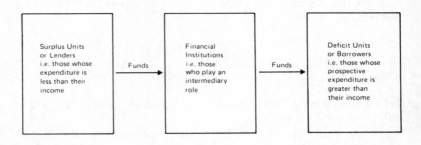

Figure 2.1. The role of financial intermediaries

It is generally agreed that the operation of financial intermediaries assists the provision of finance in at least three ways. First, they reconcile the lender's desire for liquidity (i.e. the ease of changing an asset into cash without loss) with the borrower's desire for a loan over a fixed term. Thus, for example, depositors can withdraw their deposits from building societies on demand or within a few days whereas the house purchaser borrows from building societies by way of a mortgage over a long period of time (e.g. 20/25 years). Technically this is called 'maturity transformation'. Financial intermediaries are able to provide this service because the large number of depositors with them makes it unlikely that all depositors will withdraw their funds at the same time. Second, by making loans to a large number of borrowers, financial intermediaries are able to reduce the impact of a loan default (i.e. non-payment of the loan) compared with the situation of a single lender and a single borrower. In the latter case loan default may be disastrous to the lender. Third, the financial intermediary by specialisation acquires expertise in assessing the risk involved in making the loan and also gathering information regarding safe outlets for loans which would perhaps be beyond the powers of the individual lender. By these means financial intermediaries are able to increase the flow of savings and loans within an economy and therefore increase aggregate demand. They themselves earn a profit from the service by offering interest rates on deposits lower than the charges they raise on their loans.

The link between the circular flow of income discussed in Chapter 1 and the financial flow is demonstrated in Figure 2.2 which ignores the overseas sector for ease of presentation.

Where, as before, (1) S = saving,
(2) I = Investment
and (3) $G - T$ is government expenditure less taxation i.e. that portion of government expenditure which is not covered by tax receipts and is therefore financed by borrowing.

We now move on to consider the main UK financial institutions.

2.3 The Bank of England

2.3.1 *General nature*
The Bank of England occupies a central position in the UK financial system. In addition to the fairly small ordinary banking activities it (i) assists and supervises the operation of other financial institutions and (ii) operates monetary policy on behalf of the government. For those reasons it is known as the central bank. As such it serves as an intermediary between financial institutions in London (i.e. the city)

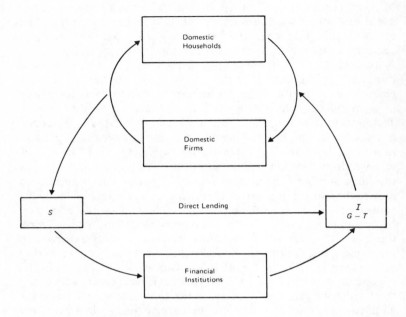

Figure 2.2. The link between the circular flow of income and the financial flow

and the government.

The Bank of England was established by charter in 1694 as a private concern and gradually assumed greater importance in the financial system over subsequent years. With its greater importance, its power to undertake independent actions became more limited and in 1946 it was nationalised. The day-to-day operation of the bank is vested in a court consisting of the Governor, the Deputy Governor, four executive directors and twelve part-time directors. In practice most decisions are taken by the Governor, Deputy Governor and the four executive directors. The Bank is clearly subservient to the political power in office and it is possible for the Treasury to issue directives to the Bank. This power has not been used because the Bank is aware of its subservient position summed up by Montague Norman (Governor from 1922-44) as '... the unique right to offer advice and to press such advice even to the point of nagging but, always of course, subject to the supreme authority of government'. Note that his statement was made prior to nationalisation of the Bank in 1946 so that it can be argued that nationalisation merely

TABLE 2.1. Bank of England: weekly return, 20 February 1980

Liabilities		Assets (£ million)	
Issue Department			
Notes in circulation	9651	Government Securities	8042
Notes in Banking Department	24	Other Securities	1633
	9675		9675
Banking Department			
Public deposits	26	Government Securities	730
Special deposits	104	Advances and other accounts	199
Bankers deposits	579	Premises, equipment and	
Reserves and other accounts	667	other securities	437
Capital	14	Notes and coins	24
	1390		1390

Source: Bank of England, *Quarterly Bulletin,* March 1980, Table 1.

regularised the existing position. The Bank of England is required to prepare weekly accounts known as the Bank Return. This return is divided into two sections, the Issue Department and the Banking Department reflecting the requirement to keep the note issue business separate from the rest of the Bank's business. In practice this is of little account since the Bank is operated as a single unit. The return for 20 February 1980 is shown in Table 2.1.

We shall now examine the functions of the Bank of England.

2.3.2 *The banking role*

The Bank of England acts as a banker to the government, other banks, overseas central monetary authorities and institutions and a restricted number of private customers. This banking role is reflected in the liabilities and assets of the Banking Department listed in Table 2.1. Public deposits represent the outstanding balance on the government's various bank accounts at the Bank of England. In addition to acting as banker to the government, any bank (subject to it possessing a satisfactory status) may keep an account at the Bank of England and many do. Two types of financial institutions however must keep accounts at the Bank of England: (i) the clearing banks who use these facilities to settle inter bank indebtedness (see section 2.4) and (ii) the discount houses (see section 2.8.1). Special deposits are deposits which the banks have been required to place at the Bank of England as part of monetary policy. As we shall discuss in Chapter 9 they are one of the means by which the Bank of England has tried to exercise control over the growth of bank deposits.

Overseas monetary authorities also keep accounts at the Bank of England in order to settle indebtedness resulting from official intervention in the foreign exchange markets (see Chapter 4). In addition, as a legacy of the old sterling area, the Bank maintains the official reserves of certain countries. Finally a restricted amount of private banking business is carried out on behalf of customers including Bank employees. This is partly due to tradition but also serves the useful function of keeping the Bank in touch with the normal commercial business of banking. Assets to match the various liabilities of the Banking Department listed in Table 2.1 consist mainly of government securities (e.g. Treasury Bills and Gilt-Edged Securities).

2.3.3 *Note issue*
The Bank of England is the sole note issuer of the government in England and Wales. This is purely an administrative function as in practice no control is exercised over the size of the note issue. From the proceeds derived from the issue of notes the Issue Department takes up governmental securities (see Table 2.1).

2.3.4 *Debt management*
In the UK total government expenditure normally exceeds total government receipts so that the resulting deficit has to be financed by government borrowing. The Bank of England has special responsibility for one source of finance, namely issues of marketable debt, i.e. those government securities which can be resold in financial markets. The two main types of securities sold are (i) Treasury Bills and (ii) Gilt-Edged Securities.

Gilt-Edged Securities consist of government bonds. Issues are in quantities of several hundred million pounds and, in order to avoid dislocating the market with such large issues, the Bank employs the following tactics. An advertisement is placed indicating the quantity of stock available and also the minimum acceptable price which will be in line with or slightly above existing market prices for similar stocks. If total applications exceed the issue (i.e. it is oversubscribed) bids are accepted in descending order of price offered. If total applications fall short of the issue, stock is allocated at the minimum price and any stock unsold is taken up by the Bank itself. To quote one example, advertisements were placed in the national press early in January for tenders to be submitted by 7 January 1981. The total size of the issue was £1,100,000,000 and the minimum tender price specified as £89.75 per £100 stock. The fixed rate of interest (coupon value) was $12\frac{1}{4}$ per cent.

After the sale is completed the Bank then fixes a price at which it is prepared to sell the stock remaining in its hands and this price is known as the 'Tap Price'. Similarly as stock comes within one year of maturity (i.e. date of redemption) the Bank will start to buy up existing holdings. By these means, the Bank's dealings in the market help to prevent the large fluctuations in the market prices of Gilt-Edged Securities which might occur if such large quantities of securities were required to be sold and purchased on a single day.

Sales of Gilt-Edged Securities are unlikely to meet the whole of the remaining deficit of the public sector, and the residual borrowing requirement (i.e. after all other sources of finance have been taken into consideration) is met by sale of Tresury Bills. These are short-term securities (maturing in ninety-one days) which are sold at a price less than the redemption value i.e. at a discount. This discount represents the profit to the holder. The amount of Treasury Bills offered for sale each week is geared to the anticipated shortfall of revenue in the following week after taking into consideration prospective sales of Gilt-Edged Securities. Sale is by tender. Prospective buyers are required to quote the price they are prepared to offer for a specific quantity of Treasury Bills indicating the day of the week they wish to take up the bills. The Bank of England accepts tenders in descending order of prices offered until the total issue is taken up. Bills are also sold via the 'Tap' at a fixed price to other government departments and foreign central banks.

The strategy followed by the Bank of England in both the Treasury Bill and Gilt-Edged Security Markets in relation to monetary policy is examined in Chapter 9.

2.3.5. *Supervision and regulation*

The Bank has a wide responsibility for supervision of the financial system. It is responsible for the conduct not only of the banks but also a wide range of city institutions such as the Stock Exchange, insurance firms, commodity traders and various other markets. The Bank is also responsible for conveying their views to the government and conversely the governments' views to them. For example, before each budget the Governor usually writes to these interests to ascertain their views on the economy and passes these on to the government.

However, it is with the banking sytem that the Bank has special responsibility. This reponsibility can be broken down into two headings (i) supervision to prevent a crisis and (ii) easing any strains that might lead to a crisis. This type of supervision and control is called prudential control. Supervision of type (i) has in the past been informal. However changes have taken place. Banks and deposit-taking institutions had to register at the Bank of England. Authorisation was made within the framework of a two-tier system consisting of (i) banks and (ii) licensed deposit-taking institutions. Financial institutions tend to think of this as First and Second Division Banking, though this type of categorisation is disputed by the Bank of England. Finalisation of the registration process took place in the spring of 1981, with appeals against the refusal to grant bank status heard in the autumn of 1981. The type of factors necessary for recognition as a bank are:

(1) high reputation and standing of the institution not only in UK financial circles but also internationally;

(2) similar requirements for the management;

(3) a wide range of banking facilities to be undertaken.

Provision was made for institutions offering highly specialised banking services to register as banks. Assets must normally be at least £5 million but in the case of the specialist institutions the figure was reduced to £250,000. Licensed deposit-takers must have assets in excess of £250,000 and attention was to be given to the fitness of their management and capital adequacy before they were granted a licence.

In addition, deposit insurance was introduced in 1981 whereby 75 per cent of individual deposits up to £10,000 in any concern will be insured. Such insurance applies to, and is finaced by, both banks and licensed deposit-takers. Sole control of both types of institutions is vested in the Bank of England (as distinct from the division of control between the Bank of England and Department of Trade hitherto practised).

The system of control is still to be finalised at the time of writing. Discussons continued between the Bank of England and the other banks for two years. The Bank of England had in mind a flexible system of supervision which would take account of the individual circumstances of the bank concerned. In July 1982, the Bank of England published a further paper setting out a general framework for measuring liquidity which will be used as a first step towards a qualitative assessment of the liquidity of individual banks taking note of a bank's particular characteristics and situation within the banking system. The system of regular discussions with the senior management of banks is being continued by the Bank of England.

The Bank's intervention to ease strains that might lead to a crisis can again be looked at under two headings. First, there is the function of the lender of the last resort. If discount houses (see section 2.8.1) are short of funds, they have the unique right to apply to the Bank of England to borrow money. The Bank will always lend money but may charge a rate above the market rate in which case the discount houses would attempt to reduce such borrowings as soon as possible. This penal rate is called minimum lending rate (MLR) and since 1978 has been fixed by the Bank as an administrative decision. Following the inroduction of the new system of monetary control in August 1981 MLR was abolished so that the lending will be carried out by the Bank at interest rates of its own choosing. The lending of last resort is important as it underpins the banking sector. As we shall see in section 2.4 the deposit banks even out their flows of cash by varying lending to the discount houses. If the banks in aggregate are short of funds they can withdraw money from the discount houses who in turn borrow from the Bank of England. Assistance is never refused but the price at which assistance is given may vary. In effect the Bank of England is indirectly lending to the banks. Nevertheless direct assistance may also be necessary in certain cases. Such an example in the UK was the so-called 'Lifeboat Committee'. Following the liquidity crisis originating in the secondary banking system (see section 2.6) in 1973 a fund was established jointly with the London and Scottish Clearing banks. The aim was to examine the balance sheets of banks in difficulties and to provide funds to support those banks whose assets were such that the institution was viable in the long term. At the peak of its operations, lending was well over £1000 million.

2.3.6. *Monetary policy*
The bank has special responsiblities for providing (i) advice on and (ii) operation of monetary policy. This function is examined in detail in Chapter 9.

2.3.7. *Sundry responsibilities*
The Bank is also responsible for operation of the exchange equalisation account, through which sterling is purchased or sold in the foreign exchange markets to influence the exchange rate (see Chapter 4, section 4.6.2). In the past the Bank was also responsible for administering the controls imposed over the purchase and sale of foreign currency by residents of the UK. These controls have now been abolished.

2.4 The banks: the deposit banks

2.4.1. *Organisation of deposit banking*

The main functions of the deposit banks include (i) operation of the payments mechanism (i.e. transmitting money between economic agents); (ii) accepting deposits; and (iii) making loans. The dominant group of deposit banks is the London clearing banks. Within this group the big four are Lloyds, National Westminster, Midland and Barclays. The London Clearing Banks own the London Clearing House through which net indebtedness of the banks to each other is settled by adjusting their balances at the Bank of England. There are of course other deposit banks, such as the Northern Ireland and Scottish Clearing Banks, and smaller banks, like the Co-operative Bank, but these together are small relative to the London Clearing Banks who conduct the bulk of the nation's retail banking.

It is an interesting question why dominance in UK deposit banking has been achieved by such a small number of firms. The answer is that economies of scale exist in banking. Potential sources of economies of scale include (i) the ability to spread risk (ii) branch rationalisation and (iii) the use of specialist Management Services. A large number of depositors means that withdrawals by single depositors are unlikely to cause any inconvenience to a bank. Furthermore national banks are able to spread risk geographically and remove the danger of the bank being seriously affected by a slump in a particular trade within a region. In addition, if various branches have different patterns of flows of funds, these will tend to cancel out for a national bank. All these factors lead to a greater public confidence in large banks. Second, the amalgamations of banking firms which occurred in the UK in the late 1960s (e.g. Martins with Barclays; Westminster with National Provincial) enabled competing branches to be closed, thus achieving economies of capital. The growth of the size of these banks has in turn enabled them to adopt specialised management functions, economic research departments and an increased use of computers. This potential for economies of scale undoubtedly accounts for the scale of British banking firms compared with that of the USA where amalgamation has been prevented by legislation.

2.4.2 *Balance sheets*

In contrast with the so-called secondary banks discussed below in section 2.6, the significant feature of the London Clearing Banks is that 85 per cent of their total deposits in January 1980 were denominated in sterling. Note also that non-sterling deposits are

TABLE 2.2. London Clearing Banks: consolidated balance sheet, January 1980

Liabilities		Assets	
		(£ million)	
Sterling		Sterling	
Sight deposits	17,300	Cash including balances at	
Time deposits	19,500	Bank of England	1,500
Certificates of deposit	1,200	Money at call	1,800
Non-sterling deposits	8,400	Bills of Exchange	
Other liabilities including		(i) Treasury	400
capital	9,200	(ii) Other	700
		Market loans	6,800
		Investments: UK	
		Government Stock	1,500
		Other	1,400
		Advances	25,800
		Non-sterling assets	8,800
		Miscellaneous sterling	
		and non-sterling	6,900
	55,600		55,600

Source: Bank of England, *Quarterly Bulletin*, March 1980, Table 3.2.

roughly equal to non-sterling assets. Their consolidated balance sheet for that date is shown in Table 2.2.

We shall now proceed to discuss the various sterling assets and liabilities listed and subsequently what factors influence the banks in determining the structure of their balance sheets.

We shall deal with the liabilities first. Sterling deposits are divided into sight and time deposits. No notice is required to withdraw sight deposits but such deposits earn no rate of interest though a notional interest may be calculated and used to offset charges for operating the account. On the other hand time deposits earn a rate of interest but notice has to be given before withdrawal is permitted. In practice this requirement to give notice is often waived. Certificates of deposit arise when a deposit is made for a fixed term and the depositor receives a certificate which indicates the nature of the deposit. The holder of such a deposit can sell such a certificate in the financial markets if he wishes to regain his money before the end of the fixed term. Thus the deposit is fixed for a term as far as the bank is concerned but realisable before that date as far as the deposit is concerned.

On the asset side cash either in the till or at the Bank of England earns no interest. Money at call or short notice is money loaned out to certain financial institutions, mainly the discount houses, which can be recalled at extremely short notice, e.g. in some cases up to mid-day for return that day. The rate of interest on such loans is of course low, certainly below that earned on Treasury Bills. Other bills of exchange mainly consist of commercial bills i.e. bills of exchange issued in connection with trade. Market loans are a new category of assets introduced in the new statistical series dating from 1975. The emphasis is that loans are made through the market to such bodies as discount houses, local authorities and various listed money brokers. This figure also includes the banks' holdings of certificates of deposits issued by other banks. The two remaining categories of sterling assets refer to loans and advances to customers and banks' holdings of stock. Loans and advances can be made in two ways: (i) by a loan for a fixed term i.e. a loan which must be repaid on a specific date; and (ii) by an overdraft i.e. the customer is permitted to overdraw his account up to a specified limit. The second method is traditionally more popular in th UK but term loans are also made. The overdraft system makes it difficult for the banks to control their lending where customers have unused overdraft facilities available and empirical studies confirm that significant unused facilities do exist. The advantage an overdraft offers to the customer is that interest is only paid to the extent that the account is overdrawn. The advantage to the banker is that the interest rate charged adjusts auto-matically with banks' rates of interest, as does the rate charged on most term loans. Term loans involve the whole of the loan being placed to the account of the borrower. Repayments are made according to a fixed scale and the borrower is charged interest whether or not he uses all the loan. Loans generally are charged at a fixed scale above the base rate in operation at the time of the loan being arranged; the exact excess over base rate depends on the circumstances of the loan.

Investments refer mainly to government securities. UK banks have been traditionally reluctant to invest directly in industry. This contrasts with the attitude taken by German banks who hold equity holdings in leading firms. Thus purchases of stocks refer mainly to central government stock and that issued by local authorities and some Commonwealth government bonds.

The question arises, what determines the proportion of assets to be held in the various categories? The first consideration is government regulation. Up to January 1981, UK banks were required to maintain at least $12\frac{1}{2}$ per cent of their eligible liabilities (roughly equal to sterling deposits and net holdings of certificates of deposits i.e. holdings less certificates issued) in the following assets:

(1) normal balances at the Bank of England;
(2) money at call;
(3) British and Northern Ireland Treasury Bills and commercial bills (subject to a maximum value of 2 percentage points out of the $12\frac{1}{2}$ percentage points);
(4) UK government and nationalised industry stocks with less than one year to maturity.

In January 1981 this figure of $12\frac{1}{2}$ per cent was reduced to 10 per cent. In August 1981 the reserve asset ratio was abolished leaving the banks free to choose their own level of holdings of balances at the Bank of England, apart from a non-operational balance equal to $\frac{1}{2}$ per cent of eligible liabilities (see Chapter 9, section 9.6). No liquidity requirements for prudential control have as yet been finalised and the banks will continue to follow existing policies and practices unless otherwise agreed with the Bank of England.

Apart from government legislation which affects asset holdings the banks also have regard to the twin motives of liquidity and profitability. Liquidity can be defined as the ease with which a financial claim can be converted into cash without loss. This involves two principles: (i) shiftability i.e. whether it is easy to transfer the claim; and (ii) capital certainty. To take one example, money at call is shiftable (i.e. on to the Bank of England via its function of lender of last resort) and is capital certain (if £100,000 is recalled £100,000 will be obtained). This contrasts with the situation for a Gilt-Edged Security. While it is shiftable because there is a well developed market for such securities it does not possess capital certainty since the market value of a bond can depart from its face value. Advances possess neither attribute as it is difficult to recall a loan at short notice! The sterling assets in the consolidated balance sheet (Table 2.2) are arranged in descending order of liquidity. Liquidity is necessary because approximately 46 per cent of sterling deposits are withdrawable on demand and most of the remainder within seven days' notice. Thus to maintain public confidence, the banks must always be able to meet withdrawals. Any failure or fear of failure to do so would lead to a 'run' on the bank as depositors endeavoured to withdraw their deposits. The aim of profitability is self-apparent. Profits are necessary to reward shareholders and provide reserves. The assets in

Table 2.2 are arranged in ascending order of profitability. At first sight it might seem therefore that profitability and liquidity are opposing forces. This is not so since the bank can only maintain profitable assets if the public has confidence in the banks, which requires them to hold an adequate stock of liquid assets. It is therefore a question of balancing the two needs.

2.4.3. *Creation of bank deposits*
Banks alter the level of their deposits by varying their holdings of assets. Thus if a loan of £100 is made to a person, on the asset side loans and advances increase by £100, while the liabilities also rise by £100 as the borrower's deposit is increased by £100. Similarly if an individual spends £100 of previously unused overdraft facilities, then assets and liabilities increase by equal amounts. Loans and advances increase by £100 and when the person to whom the cheque is made out deposits the cheque with his bank, his (not the borrower's) deposit will increase by £100. Banks are able to create deposits in this way because the public is willing to accept bank deposits as a means of payment; in other words bank deposits are generally acceptable as money by the public. This process is demonstrated in Table 2.3.

In Table 2.3 column 1 represents the situation before the loan of £100 is made, column 2 the situation after the loan of £100 is made. Note that deposits have risen by £100, demonstrating the truth of the old adage that every loan creates a deposit. A similar process arises if banks buy financial securities. In this case the increase in liabilities (deposits) is matched on the asset side by a corresponding increase in investments. By buying financial securities and/or increasing their loans banks acquire profit-earning assets thereby increasing their total profits.

It might appear that banks have a seemingly unlimited ability to create deposits, but two points should be borne in mind. First, total lending by banks (to public and private sectors either directly or indirectly through purchase of securities in financial markets) can only increase if their total deposits increase. Second, the level of bank

TABLE 2.3. Creation of bank deposits: ABC Bank Ltd

	Liabilities			Assets	
	1	2		1	2
			Other assets	500	500
Deposits	1000	1100	Loans and advances	500	600

deposits and therefore total lending is restricted because deposits are normally constrained (either by law or custom) to a specific ratio of defined reserve assets. As noted above banks retain the confidence of their customers by holding a stock of reserve assets. Hence in practice banks will always maintain some minimum reserve asset ratio (Reserve Assets/Total Deposits) to meet withdrawals of deposits by customers. If this ratio were 10 per cent of total deposits then their ability to create deposits would be limited to a maximum of ten times the amount of reserves held. More formally the maximum amount of deposits could be created is given by:

$$D = \frac{R}{\alpha} \qquad (2.3)$$

where (1) D = bank deposits
       (2) R = reserve assets
       (3) α = the reserve ratio

Banks may choose to hold excess reserve assets (i.e. above the minimum level) as an additional safety margin to meet unanticipated withdrawals so that equation (2.3) prescribes the *maximum* amount of depoists that can be created.

It should be noted finally that transfers between customers of different banks do not influence the ability of the banking system as a whole to make loans. If the two persons (i.e. the borrower and the recipient of the cheque) do not use the same bank, an adjustment of cash (i.e. balances at the Bank of England) will take place between the banks. To illustrate this, consider the example of Mr. Jones who banks with Barclays and Mr. Smith who banks with Lloyds. Mr. Jones writes out a cheque for £100 in Mr. Smith's favour. The result as far as total liabilities are concerned is that total deposits at Barclays fall by £100 while those at Lloyds increase by £100. As indicated earlier the banks use their deposits at the Bank of England to settle inter-bank indebtedness so that the corresponding asset changes are (i) a rise of £100 in Lloyd's balance at the Bank of England and (ii) an equivalent fall of £100 in Barclays' balance there. So nothing has changed in the banking sector as a whole. Total deposits remain the same, as do total balances at the Bank of England. All that has happened is that the distribution of assets and liabilities between banks has changed.

2.5 The savings banks

Originally the savings banks operated to provide an outlet for small savings similar to that now provided by the Building Societies. However, as we shall discuss in section 2.5.2 this role has changed dramatically for the Trustee Savings Banks in the 1970s.

2.5.1. *National Savings Banks*

This savings bank originated as the Post Office Savings Bank in 1861 but changed its name to the National Savings Bank in 1969. Its main function is to transfer savings from the private sector (essentially by small savers) to the government. The NSB operates two accounts on behalf of small investors, ordinary and investment accounts. Investment accounts are available to the saver who has at least £50 in his ordinary account.

2.5.2 *Trustee Savings Banks (TSBs)*

The Trustee Savings Banks operate in a similar manner to the NSB, providing saving outlets for small savers in the form of savings and investment accounts. In addition they operate current account facilities enabling the provision of a wide range of banking facilities including cheque cards, overdraft facilities and term deposits. The power to provide such banking services was given by the Trustee Savings Bank Act in 1967 which also stimulated amalgamation. At the apex of the TSBs is the Central Trustee Savings Bank Ltd which acts both as a bank to the TSBs and provides clearing facilities for member banks since it is a member of the clearing house.

2.5.3 *The National Giro*

The National Giro operates a money transfer system through post offices. The system is relatively small. In order to broaden its appeal the National Giro has offered industrial and commercial customers relatively attractive terms for wage payments to be made via the giro system. It also offers customers a means to borrow via a finance house rather than directly from the giro.

2.6 Other banks: the secondary banking system

Although secondary banks are a very heterogeneous group they contrast in three main ways with the operation of clearing banks. First, the majority of their business is in foreign currency. For January 1980 sterling deposits only accounted for 20 per cent of total deposits of the combined group of these banks. There are differences between the individual groups of banks but the general principle that foreign currency deposits from the larger proportion of their business applies in all cases. Second, the involvement in the payments mechanism is minimal; for the group as a whole sight deposits came to only 24 per cent of total sterling deposits or a mere 5 per cent of total business at January 1980. These other banks are then best considered to operate in the manner of other financial intermediaries, i.e. they accept deposits of money and make loans in various ways. Third, the size of their deposits is large, a minimum acceptable deposit being in the range of £50,000 to £100,000. They are therefore considered to be 'wholesale' as opposed to 'retail' bankers.

In contrast to the clearing banks, these banks are far more concerned with 'matching' their asset and liability structures both with regard to their maturity and their currency. For example, if a bank accepts a $ deposit expiring on 1 May 1985, it will endeavour to match this with a corresponding asset maturing on the same date. As we have seen, because the clearing banks operate in the retail side of the business, accepting large numbers of small deposits, liquidity rather than 'matching' is their guiding principle.

The banks included in the 'secondary' banking system are:

(1) accepting houses
(2) overseas banks
(3) other British banks
(4) consortium banks.

For the purposes of this book, the accepting houses, otherwise known as merchant banks, are the most important. These are diverse institutions who enter into the following types of business. First, they accept (i.e. guarantee) bills of exchange on behalf of their customers, that is, they sign the bill. In effect they sell their good name which is well known as opposed to that of the trader which may not be as well known. In fact not many bills are held in their portfolio and they are generally sold to the discount houses. Second, they offer financial advice to customers, with respect to raising finance, dividend policies and also take-overs, both initiating such bids and offering defence against bids. Third, they are heavily involved in raising new capital by firms and offering advice on such matters as (i) drawing up the prospectus, (ii) pricing new share issues and (iii) arranging for new issues to be underwritten. Fourth, they manage portfolios on behalf of their customers though they themselves rarely hold shares. They have also assisted in the establishment and management of unit trusts (see section 2.7.4). Fifth, they conduct ordinary banking business already discussed, especially with regard to foreign currency business and participation in the Eurocurrency markets (see Chapter 14). Apart from liquid asset holdings, domestic sterling business consists mainly of advances to the private sector, interbank loans (see section 2.8.2) and loans to local authorities. Sixth, different accepting houses undertake different specialist functions. Some are involved in the gold bullion market, others in commodity dealing, factoring and export finance.

The other banks which comprise the remainder of the secondary banking system can be dealt with more quickly. Overseas banks have been attracted to set up branch offices in London as a major international financial centre for a variety of reasons. For example, to serve the needs of their domestic customers, the growing attraction of the Eurocurrency markets (see Chapter 14). Other British banks include those whose head offices are in Britain but whose main business is overseas. Consortium banks, a relatively new phenomenon, developed in the 1970s. These are independent units whose shareholders are banks from different countries. Business includes lending to large multinational companies.

2.7. Non-bank financial intermediaries (NBFIs)

In contrast with clearing banks, non-bank financial intermediaries have only a very limited role to play in the payments mechanism and in fact maintain their balances at deposit banks, not the Bank of England. Thus unlike the liabilities of clearing banks, those of NBFIs are not generally accepted as a means of payment. The main function of the NBFIs is therefore to lend money deposited with them. In order to demonstrate this difference a simple numerical example is shown in Table 2.4 on the assumption that the NBFI maintains a reserve ratio of 5 per cent cash (in the till and at the bank) and 15 per cent government stock. Column 1 shows the original position, column 2 shows that after a new client has deposited £100 and column 3 shows that after the NBFI has increased its lending and maintained its reserves (both cash and government stock) at the prescribed ratios of 5 and 15 per cent respectively.

TABLE 2.4. Illustration of NBFI activities

	Liabilities				Assets		
	1	2	3		1	2	3
	£	£	£		£	£	£
Deposits	1000	1100	1100	Cash	50	150	55
				Government stock	150	150	165
				Loans	800	800	880
	1000	1100	1100		1000	1100	1100

It can be seen that the expansion of lending i.e. movement from column 2 to column 3 has not led to an expansion in deposits merely a re-arrangement of assets. Thus cash has fallen by £95 while holdings of government securities have increased by £15 and loans by £80. As mentioned earlier this situation contrasts with lending by banks which increases the level of their deposits; i.e. banks are able to create credit whereas NBFIs only transmit credit. This argument needs a slight caveat in that if funds loaned out by the NBFI return to th e NBFI in the form of further deposits then the act of lending will in fact have increased deposits.

The growth of certain NBFIs, especially Building Societies, has been considerably faster than that of the clearing banks and it is an interesting question whether this has been to the detriment of the banks in any way. The traditional answer was 'no'. It was held that part of the deposits of a NBFI would be at a bank and the remainder (i.e. that portion lent out by the NBFI) would be held as bank deposits by the borrower or persons to whom the borrower made payments. This argument needs to be hedged in several respects. First, if the major portion of the reserves of a NBFI is held in the form of government stock rather than deposits at a bank, it will therefore be lost to the bank. Second, the portion of reserves held at banks is likely to be held in the wholesale market earning rates of interest rather lower than at the retail end. Finally, those who receive payments from the borrower of funds may also use a proportion of the funds to purchase government stock thus removing more funds from the banking system. As the NBFIs grow larger so these losses to the clearing banks will become larger in aggregate. Hence it is a reasonable conclusion that the growth of NBFIs has probably been to the detriment of the banks. In other words the banks and NBFIs are in fact in competition with each other.

Having indicated the way in which NBFIs function we will now examine the various types of NBFI in operation in the UK, noting the high degree of specialisation of business adopted by each group of NBFI.

2.7.1 *Building Societies*
Building Societies operate in the traditional manner of NBFIs accepting deposits, virtually withdrawable on demand, from a wide range of small savers. They make loans for the purpose of house purchase for periods ranging from fifteen to twenty-five years, and are the dominant institution providing finance in the market for new or existing houses. The interest rate charged on mortgage loans is not fixed but is adjusted throughout the period of the mortgage. However

this entails administrative costs and Building Societies tend to change their rates less frequently than the changes which occur in other market rates i.e. they are 'sticky'. Thus levels of interest rates that Building Societies give on deposits and charge on mortgages tend to be lower than other market rates when interest rates are rising and higher when they are falling.

2.7.2 *Finance houses*
These houses are institutions which have traditionally been associated with hire purchase and instalment credit. Other uses of funds take the form of providing loans to firms who hold stocks, to subsidiaries engaged in the factoring business and to provide assets leased out to companies. Sources of funds are (i) deposits (ii) discounted bills and borrowing and (iii) isued share capital. Banks themselves are heavily involved in the provision of finance for the finance houses.

2.7.3 *Insurance companies and pension funds*
The business of insurance is that of spreading risk. Thus persons pay insurance companies a premium in return for the promise of a sum of money in the event of, for example, death, a car crash, fire, etc. Pension funds accept premiums now in return for the promise to pay a pension at a later date. Thus both types of business are faced with the twin problems of what to do with their funds and yet ensure ability to meet their commitments. Adequate liquidity is essential but in view of the long-term nature of their liabilities, they are able to purchase long-term assets. In addition diversification spreads the risk. Types of assets purchased include government stock and equities, and because of the volume of available funds these institutions tend to dominate the stock market. Insurance companies also provide finance for mortgages. Both these types of institution are dominant in raising finance by companies through new issues.

2.7.4 *Investment and unit trusts*
Both of these types of financial institution are concerned with spreading the risk involved in share ownership. Instead of holding shares directly, individuals own a share in a financial institution which itself holds a wide range of shares. In this way the risk inherent in specialisation (i.e. that of the company failure) is reduced. As such they increase the attraction of holding equities and thus facilitate raising finance through new issues of equities by companies. The two types of institution differ in the follwing respects. In American terminology an investment trust is close-ended since it can only expand by issuing new share capital or loans. Existing shares or loan

stock can only be sold via the stock exchange. On the other hand unit trusts are open ended in that the size of a trust expands or contracts as more units are sold to or redeemed directly from the trust. Units are not transferable between persons and the price of units is based on a valuation of the trust.

2.8 The London money markets

The London money markets are markets for short-term funds, mainly among financial institutions. The traditional market is the discount market but alongside this other money markets have developed since the 1950s. These are called the parallel or complementary markets. In this section we consider only the domestic sterling money markets, leaving discussion of Eurocurrency markets to Chapter 14. It should be noted that the small size of the traditional discount market belies its importance because it is one of the markets through which the Bank of England implements monetary policy.

2.8.1 *The discount market*

This market dates back at least 150 years but over the years the nature of its business has changed. Originally small country banks used the London market to discount bills because they lacked sufficient funds to discount all the bills presented to them by customers. With the growth of London as an international finance centre, the London discount market was increasingly used for discounting commercial bills. During the slump of the 1930s, the main business became discounting Treasury Bills. This process continued until by 1959 the commercial bill was described by the Radcliffe Report (1959) as having only 'vestigial' importance to the discount houses[1] Subsequently the importance of Treasury Bill business has declined and that of discounting commercial bills increased. Significantly the market has also become interested in certificates of deposit, and short-term government stock.

The main participants in the discount market are (i) the discount houses, (ii) the banks and (iii) the Bank of England. There are eleven discount houses and all are members of the London Discount Market Association. They borrow money and hold financial securities. The main source of their funds is money at call or short notice borrowed from the clearing banks; this accounted for 88 per cent of their funds in January 1980. Borrowing by this method is secured since a discount house lodges with the bank the bills plus a margin above market value as collateral security.

1. Report on the Working of the British Monetary System.

As we discuss in Chapter 9, section 9.6 the new system of operating monetary policy requires greater intervention in the money markets by the Bank of England. This will require an adequate supply of commercial bills. In this connection the Bank of England has extended the list of banks whose acceptances are eligible for re-discount at the Bank of England. At the same time it was thought necessary to link eligibility to the existence of an adequate supply of funds for the discount market. Consequently each eligible bank has undertaken to ensure that it will maintain with the London discount houses and with approved money brokers and gilt-edged jobbers secured call money equal to: (i) on average 6^1 per cent of that bank's eligible liabilities, (ii) not less than 4 per cent of that bank's eligible liabilities on any particular day.

Another source of funds is the Bank of England and discount houses have the sole right of access to the Bank as lender of last resort function. In January 1980 the main asset held consisted of bills discounted (Treasury Bills, local authority and commercial bills) which accounted for two-thirds of total assets. Other assets held include certificates of deposit, UK local authority bonds and UK government stock mainly with less than five years to maturity. The Bank of England has recently set out a system of prudential regulation for discount houses. This limits the size of each house's balance sheet by restricting the quantity of assets held to 40 times its capital base.

The profit of the discount houses comes from two sources: (i) dealing profits and (ii) the margin between the yield on the securities and the cost of funds borrowed.

There are other participants in the markets such as some money brokers, and other discount brokers but they do not have privileged access to the Bank of England.

What is the importance of this market? First of all, it provides an easy method for banks to dispose of surplus cash. If one bank has a surplus it can increase its loans of money at call. Conversely if another is short of cash it can withdraw call money from the market. Thus the market enables banks to economise on cash holdings. Second, the market acts as a buffer between the Bank of England and the banks. If the Bank of England wishes to restrict credit, it can ensure that the banks in total are short of cash so that the consequent withdrawals of call money force the discount houses to borrow from the Bank of England. By imposing penal borrowing rates the Bank can discourage credit expansion. Third, up to 1981, this market was a market for reserve assets.

1. This was reduced to (i) 5 per cent in 1983 and (ii) $2\frac{1}{2}$ per cent on any particular day.

Nevertheless the question remains as to whether the existence of the discount houses is really necessary. The UK is the only country where the central bank does not deal directly with the banks. Clearly, the functions served by the discount houses could be undertaken by the banks. Probably the best argument for the current system is that it has worked up to now.

2.8.2 *The parallel or complementary markets*

The main growth of the parallel money markets has been since the mid-1950s and in essence they are markets for clearing bank deposits. These markets are different from the traditional discount market in several important respects. First, lending is not secured in the way that borrowings by discount houses from the banks are secured by the value of securities offered as collateral. Second, there is no lender of last resort to avoid the danger of market collapse. Third, there is no direct intervention by the authorities in the parallel markets. Nevertheless some financial institutions (e.g. the discount houses and banks) operate in both markets so that financial conditions will tend to be similar in both. Thus if interest rates rise in the traditional discount market, they will also tend to rise in the parallel markets; coversely they will tend to fall in both markets.

The major parallel money markets are (i) the local authority market, (ii) the interbank market and (iii) the market for certificates of deposits. Two minor markets also exist, namely (i) for finance houses and (ii) the inter-company market.

The local authority market is probably the oldest of these markets and dates back to 1955 when local authorities were forced to borrow in the market rather than via the Public Works Loan Board (PWLB) which up to that time was the sole source of funds for local authorities. The three main forms of money market borrowing by local authorities are (i) temporary money from two days to 364 days (ii) local authority bonds with one year being a popular maturity and (iii) bills. In one sense lending is secured i.e. by the rates of the local authority. There is also a type of lender of last resort i.e. the PWLB.

The interbank market is probably the most important of the markets. The loans in this market are completely unsecured and are for periods varying from overnight up to five years, although the short end of the market is the dominant sector. Interest rates are volatile particularly in the very short end of the market but the market has assumed such importance that the London Interbank Offer Rate (LIBOR) for three months tend to be regarded as the representative cost of money in London. The main participants in the market are the clearing banks, secondary banks and also to some extent other financial institutions such as insurance companies and pension funds as well as industrial and commercial companies. A lot of the business passes through specialist brokers but some lending and borrowing is organised directly between banks. The market serves three main purposes. First, to even out receipts and flows of money. This is an example of matching assets and liabilities already discussed with reference to the secondary banking system. Second, it enables the participants to take a view with respect to future rates of interest. Thus if an agent expects rates to fall, it will be advantageous to borrow temporarily the necessary funds in the interbank market rather than to seek out term deposits at higher rates of interest. Finally, it enables a bank to accept a deposit from a less well known name and then pass it on with the advantage of its own well known name.

The other major parallel money market is that for certificates of deposit. The nature of certificates of deposit has already been discussed. One of their attractions is that they can be sold so that the depositor maintains liquidity. This sector of the money market provides a secondary market for certificates of deposit ensuring the property of liquidity. The main dealers are the banks and discount houses. Certificates of deposit may be dominated in sterling, dollars or German marks. In January 1981 a new market was opened for certificates of deposit dominated in terms of Special Drawing Rights (see Chapter 14). The basic appeal of such a new security is as a hedge against exchange rate changes because Special Drawing Rights are valued in terms of a mixture of currencies.

Finally the two minor markets require little discussion. The finance houses attract deposits mainly from the banks for their hire purchase business. The intercompany market[1] started around 1965 when restrictions on bank lending were imposed by the government as part of its monetary policy. One way around these restrictions was for companies to borrow from each other. The attraction for the lender is that he earns a rate of interest on funds otherwise lying idle. Business is usually conducted via specialist brokers.

2.9 London financial futures market

In September 1982 a new financial market opened in London; The London International Financial Futures Exchange (LIFFE). In this section we examine the nature and role of this market.

LIFFE is run by a Board of Directors representative of a wide spectrum of city institutions though it is likely that the Bank of England will exercise overall supervision and control. Access to the market is limited to members who in the main come from financial

---

1. This market has now ceased to operate.

institutions such as banks, discount houses, stock exchange firms etc. Consequently dealing by outsiders must be made through a member. Dealing is through the method of 'open outcry' with members standing around a pit indicating offer and acceptance of bids.

The exchange deals in the following securities.

Currencies (all against the $)	Unit of Trading
Sterling	25,000
Swiss Franc	125,000
Deutsche Mark	125,000
Yen	12.5m

Interest rates

Sterling 3 month time deposit	£250,000
Sterling long-dated gilt-edged security	£50,000
Euro-dollar 3 month time deposit	1m$

The nature of a futures contract is that the price is agreed now but the contract is scheduled to operate at a future date. The role of such contracts is to hedge against uncertainty inherent in economic life. To demonstrate this role we consider the example of a company due to receive a payment of £500,000 on 1st January. At the present moment (say 1st December) the company treasurer foresees no immediate use for the funds and plans therefore to invest the £500,000 in a short-term financial security (e.g. a sterling certificate of deposit, or a Treasury Bill). He is unsure what the rate of interest will be on the 1st January but can obtain a hedge against interest rate changes by purchasing a futures contract in respect of a sterling 3 month time deposit. If on the 1st January interest rates have risen, the futures contract will appear less desirable so its price will fall. Consequently when the contract is sold on 1st January, a loss will be incurred but the company will obtain a higher rate of interest than envisaged on the security purchased that day. Similarly if interest rates have fallen the price of the futures contract will rise. This gain will offset the lower rate of interest obtained from the security purchased on the 1st January. Therefore by using the financial futures market the company treasurer is able to lower the range of the prospective returns on the investment carried out later. The degree of the success of the hedge will depend on two factors. First, how closely movements in the return on the futures contract match movements in the return on the financial instrument to be purchased. In this connection it is important to note the limited range of assets traded in the market. Second, how costly the transaction is. In a similar way, traders can hedge against exchange rate changes by entering into futures contracts for the currencies specified above.

One role of the market is therefore to enable economic agents to hedge against future changes. Experience in other financial futures markets suggests that, although futures contracts have a specified time, at least 90% are terminated before the delivery date. This indicates that this type of market is mainly used for covering risks rather than taking delivery of the contract concerned. Of course the market also provides a vehicle for speculators to attempt to gain from 'beating' the market.

2.10 Concluding remarks: the Wilson Committee Report[1]

In early 1977, the so-called Wilson Committee was established to review (i) the financial institutions and their supervisory arrangements and (ii) the provision of funds for industry and trade. On the provision of funds, the committee expressed general satisfaction with the UK financial system and put forward the view that the main reasons for Britain's relatively poor investment performance arose from the unwillingness of UK firms to undertake the required expenditure. The committee was divided over whether to set up a new public or semi-public institution to provide finance for industry. On the other hand the committee was agreed that a re-discount facility for some of the banks medium-term lending to industry was desirable. The rationale behind this suggestion was that strict application of monetary policy may prevent the banking sector from meeting the financial requirements of industry. The solution arrived at by the committee is for the government to issue additonal gilt-edged stock to the banks and use the proceeds to re-finance bank lending.

With regard to the financial institutions, the report provides excellent reading on the nature and functions of the financial institutions and relevant markets. The committee drew attention to the growing importance, if not dominance, of the pension funds in the capital markets. The general tenor of their recommendations concerning the operation of pension funds was greater disclosure of information to members and more representation for members on

1. Committee to Review the Functioning of Financial Institutions, Cmnd 7937, HMSO.

the governing bodies. Regarding banks, the committee was opposed to nationalisation and felt generally satisfied with their performance. A minor qualification was made in that some anxiety was expressed that ownership of the clearing house by the banks could be used to restrain competition from potential newcomers. The committee accepted that it had received no evidence that this had actually occurred in the past.

The Wilson Committee did make significant recommendations with respect to the operation of the building societies.First, they felt that the cartel for recommending deposit and mortgage rates should be abolished in order to stimulate competition amongst the various societies. Second, it was argued that the societies should pay tax at the full rate of corporation tax rather than at the reduced rate of 40 per cent. Third, it was argued that the composite rate arrangement should be ended. This arrangement enables the building societies to pay interest to depositors net of tax, the societies themselves accounting for the basic tax due by their depositors. This particular proposal was part of a wider suggestion that all deposit-taking financial institutions should be treated in the same way for tax purposes.

This review of the Wilson Committee Report has been brief and has only touched on some of the recommendations which are of particular relevance to the institutions discussed in this chapter. The interested reader is recommended to read sections of this report, particularly those dealing with the operation of financial institutions and markets.

3 The Role of Money

3.1 Introduction

Having discussed the nature of UK financial institutions in Chapter 2 we are now in a position to examine the role of money i.e. how money affects the level of economic activity. Clearly at the present time this topic is the subject of considerable controversy and we will indicate some of the main areas of disagreement. We begin by considering the nature and functions of money. Precise definitions of official UK money aggregates are provided in the Appendix A to this chapter.

3.2 The nature of money

Money can be defined as anything which is generally acceptable as a means of payment. The emphasis is on the concept general acceptability. Money could consist of any asset, for example, precious metals, shells, cattle and in prisons even cigarettes have served as money. In the UK today money can be considered to be notes and coins together with bank deposits; note that cheques are merely the means of transferring bank deposits from one person to another and should not be considered as money.

3.2.1 *The functions of money*

Money is normally considered to serve four functions: (i) a medium of exchange; (ii) a store of value; (iii) a unit of account; and (iv) a standard for deferred payments.

(i) *Medium of exchange.* In a modern economy, most transactions are settled in money. Workers receive wages in money and buy goods from shops with the money received. It is in its function as a medium of exchange that money serves its most important use. The only alternative to money is direct barter of goods for goods which is sometimes but not often used e.g. free accommodation for workers in certain jobs where accommodation is provided in return for labour services.

The problem with barter is that it requires what is known as double coincidence of wants i.e. the person selling the good requires another person willing to exchange the commodity required. Barter involves both parties offering the precise quantity and quality of the commodity concerned required by the other party. This is a very onerous requirement not helped by the fact that some commodities are not readily divisible (e.g. how do you exchange half a cow?). The use of money as a medium of exchange has greatly assisted specialisation of labour and trade and therefore the growth of modern economies.

(ii) *Store of value*. Closely connected with the function money serves as a medium of exchange is its use as a store of value. Exchange is not instantaneous, and an economic agent may wish to hold money to buy a good in a month's time. Money allows independence between the timing of receipts of income and making payments. Of course money is just one form in which wealth can be held and the reasons why money is held rather than other assets (e.g. building society deposits) are examined in section 3.4 which deals with the demand for money.

(iii) *Unit of account*. Money also serves as a unit of account i.e. a yardstick in which the value of other commodities and services is measured. For example, company accounts are valued in terms of money. Consider the difficulties of evaluating purchases of various types of materials for car manufacture and subsequent sales of cars other than in monetary terms. Relative prices are easily measured through the use of money. If for example, the price of commodity X is £3 per unit and Y is £1.5 per unit the price of X in terms of Y is 2. Use of money prices enables the relative price of X to be evaluated instantaneously not only in terms of Y but also relative to all other commodities. As we saw in Chapter 1 national output is measured in terms of money rather than in terms of physical output of commodities produced.

(iv) *Standard for deferred payments*. Finally money serves as a standard for deferred payments. Often goods are purchased now with a promise to pay at a later date. An extreme example is the case of house purchase by means of a mortgage. The use of money facilitates this type of transaction and also the payment of interest on deferred payments.

3.2.2. *The properties of good money*

In order to serve these functions money must be endowed with certain properties and it is only against the background of these functions that the desirable properties of money can be considered. These properties are discussed below.

(i) *Stability of value.* If money is to serve as a 'yardstick' then its value should ideally be constant. Recent years have seen persistent inflation which reduces the usefulness of money in all functions. The least affected is that of a medium of exchange, which is only seriously adversely affected by extremely rapid inflation i.e. hyper-inflations. In contrast fairly moderate inflation makes money a less attractive asset to hold as a store of value compared with other assets such as antiques and gold. Inflation also reduces the efficiency of money as a unit of account as evidenced by problems involved in interpreting company accounts over a long run of years and also the divergence between real and nominal GNP examined in Chapter 1.

(ii) *Uniformity.* Clearly money must be of uniform quality to be acceptable. One example of the problem of monies of different qualities circulating together is the circulation of metal coins whose metallic value exceeds their monetary value. Such coins will be used as metal rather than money. This is just one illustration of what is known as Gresham's Law i.e. bad money drives good money out of circulation. In more general terms if two types of money circulate together and one is less attractive than the other the more atttractive asset will be held and the less attractive passed on as money.

(iii) *Portability.* Money must be easily transferable to fulfil its functions. Thus the use of bank deposits with transferability through the cheque system is an admirable monetary system.

(iv) *Divisibility.* Again this requirement is self evident and, as has already been indicated, is one of the problems experienced in direct barter.

(v) *Acceptability.* This is the main requirement as indicated at the beginning of this chapter. Anything can serve as money provided it is generally (i.e. widely) acceptable as a medium of exchange. Acceptability is different from the laws of what constitutes legal tender which only define in what quantities notes and coins are legally acceptable.

(vi) *Durability.* Durability means a good or asset can continue to exist for more than a short period of time. Thus once created a bank deposit will remain in the account of a person until such time as he uses it to make a payment. Contrast this with the situation of an asset which deteriorates (e.g. a melon) and therefore its potential for use as money is extremely limited.

(vii) *Scarcity*. Finally, the supply of an asset to be used as money must be controlled. If every person can create the asset it would not be acceptable. In a modern economy money (i.e. notes and coins) is created by the state and a limited number of financial institutions (i.e. the banks who create deposits).

The astute student will note that the initials of these properties from a mnemonic SUPDADS or PASSDUD!

3.2.3. *The quantity of money*

The problem we are interested in here is how easy it is to identify money in practice. The underlying distinction between money and other assets is the function money serves as a medium of exchange. Notes and coins and deposits with the banks clearly serve as a medium of exchange and are therefore money. Many other assets serve as a store of value, especially deposits, with the non-bank financial intermediaries examined in Chapter 2. Some of these assets are extremely liquid (e.g. deposits with building societies can be withdrawn on demand or within days) but they have to be changed into money before they can be used as a medium of exchange. For this reason these extremely liquid assets are termed 'near money' and the use of the term 'money' is restricted to assets which can be used as a medium of exchange, i.e. notes and coins and bank deposits. Nevertheless our concentration on bank deposits together with notes and coins as money does not imply that there is no ambiguity in the definition of money, especially on the margin. For example, time deposits with banks for which notice of (i) withdrawal or (ii) transmission by means of a cheque is required in principle (if not in practice) are termed money within a broad definition of money whereas deposits with a building society withdrawable on demand, but not chequable, are not classed as money. We discuss the current UK official definitions of money in Appendix A to this chapter.

In fact bank deposits form the major part of the money supply. Further, as we noted in Chapter 2, section 2.3.3, notes and coins are supplied through the Bank of England according to public demand so that subsequent discussion of the control of the money supply will concentrate on the control of the creation of bank deposits.

3.3 The supply of money

Much of current government macroeconomic policy is directed towards control of the money supply so, as a prerequisite to the study of monetary policy, it is necessary to examine the money supply process. In fact two extreme theories have been put forward, one emphasising the supply of bank deposits and the other the role of the demand for bank lending leading to the creation of bank deposits. Of course there is an over-simplification and many economists would take an eclectic or compromise position accepting elements of both theories. Nevertheless it is convenient for the purposes of exposition to assume the existence of these two extreme theories.

3.3.1 *Supply side theories*

In this section we refer back to the analysis of Chapter 2, section 2.4.3. To recapitulate we demonstrated that banks could create bank deposits by expanding the asset side of the balance sheet by either making loans or purchasing securities. The incentive to increase total assets held is that such assets earn a return and thus increase the profitability of the bank. The restraint on the expansion of assets is the requirement to maintain a specified proportion of assets relative to deposits (i.e. a reserve ratio) in the form of reserve assets which ideally would be under the control of the government or central bank. It should also be remembered that it is not essential that a reserve ratio is specified provided the banks themselves work to a customary ratio. To sum up, in this view of the money supply process the creation of bank deposits depends on the supply of reserve assets available to the banks (see Figure 3.1).

In Chapter 2, section 2.4.3 we noted the possibility that in practice banks will hold excess reserves to provide for unforeseen withdrawals of deposits. The opportunity cost of holding excess reserves is the loss of interest receipts which could have been earned if more profitable assets (i.e. financial securities, loans and advances) had been held. It is reasonable to assume that as the rate of interest rises, banks will be less willing to hold excess reserves because of the greater loss of potential earnings. Consequently the money supply will be positively related to the rate of interest (see Figure 3.3) up to the point where deposit creation is constrained by the minimum reserve requirements. Any additional creation of deposits after that point will require banks to obtain additional reserves assets. Nevertheless this is only a minor qualification to the basic idea that creation of money depends on the quantity of reserve assets in existence. The direction of causation is therefore that indicated in Figure 3.1.

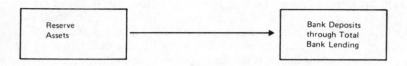

Figure 3.1. Relationship between creation of bank deposits and reserve assets

It remains to explain what determines the supply of reserve assets available to the banks and in order to do this it is necessary to examine how the government finances its expenditure. The public sector borrowing requirement (PSBR) refers to the amount of money the public sector has to borrow after taking into consideration its total expenditure and revenue. The public sector consists of central and local government together with the public corporations (mainly industrialised industries). Total expenditure includes not only expenditure on goods and services but also all current grants to firms and persons, interest payments on money borrowed, and the financing of losses of nationalised industries. Similarly total revenue refers to taxes, repayment of grants, interest received, and profits made by nationalised industries and other public corporations. Finally, it remains to emphasise that the public sector borrowing requirement refers to net borrowing by the public sector from other sectors; all transactions within the public sector having been netted out. In addition to the domestic influences on the PSBR described above there is also that portion arising from intervention in the foreign exchange market. The reasons for and method of intervention are described in the following chapter and it is only necessary to note here that if the Bank of England is selling sterling on the foreign exchange market (i.e. there is an overall balance of payments surplus) then it must raise the sterling which it intends to sell; this is additional to the money the government needs to borrow to finance the gap between its total expenditure and revenue arising from domestic policy considerations (i.e. the PSBR is increased). Similarly if the Bank of England is buying sterling on the foreign exchange market (i.e. there is a balance of payment deficit) it obtains money which the government can use to finance the gap between its expenditure and revenue (i.e. the PSBR is reduced).

In order to examine the connection between the PSBR and the supply of reserve assets available to the banks it is necessary to look at the effect of government expenditure to the private sector on the reserves held by the deposit banks at the Bank of England. Any payment by the government will raise banks' balances at the Bank of England. The recipient of the cheque will lodge the cheque at his bank so that his deposits rise i.e. the money supply increases. On the asset side of its balance sheet the deposit bank will receive a cheque drawn on the Bank of England so quite naturally its balance at the Bank of England will rise. Conversely when a member of the private sector makes a payment to the government, his bank deposit will decrease (i.e. the money supply decreases) as does the bank's balance at the Bank of England. Thus banks' balances (and therefore their reserves) at the Bank of England will increase to the extent that payments by the government to the private sector exceed payments by the private sector to the government. Conversely banks' reserves will fall if payments by the private sector to the government exceed payments to the private sector by the government. The government can finance the PSBR by selling securities which are either marketable (e.g. bonds, Treasury Bills, etc.) or non-marketable (e.g. National Savings). Finance obtained from these sources will not affect the money supply since payments to the government exactly cancel out payments by the government. On the other hand if the PSBR is financed by money creation (i.e. writing out cheques not matched by a corresponding sale of securities) then banks' reserves will increase. This analysis can be prescribed more formally using the following identity to describe the method of financing the PSBR.

$$PSBR = OMO + NMD + BPF + \Delta H \qquad (3.1)$$

where   (i) OMO = sales of marketable securities (termed open market operations)
      (ii) NMD = sales of non-marketable debt
      (iii) BPF = finance obtained through a balance of payments deficit
and   (iv) ΔH = change in banks' reserve assets.

Identity (3.1) is sometimes called the government budget constraint.

Re-arranging (3.1) gives:

$$\Delta H = PSBR - OMO - NMD - BPF \qquad (3.2)$$

showing that the change in banks' reserves is dependent on the method of financing the PSBR. The direction of causation is shown in Figure 3.2 which completes Figure 3.1.

Figure 3.2 brings out the essence of the supply side approach to the determination of the money supply; a PSBR not fully financed by sales of debt will lead to a change in banks' reserve assets and ultimately to a change in the money supply.

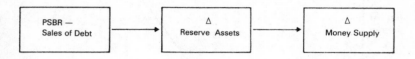

Figure 3.2. Relationship between PSBR, reserve assets and the money supply

3.3.2 *The role of bank lending*
The essence of this alternative is that it is the demand for bank loans which 'drives' the money supply process. It is argued that the demand for bank loans is relatively unresponsive (inelastic) to interest rate changes at least in the short run. An increase in the demand for bank loans is followed by a corresponding increase in the supply of loans from the banks, i.e. the banks are passive in this process. As examined in Chapter 2 the level of bank deposits and therefore the money supply increases. The whole process does however depend on the banks' ability to acquire reserve assets to validate the increased level of deposits. There is considerable evidence that the banks were able to do this under the old reserve regulations which operated until spring 1981. One method employed by the banks was to switch lending to the discount houses from market loans (which were not reserve assets) to money at call (which was a reserve asset).

3.3.3 *Concluding remarks*
Probably the truth lies somewhere between these two extremes so that the money supply is determined by both demand and supply influences. In the following sections we shall assume that the money supply is partly determined by the authorities and partly by the demand for loans and that the quantity of money is responsive to interest rate changes. The shape of the money supply curve is shown in Figure 3.3.

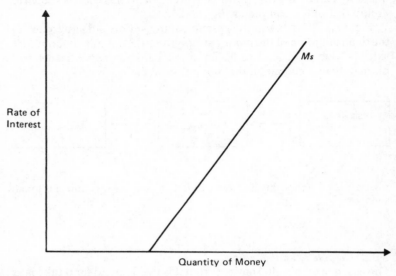

Figure 3.3. The money supply curve

3.4 The demand for money

The concept of the demand for money, or liquidity preference as it is sometimes called, owes much to the work of Lord Keynes. It is important to note that the demand for money, unlike the demand for consumer goods such as butter, is a demand to hold an asset not to consume a good. Consequently it is necessary to explain the factors which determine the quantity of money people wish to hold.

It is customary to distinguish three motives for holding money; (i) the transactions motive, (ii) the precautionary motive and (iii) the speculative motive. The first two are relatively easy to discuss. The transactions motive arises because receipts of income and payments are not precisely synchronised so that the transactor holds money balances to finance expenditure between receipts of income and making payments. For example, many salary owners are paid once a month and hold money balances to finance their transactions such as purchases of food, petrol, entertainment, etc. throughout the period up to the next pay day. Similarly firms will hold money balances to meet current expenditure. Money holdings for this motive will be larger the higher the level of expenditure undertaken and income received. The precautionary motive also depends largely on the level of income and expenditure. As the future is uncertain it is likely that the transactors will hold money balances above the minimum required to finance known current expenditure in order to meet for unforeseen circumstances. The amount of money held for this reason will depend on (i) fluctuations in income and expenditure and (ii) the volume of expenditure. Thus for both the transactions and precautionary motives the quantity of money held will vary directly with income i.e. as income increases so will the quantity of money demanded for transactions and precautionary purposes.

Money is used not only as a medium of exchange but also as a store of value. One reason for holding money as a store of value is for speculative purposes. The quantity of money held for this motive depends primarily on the rate of interest. The idea behind the speculative motive is that the choice facing speculators is to hold money or bonds. Now as we have seen in Chapter 2, section 2.1 the price of bonds and the rate of interest move in opposite directions. If the rate of interest rises bond prices will fall and bond holders will incur a capital loss. Conversely if the rate of interest falls, bond prices will rise and bond holders will obtain a capital gain. Thus bonds will be more attractive to hold if interest rates are expected to fall and money more attractive if interest rates are expected to rise. How do speculators judge the likely future course of interest rates? One explanation is based around the existing level of interest rates. The higher the rate of interest at present, the more likely it is to fall in the future and the more attractive bonds are to hold compared with money because of the anticipated capital gain. Conversely the lower the present rate of interest the less attractive bonds are to hold. It is likely that speculators will have different expectations about how the rate of interest will change. However, it can be argued that the higher the present rate of interest, the greater will be the number of speculators who believe that the interest rate is likely to fall. Consequently the demand for bonds will be larger or equivalently the demand for money smaller. Conversely the lower the current rate of interest, the greater will be the number of speculators who believe that interest rates will rise. Consequently the demand for bonds will be smaller or equivalently the demand for money will be larger. For these reasons the demand curve for money will be downward sloping with respect to the rate of interest. This is illustrated in Figure 3.4.

At interest rate r_1 the quantity of money demanded is M_1. As the rate of interest falls to r_2 the quantity of money demanded increases to M_2.

The demand curve shown in Figure 3.4 is drawn on the assumption that income and therefore the quantity of money demanded for transactions and precautionary motives remains

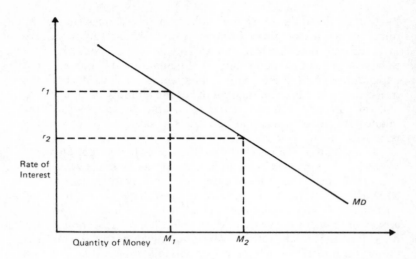

Figure 3.4. The demand curve for money

constant. If income rises so will the quantity of money demanded for transactions and precautionary motives so that the demand curve in Figure 3.4 will shift outwards (i.e. to the right). Conversely a fall in income will reduce the transactions and precautionary demand for money and will cause the demand curve to shift inwards (i.e. to the left).

The speculative motive is not the only reason for holding money as a store of value. First, quite simply, the higher the rate of interest the higher the opportunity cost i.e. the greater the interest on bonds given up to hold money. Second, money is capital certain whereas the capital value of bonds fluctuates according to the rate of interest i.e. there is a risk inherent in the holding of bonds. Economic agents require a return on bonds to overcome their dislike of risk i.e. in technical jargon they are 'risk averse'. The higher the rate of interest the more they overcome their risk aversion and the more bonds (and therefore less money) they wish to hold. Consequently both these reasons for holding money also predict that the quantity of money demanded will increase as the rate of interest falls.

The slope of the demand curve for money depends on the existence or absence of close substitutes for money. If close substitutes existed a slight rise in the rate of interest would cause a large movement out of money into other assets to take advantage of the higher return provided by them. Conversely a fall in the rate of interest would lead to a large movement out of these other assets into money. This would mean that the money demand curve shown in Figure 3.4 would be relatively flat. In the limiting case of perfect substitutablity of money for other assets the demand curve would be horizontal. Conversely a low substitutability of money for other assets would lead to a relatively steep money demand curve. In the limiting case of no substitutes the money demand curve would be vertical (i.e. the money demand curve would be perfectly inelastic with respect to the rate of interest.)

Types of assets which might be close substitutes for money are bonds and deposits with non-bank financial intermediaries. One way to check the degree of substitutability of these assets for money is to look at the empirical evidence on the demand for money. If empirical studies show that the quantity of money demanded is very responsive to interest rate changes these assets are close substitutes for money and vice versa. In fact the evidence suggest that the demand for money does depend on the rate of interest in the manner specified above but that the degree of responsiveness (i.e. elasticity) is quite low. Consequently empirical evidence suggests that there is a quite low degree of substitutability between money and bonds i.e. that vertical and horizontal demand for money curves do not exist in the real world.

In the analysis so far money has been considered to be a substitute for financial assets. However Milton Friedman in his restatement of the Quantity Theory of Money has argued that money is a substitute for a wide range of assets. In his view money is not a particularly close substitute for any asset. Money is regarded as being unique in that it is a temporary abode of purchasing power which can be used to purchase any other type of asset, not just financial assets. Consequently the quantity of money demanded will depend on the rate of return not only on financial assets but also on real assets. How are we to measure the return on real assets? To do this the concept of a rate of interest must be broadened to include the return on assets other than financial assets. Returns on holding real assets such as, for example, houses or consumer durables consist of a stream of future services and this can be related to the cost of the asset in the form of a rate of interest. This reasoning can be applied to all assets which are not consumed immediately though in most cases it must be recognised that these rates of interest are implicit rather than explicit since they are not quoted in any market. One particular component of the return on real assets is the rate of inflation. In times of inflation real assets such as gold or antiques whose prices change in line with inflation may prove to be more attractive than either bonds or money

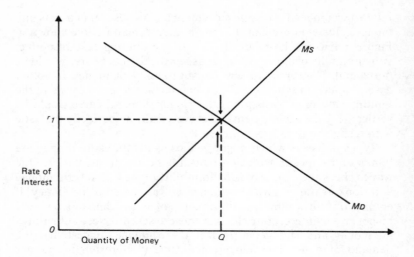

Figure 3.5. The determination of the equilibrium rate of interest

which are fixed in nominal terms and whose real value declines with inflation.

3.5 Interest rates

There are two main approaches to the theory of interest rates; (i) monetary theory and (ii) loanable funds theory. These theories are surveyed in sections 3.5.1 to 3.5.3 while in section 3.5.4 we discuss the reasons why interest rates differ.

3.5.1 *Monetary theory of interest rates*

In Keynesian analysis the rate of interest is determined by the demand for and supply of money. The equilibrium rate of interest will occur where the quantity of money demanded is equal to that supplied. This is demonstrated in Figure 3.5 (a combination of Figures 3.3 and 3.4).

The equilibrium rate of interest is Or_1. At this rate both the quantity of money demanded and that supply are equal to OQ. At a rate of interest above Or_1 the quantity of money supplied would exceed the quantity demanded. Economic agents would try to dispose of their excess money balances by purchasing bonds i.e. the substitute for money. This would cause bond prices to rise and the rate of interest to fall. Alternatively economic agents might deposit some of their excess money holdings with NBFIs. As their deposits increased NFBIs would wish to expand their scale of lending and in order to do this they would lower their rates of interest. The effect therefore would be the same whether the excess money balances were used to buy bonds or were deposited with NFBIs. Similarly if the market rate of interest is less than Or_1 the quantity of money demanded would exceed that supplied. Agents would try to get hold of extra money balances by selling bonds (i.e. the substitute for money) and/or withdrawing deposits from NFBIs. This would cause bond prices to fall and the rate of interest to rise. The chain of reaction is indicated on Figure 3.5 by the arrows.

The rate of interest will change following changes in (i) the supply of money, (ii) the general price level or (iii) the demand for money.

Changes in the money supply
An increase in the supply of money (due, for example, to an increase in the reserve base) will cause the rate of interest to fall. This is demonstrated in Figure 3.6.

The original supply curve of money is M^S_1 with the corresponding equilibrium level of the rate of interest Or_1. An increase in the supply of money (M^S_1 to M^S_2) causes the equilibrium rate of interest to fall to Or_2. The adjustment process is essentially the same as that described above. At the original rate of interest Or_1 there is an excess supply of money equal to AB so that bond purchases and/or deposits with NFBIs would cause the rate of interest to fall. The converse would occur for a decrease in the supply of money i.e. a rise in the rate of interest would occur.

Changes in the general price level
So far we have discussed the demand for and supply of money without mentioning the price level. When we discussed the demand for money we indicated the role of the transactions and precautionary motives. Clearly these motives are a demand for money expressed in terms of purchasing power or more technically real money balances. In fact it is normally held that the total demand for money is a demand for real money balances. The problem is how to measure the real quantity of money and the method usually used is to divide the nominal quantity of money (i.e. the number of £s) by a general index of prices. Regardless of the method of measurement an increase in the price level, given the nominal quantity of money, will reduce the real value of the money supply leading to an excess demand for money at the original rate of interest. Economic agents would try to obtain extra money balances by selling bonds and/or withdrawing deposits from non-bank financial intermediaries

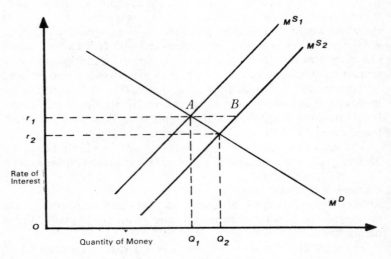

Figure 3.6. An increase in the supply of money

causing the rate of interest to rise. In terms of Figure 3.6 this can be demonstrated by a shift to the left of the money supply curve.

Thus interest rates will rise if (i) the nominal quantity of money supplied is reduced given the price level or (ii) the price level rises given the nominal quantity of money. Conversely the rate of interest will fall if either (i) the nominal quantity of money is increased given the price level or (ii) the price level falls given the nominal quantity of money.

Changes in the demand for money

The effect of an increase in the demand for money is to cause the rate of interest to rise. For example, if GNP increased this would lead to an increase in the demand for money (i.e. for transactions and precautionary purposes) causing the demand curve to shift to the right. This is demonstrated in Figure 3.7.

The original money curve is M^D_1 with the corresponding equilibrium rate of interest Or_1. The new money demand curve is M^D_2 so that the rate of interest rises to Or_2. The reason for the increase in the rate of interest is the familiar one that there is an excess demand for money at the original rate of interest Or_1 or equal to AB. This provokes bond sales and/or withdrawals from NFBIs and therefore leads to an increase in the rate of interest.

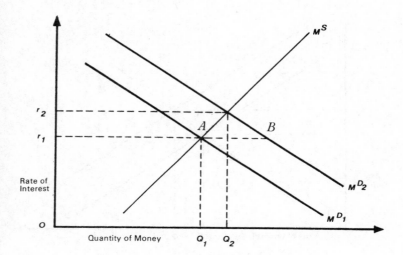

Figure 3.7. An increase in the demand for money

3.5.2 *Loanable funds theory*

The analysis we have so far discussed is essentially Keynesian in nature. The rate of interest is determined by monetary forces namely the demand for and supply of money. There is however another alternative explanation of the rate of interest, which considers the demand for and supply of loanable funds. The demand for loanable funds arises from firms and individuals who wish to borrow to finance their expenditure mainly for the purpose of investment. On the other hand the supply of loanable funds is provided by those who wish to save and who are willing to lend their savings. The determinants of demand and supply can be summed up in the catch phrase 'productivity and thrift'. Productivity shows how profitable borrowing is and thrift the propensity to save. The rate of interest in this theory equates the demand for and supply of such funds. The supply of loanable funds is considered to be a positive function of the rate of interest since a higher rate of interest is necessary to induce people to save more and abstain from consumption, i.e. the supply curve in Figure 3.8 slopes upwards. In Chapter 1, section 1.3.1 we showed that investment declines as the rate of interest increases. Consequently the demand for loanable funds is a negative function of the rate of interest, i.e. the demand curve in Figure 3.8 slopes downwards.

The equilibrium rate of interest (i.e. r_1) occurs where the quantity

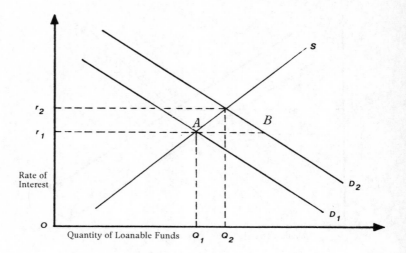

Figure 3.8. An increase in the demand for loanable funds

of loanable funds demanded equals that supplied. Changes in either the demand or supply of loanable funds will alter the rate of interest. For example, an increase in the demand for loanable funds will shift the D curve to the right to D_2 causing the equilibrium rate of interest to rise to r_2 because there is an excess demand for loanable funds, equal to AB at the original rate of interest Or_1. Competition amongst would-be borrowers will force the rate of interest up to Or_2 at which point the demand for and supply of funds will again be equal to each other. In a similar manner an increase in the supply of loanable funds would cause the equilibrium rate of interest to fall.

3.5.3 *Reconciliation of the monetary and loanable funds theory*
Is it possible to reconcile these two theories about how the rate of interest is determined? The demand for and supply of money emphasises the role of stocks, and provides an explanation of the rate of interest in terms of equilibrium between the supply of and demand for stocks. As such it is a short-run theory. In contrast the loanable funds theory is concerned with flows of funds and the determinants of the flows (productivity and thrift) both of which are long-run phenomena. Thus a possible reconciliation of the two theories lies in the different time horizons implicit in them. In the short run the monetary explanation is dominant and it is possible for the market

for loanable funds not to be in equilibrium. However in the long run full equilibrium will require both markets to be in equilibrium and the flows will probably dominate the situation.

3.5.4 *Differing rates of interest*

Up to now we have assumed a single rate of interest but casual observation suggests that this is not true. For example, mortgage rates of interest are different from those charged by hire purchase firms. Consequently it is necessary to interpret 'the' rate of interest discussed above as referring to the average level of interest rates or perhaps an index of the level of interest rates. We now examine what determines differences in interest rates within that average level.

Some of these differences can be attributed to differences in risk both with respect to the purpose for which the loan is required and also the standing of the borrower. For example, a major industrial company is able to achieve access to borrowing at lower rates of interest than smaller companies because it offers a lower risk of default. Similarly loans for house purchase are secured by a safe asset (i.e. the house) and consequently are charged at lower rates of interest than hire purchase loans where the quality of the assets is more suspect. Again differences in the treatment of tax play a role in the differences between interest rates. For example, the Building Societies have an arrangement whereby they pay tax to the Inland Revenue so that the recipient of the interest on deposits with Building Societies pays no further tax as long as he is paying income tax at the standard rate.

The term structure

However, even after allowing for these factors, significant differences still remain and these may be attributed to the term or duration of loan. The differing rates of interest due entirely to differences in the term of borrowing are called the term structure of interest rates. The term structure can be depicted graphically and is called the yield curve, but again it must be stressed that drawing a yield curve is only permissable for similar assets with different terms of maturity e.g. UK Government stock with, for example, five, six years, etc. to maturity.

Yield curves (the term yield to maturity was discussed in Chapter 2, section 2.1) may take a variety of shapes but the most common is of the form shown in Figure 3.9. At other times the yield curve has been relatively flat or even sloped downwards. We wish to indicate three explanations of the yield curve: (i) expectations theory; (ii) liquidity premium; and (iii) preferred market habitat.

First, the expectations theory predicts that given perfect foresight

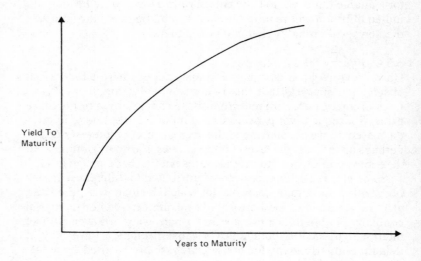

Figure 3.9. Yield curve

the long-term interest rate will be an average of the current short term rate and future expected short-term rates. Consider, for example, a one year rate: amongst other options open to the borrower and lender are four three-month loans. Thus the one-year rate should equal the average of the current three-month rate and the expected three-month rate for the subsequent quarter. Assuming that (i) arithmetic averages approximately the true situation, [1](ii) the current three-month rate is 5 per cent and (iii) is subsequently expected to be 6 per cent for the next two quarters and 7 per cent for the last quarter. The average rate would then be 6 per cent i.e.

$$\frac{(5 + 6 + 6 + 7)}{4}$$

If the one-year return is more than 6 per cent funds will flow out of the short market into the long market thus raising short-term rates and lowering long-term rates until consistency between the two rates is established. The converse would apply if the long-term rate were

1. The true average should involve geometric means but we have taken the arithmetic mean as an approximation.

lower than the average of the actual and expected short-term rates. The expectations theory predicts that the yield curve would slope upwards if interest rates were expected to rise—in our example the one year rate is greater than the short-term rate. On the other hand the yield curve would slope downwards if interest rates were expected to fall. If no change is expected in future rates of interest the yield curve would be horizontal.

The expectations theory does not predict that one yield curve shape will be dominant; over long periods of time interest rates cannot on average rise more than they fall. It therefore fails to explain why upward sloping yield curves are more common than other types of yield curve. However as soon as we relax the assumption of perfect foresight, an alternative explanation comes into the analysis. Long-term lending involves a risk of the investor incurring capital losses on an asset because of unforeseen rises in interest rates and therefore falls in the value of the security should he need to encash it before maturity. The lender will therefore expect a premium in the interest rate over and above the short-term rate before he is willing to lend for a longer period. Similarly the borrower will be willing to pay this premium to avoid having to go to the market more frequently. Thus the existence of a liquidity premium will ensure that the normal yield curve will slope upwards, i.e. consistent with empirical evidence. However this shape would be modified in the light of expectations of future interest rate changes. If interest rates were expected to rise then the yield curve would slope upwards more steeply than normal. If they were expected to fall, the yield curve would slope upwards less steeply,or if the expected fall was quite large the yield curve would slope downwards. Thus a combination of the expectations and liquidity theories is capable of explaining all types of yield curve observed in practice.

The preferred market habitat theory stresses market segmentation of financial markets i.e. the assets traded in the markets are not perfect substitutes so that arbitrage will not ensure strict equality between current rates and future expected rates in the manner described above. In its extreme form, the theory suggests that no switching at all between the various assets is possible so that rates of interest in the various markets represent demand and supply conditions in that market. Higher long-term rates reflect the situation that there is an inbalance between demand and supply since borrowers prefer to borrow long and lenders lend short. The extreme version of the preferred market habitat is however inconsistent with the alternative shapes of the yield curve observed unless the various transactors' preferences change remarkably quickly.

To sum up, therefore, the term structure of interest rates reflects the influence of expectations, liquidity premiums and market segmentation.

3.5.5 *Concluding remarks*
As we have noted in section 3.5.4 there is no such thing as 'the' rate of interest. Our explanation of the rate of interest in sections 3.5.1 to 3.5.2 must therefore be taken to refer to the average level of interest rates. For example, an increase in the money supply will lower the average level of interest rates. Subsequently when we discuss the rate of interest it should be remembered that in fact we are using the term 'the' rate of interest as a convenient short hand for the average level of differing rates of interest.

3.6 Money and economic activity

3.6.1. *The Keynesian view*
In this section we shall consider the connection between money and economic activity in quite general terms without discussing how the effects of monetary changes will be divided between real output and price changes. This topic will be examined in Chapter 5 on inflation.

The Keynesian view on the relationship between money and economic activity follows on quite naturally from the discussion of the previous section. Changes in the money supply initially affect the rate of interest. The consequent change in the rate of interest affects aggregate economic activity by causing changes in investment. In Chapter 1, section 1.3.1 we indicated that one of the determinants of investment is the cost of borrowing funds i.e. the rate of interest. A reduction in the rate of interest will lead to an increase in investment (i.e. aggregate demand) and therefore a rise in real output (assuming the existence of unemployment and the absence of any supply side constraints as per Chapter 1). The size of the increase in national income will itself depend on the size of multiplier. The whole process can be illustrated using the 45° line diagram of Chapter 1 (see Figure 3.10).

Investment increases from I_1 to I_2 (ΔI) following a reduction in the rate of interest (Δr). This causes an increase in national income from Y_1 to Y_2 (ΔY). Conversely a reduction in the money supply will lead to a reduction in real income via a reduction in investment due to the rise in the rate of interest.

Thus the Keynesian view of how money affects economic activity can be illustrated by a simple flow diagram (Figure 3.11).

This transmission mechanism can be broadened if consumption

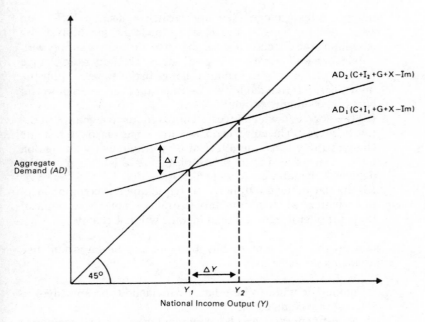

Figure 3.10. An increase in the supply of money

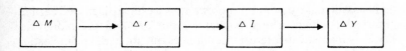

Figure 3.11. The transmission mechanism

(especially consumer durables) is also affected by interest rate changes. This does not however alter the basic hypothesis that changes in the money supply affect real economic activity via changes in the rate of interest. Within the transmission mechanism the importance of money depends on:

(1) the degree to which the rate of interest changes following a change in the money supply. This will depend mainly on how responsive (i.e. elastic) the demand for money is with respect to the rate of interest. The lower the responsiveness the more

interest rates change (see arguments in section 3.5). The interested reader can prove this statement for himself by examining the effects of a given change in the money supply with money demand curves of varying slopes. The larger the change in the rate of interest following a change in the money supply the more likely it is that money will be important i.e. have a powerful effect on economic activity.

(2) the degree to which investment responds to a change in the rate of interest. The more responsive investment is to interest rate changes the greater the effect of a given monetary change on national income, i.e. in terms of Figure 3.10 the more the aggregate demand curve will shift upwards.

(3) the size of the multiplier. This requirement is common to all disturbances whether monetary in origin or not. For example, if the multiplier is zero national income will not change.

To sum up the argument so far, for money to be important two requirements are necessary:

(i) money demand to be relatively inelastic (unresponsive) to interest rate changes; and
(ii) investment (and/or other components of aggregate demand) to be fairly responsive (i.e. elastic) to changes in the rate of interest.

Both these requirements are necessary; failure of either in Keynesian analysis will make money unimportant. As we have discussed earlier empirical evidence suggests that (i) the demand for money is relatively inelastic to interest rate changes but not perfectly inelastic, and (ii) investment and spending on consumer durables do respond to interest rate changes but the degree of response is quite low. However, the view that money affects aggregate demand only through changes in the interest rate has itself been criticised by monetarists. They dispute the view that monetary changes influence the real economy only via changes in the rate of interest. Why should money not be a substitute fo real assets as well as financial assets such as bonds? This view is enshrined in the quantity theory approach to which we now turn.

3.6.2 *The quantity theory approach*
The original quantity theory has a long history dating back at least to the middle of the seventeenth century but perhaps received its most well known exposition at the beginning of this century by an

American economist, Irving Fisher. In this version of the quantity theory money is viewed as a substitute for goods. Any agent who has excess money balances will try to get rid of these balances by spending them on goods. Society as a whole cannot get rid of money balances in this way since money spent by one individual is merely received by another member of that society (assuming no foreign trade). If we assume that the economy is at full employment, then the extra demand created by agent's attempts to get rid of excess money balances will cause prices to rise consequently bringing about equality between the amount of money in existence and the demand for it. In other words excess money balances will be eliminated due to the price rises causing a reduction in real balances held.

We now analyse the quantity theory more formally. The basic equation of exchange is:

$$MV = PT \qquad (3.3)$$

where (1) M = the quantity of money
      (2) V = the velocity of circulation (the average number of times money exchanges hands to finance all transactions)
      (3) P = the average price per transaction
and (4) T = the total number of transactions per time period.

V was considered to be fixed by institutional factors which were thought to change slowly over time. Thus for practical purposes V could be assumed to be constant.

At the time of the formulation of this version of the quantity theory economists believed that the economy tended to move towards a full employment equilibrium. Therefore T could also be considered a constant. The quantity of money theory was held to be exogenous i.e. independent of V, T or P. The combination of these assumptions led to the well known prediction of the traditional quantity theory that changes in the money supply lead to proportionate changes in the price level. In other words a 10 per cent increase in the money supply will produce a 10 per cent increase in the average price per transaction when equilibrium is re-established. However it is important to realise that this prediction does refer to equilibrium situations.

This analysis can easily be demonstrated by a simple rearrangement of (3.3) above.

$$P = / \frac{V}{T} / M \qquad (3.4)$$

Since both V and T are constant

$$\frac{V}{T}$$

is a constant and (3.4) may be written.

$$P = \alpha M \qquad (3.5)$$

where α is some constant.

Money affects real output only in the short run; in the long run it is argued that changes in money are entirely reflected by proportionate changes in the average price per transaction P. Empirical evidence suggests that the quantity theory is more applicable to the long run than the short run. In the long run, the economy tends to full employment whereas in the short run quite clearly periods of unemployment are observed. This helps to account for the eclipse of the quantity approach by Keynesian liquidity preference analysis from the late 1930s through to the 1950s.

In the 1960s however Friedman's restatement of the quantity theory gained credence. As we examined in section 3.4, Friedman argued that the choice with regard to liquidity preference was not just between money and finacial assets but should be extended to permit substitution between money, finacial, and real assets. Consequently an increase in money would affect aggregate demand directly as the money was substituted not just for bonds but also (i) new real assets especially consumer durables and (ii) existing real assets. In fact, as we shall see in Chapter 5, it is held that in the long run changes in the money supply will only affect prices not real output, i.e. the analysis is in the quantity theory tradition.

APPENDIX A

UK Definitions of the Quantity of Money

A3.1 Money supply

There are three official definitions of the UK money supply in current use. These refer to M1 (narrow definition) sterling M3 and M3 (broad definition). Sterling M3 is used for the purpose of calculating and publishing monetary targets. M1 is defined as the sum of:

(1) notes and coins in circulation with the non-bank private sector; and
(2) sterling sight deposits held by the private sector with the monetary sector (see section A3.2).

Sterling M3 is defined as the sum of:

(1) M1;
(2) sterling deposits (both sight and time) held by the public sector with the monetary sector; and
(3) sterling time deposits held by the private sector with the monetary sector.

M3 is defined as:

Sterling M3 plus all deposits held by UK residents with the monetary sector in currencies other than sterling.

Note the exclusion from these definitions of:

(i) sterling deposits held by non-residents with the UK monetary sector;
(ii) foreign currency deposits held by residents with overseas banks and monetary institutions.

A3.2 The UK monetary sector

This sector includes:

(i) all recognised banks and licensed deposit-takers
(ii) the National Giro
(iii) the Trustee Savings Banks
(iv) the banking department of the Bank of England
(v) banks resident in the Channel Islands and the Isle of Man
who opt to join the cash deposit scheme.

A3.3 Eligible liabilities

The basis of the calculation of the banks' (i) cash deposit (see Chapter 9,section 9.6) and (ii) any special deposit liability (see Chapter 2, section 2.3.2) is eligible liabilities. Calculations of total eligible liabilities is designed to represent an institution's net deposit liability after allowing for holdings of similar assets.

The institution's total eligible liabilities are defined as:

(1) all sterling deposits from UK non-bank residents and overseas residents with an original maturity of less than two years plus funds temporarily held in suspense accounts
(2) net sterling deposits from UK banks
(3) net issues of Certificates of Deposit
(4) net sterling liabilities to an overseas office
(5) net liability in currencies other than sterling
(6) 60 per cent of transit items
less
(7) funds (other than those covered in category 2 above) lent to other institutions in the monetary sector
less
(8) secured money at call placed with money brokers and gilt-edged jobbers on the Stock Exchange.

A3.4 Domestic Credit Expansion

Domestic Credit Expansion (DCE) in any period is equal to the increase in the money stock after adjustment for a change in money balances due to the overall balance of payments situation. It is therefore a special kind of credit in that it only incorporates credit which leads to monetary expansion. It is used as an indicator of domestically generated credit which directly leads to an increase in sterling M3. The two principal components of DCE are (i) that portion of the PSBR which is not financed by purchase of debt by the UK private sector other than the monetary sector and (ii) the increase in the stock of lending to the private sector by the monetary sector.

Note that although the money stock is calculated from the liabilities side of the balance sheets of the institutions within the monetary sector, DCE is calculated (explicitly or implicitly) from the asset side. The relationships between the PSBR,DCE and sterling M3 are shown below:

1 PSBR
2 − purchases of securities by the UK non-bank private sector
3 + sterling lending by institutions within the UK monetary sector to the UK private sector
4 + overseas lending in sterling by institutions within the UK monetary sector.
  = DCE
5 + change in external foreign currency finance of the public sector (− = increase)
6 + change in overseas sterling deposits (− = increase)
7 + change in banks' foreign currency deposits net of foreign currency assets (− = increase)
8 + change in banks' non-deposit liabilities (− = increase)
  = change in sterling M3.

Items 5, 6 and 7 are broadly speaking the counterpart of the current account plus surplus/deficit plus net capital flows to the UK private sector in the balance of payments account.

A3.5 Private sector liquidity

Two measures of private sector liquidity (PSL 1 an PSL 2) are published in the official statistics. The cut-off in the definition of what constitutes liquid assets as opposed to non-liquid assets is bound to be arbitrary. In principle liquid assets are defined as sterling assets within one year of maturity or realisable in one year without loss. In practice because of the lack of adequate statistics it is necessary in most cases to modify the definition to assets with an original maturity of less than one year plus realisable assets.

It is helpful to consider private sector liquidity being compromised of four blocks:

(1) money. The customary definition of sterling M3 is used to define private sector liquidity save for the exclusion of (i) time deposits and certificates of deposit with an original maturity of more than two years (no other deatils of the split are available) and (ii) all public sector deposits;
(2) other money market instruments including Treasury Bills, bank bills, deposits with local authorities and deposits with finance houses, less finance houses' holdings of money and

other money market instruments;
(3) savings deposits and securities including shares and deposits with building societies and national savings securities, less building societies' deposits with monetary institutions;
(4) certificates of tax deposit.

In general terms, apart from some minor differences in definitions, PSL1 consisit of blocks (1), (2) and (4) whereas PSL2 consists of all four blocks.

4 International Economy

4.1. Introduction

In Chapter 1 we discussed how a change in the level of exports or imports will affect domestic output. Initially it was assumed that exports were autonomously determined (i.e. independent of changes in the level of domestic income and output), while imports depended on the level of domestic demand. In this chapter we will examine more fully the determinants of the level of exports and imports and the nature of international transactions. We will begin our discussion by examining the nature of a country's balance of payments.

4.2 Balance of payments accounts

4.2.1 *Nature of the balance of payments*

A country's balance of payments account record all economic transactions undertaken between its residents and those of foreign countries during a given period (e.g. a year). Thus, for example, British manufacturers who export to the US eventually require payment for their goods in sterling. American importers can either: (i) pay British manufacturers in dollars who in turn exchange them for sterling; or (ii) exchange dollars for sterling and pay British manufacturers for their goods in sterling. All receipts from non-residents are termed credits and give rise to: (i) supplies of foreign currency (i.e. dollars in the above example) and (ii) a demand for domestic currency (i.e sterling in the above example). In contrast debit items result from payments by residents to non-residents (e.g. UK imports from America) and give rise to: (i) a demand for foreign currency and (ii) supplies of domestic currency.

Credits and debits in the balance of payments can arise from two types of transactions: first, transactions in goods and services which are recorded in the current account; second, transactions in capital assets (both real and financial) which are recorded in the capital account. The sum of the current and capital accounts shows what is called the balance for official financing i.e. the net balance of all transactions between residents and non-residents.

4.2.2 *Current account*
The current account of the balance of payments records all trans-actions of current purchases of goods and services. In the UK the current account is subdivided into: (i) the balance of 'visible' trade, which measures the difference between the value of goods exported and those imported (e..g. raw materials, foodstuffs, manufactured goods, etc.); and (ii) the 'invisible' balance (i.e. services), which includes expenditure on such items as tourism, shipping, banking, insurance, and other invisible items such as property income (e.g. interest and dividends on loans and investments) and transfers (e.g. government aid and EEC contributions). The current account will be in deficit when the total value of imported goods (i.e. all visibles) and services (i.e. all invisible items) is greater than the total value of goods and services exported, and vice versa. A deficit corresponds to a situation where expenditure made to non-residents is greater than receipts from abroad. Conversely a surplus occurs when payments to non-residents are less than receipts from abroad. In order to give some idea of the magnitude and importance of the various components of the current account Table 4.1 shows the UK balance of payments on current account in 1980.

In 1980 there was a visible trade surplus of £1,178 million. This surplus was supplemented by a surplus of £2,028 million on the invisible balance leaving an overall balance of payments surplus of £3,206 million on current account. It is interesting to note that the balance of earnings from interest, profits and dividends corresponds to the concept of net property income from abroad discussed in Chapter 1.

4.2.3 *Investment and other capital flows*
This section of the balance of payments is loosely termed the capital account and records the borrowing and lending of funds by residents from and non-residents of that country. Capital transactions include: (i) short-term capital movements (e.g. purchases of short-term assets such as Treasury Bills and other money market assets); and (ii) long-term capital movements (e.g. borrowing and lending by individuals and firms, investment in new plant and machinery, purchases and sales of existing real and financial assets, etc.). The net capital flow can be positive (i.e. an inflow of funds to the domestic country) or negative (i.e. an outflow of funds from the domestic country). For example, if borrowing exceeds lending of funds abroad a net capital inflow will occur. In the UK the difference between the

TABLE 4.1. UK balance of payments on current account, 1980
(£ million)

	Receipts from abroad (exports)	Payments to non-residents (imports)	Balance (+ Surplus) (− Deficit)
Visible (goods)	47,389	46,211	+1,178
Invisibles { services	15,809	11,621	+4,188
property income	8,204	8,242	− 38
transfers	1,751	3,873	−2,122
	25,764	23,736	+2,028
Total	73,153	69,947	+3,206

Source: Central Statistical Office (1981), United Kingdom Balance of Payments (Pink Book), (London: HMSO), Tables 1.1 and 1.2.

balance on the current account and the net capital flow is known as the total currency flow or the balance for official financing. In 1980 this balance was £1,192 million (see Table 4.2).

TABLE 4.2 UK overall balance of payments, 1980
(£ million)

Current account balance	+3,206
Balance of investment and other capital transactions (including the balancing item[a])	−2,014
Balance for official financing	+1,192

Source: Central Statistical Office (1981), United Kingdom Balance of Payments (Pink Book), (London: HMSO), Tables 1.1 and 1.2.
Note: (a) The balancing item reflects errors and omissions in recording international transactions.

The surplus of £3,206 million on the current account was partially offset by a deficit of £2,014 million on the capital account, leaving a positive balance for official financing of £1,192 million.

4.2.4 *Official financing*
The official financing section of the balance of payments shows either: (i) how any deficit on the combined current and capital accounts has been financed, or alternatively (ii) how any surrplus on the two accounts has been used.

A deficit (i.e. where total debits exceed total credits) can be financed officially by: (i) running down a country's gold and foreign exchange reserves; and/or (ii) borrowing from abroad (e.g. from foreign central banks or the International Monetary Fund). Conversely a surplus (i.e. where total credits exceed total debits) allows a country to: (i) build up its gold and foreign exchange reserves; and/or (ii) reduce its liabilities (i.e. repay previous borrowings) with official foreign monetary authorities.

In 1980, the UK received an allocation of Special Drawing Rights (see Chapter 14) of £180 million making a total surplus (including SDRs) of £1,372 million. As shown in Table 4.3 this surplus was used to: (i) add to official reserves (£291 million); (ii) repay previous borrowings of (£1.081 million).

It is important to note that as a financial statement the overall sum of the balance of payments is zero (i.e. it always balances) since the sum of the current and capital accounts is always matched by an

TABLE 4.3. Official financing

(£ million)

1. Balance for official financing	1,192
2. Allocation of SDRs	180
Total official financing	1,372
3. Additions to official reserves	291
4. Repayment of previous borrowing	1,081
	1,372

Source: Central Statistical Office (1981), United Kingdom Balance of Payments (Pink Book), (London: HMSO), Tables 1.1 and 10.1.
Note that in the presentation of the accounts items 3 and 4 are shown with negative signs so that the overall total balances to zero.

exactly equivalent balance (but one with an opposite sign) in the official financing section. It is also important to realise that this does not imply that the balance of payments is in equilibrium. Clearly a deficit on the combined current and capital accounts cannot be financed indefinitely by running down official reserves because in the limit official reserves will run out. Equilibrium is not ensured when the sum of the current and capital accounts is zero since the authorities may be concerned with the composition of the accounts. For example, for reasons examined in Chapter 6 (section 6.5) it is not possible for a current account deficit to be financed indefinitely by a capital account surplus. The concept of equilibrium in the balance of payments is discussed further in Chapter 6, section 6.5.

Table 4.4 shows a useful summary of our discussion so far with respect to the nature of the balance of payments, while Table 4.5 shows the main components of the UK balance of payments as percentages of GNP (at factor cost) over the period 1972-82.

4.3 The determination of the level of imports
The main determinants of the demands for imports are: (i) income; (ii) relative prices (i.e. the price of domestically produced goods relative to the price of similar goods produced abroad); and (iii) other factors such as tastes, quality of the goods, delivery dates, etc.

First, changes in domestic aggregate income will affect the level of imports into a country. This relationship between imports and national income was discussed in Chapter 1, section 1.3. To recapitulate, as domestic income rises, aggregate demand will increase and

TABLE 4.4. The balance of payments

	£	£	£
Current account:			
Value of exports (credits)			
− value of imports (debits)			
	———		
= balance of trade			
+ value of invisible exports (credits)			
− value of invisible imports (debits)			
		———	
= balance on current account			
Investment and other capital flows:			
Inflows of capital (credits)			
− outflows of capital (debits)			
		———	
= balance on the capital account			———
Balance for official financing			
(= sum of current and capital account			
balances)			
			———
Official financing:			
Changes in reserves			
(decreases if balance for official financing is negative,			
increases if positive)			
Changes in official borrowing			
(increases if balance for official financing is negative,			
decreases if positive)			
			———
Total (= balance for official financing,			
but with opposite sign)			
			———

some portion of this increase in demand will be met by imported goods i.e. the marginal propensity to import is greater than zero. Conversely as aggregate demand decreases the quantity of imports will also decrease. The relationship between aggregate demand and imports may not be proportional since during a period of boom domestic bottlenecks may appear as the economy approaches a situation of full employment causing imports to rise more than proportionately to the increase in aggregate demand.

Second, the level of a country's imports will be influenced by the price of imported goods and services relative to those of home produced substitutes. Because the prices of goods are measured in the currency of the countries in which they are produced (e.g. US

TABLE 4.5 UK balance of payments, 1972–82 (percentage of GNP at factor cost)

	1972	1973	1974	1975	1976	1977	1978	1979	1980	1981	1982
Current balance	0.4	-1.5	-4.3	-1.6	-0.7	0	0.8	-0.4	1.7	3.0	2.3
Total investment and other capital transactions	-1.2	0.3	2.1	0.2	-2.6	3.2	-2.9	1.3	-1.0	-3.5	-1.2
Balancing item	-1.4	0.1	0.1	-0.1	0.2	2.4	1.3	0.1	-0.1	0.1	-1.6
Total official financing	-2.0	-1.2	-2.2	-1.5	-3.2	5.7	-0.8	1.1	0.7	-0.3	-0.5
Net transactions with overseas monetary authorities and foreign currency borrowing (net)[a]	0.8	1.5	2.3	0.8	2.4	1.7	-0.8	-0.5	-0.6	-0.8	-0.1
Change in official reserves	-1.2	0.3	0.1	-0.7	-0.7	7.4	-1.6	0.6	0.1	-1.1	-0.6

Source: Central Statistical Office (1983), United Kingdom Balance of Payments (Pink Book), (London: HMSO), Table 1.3, National Income and Expenditure (Blue Book), (London: HMSO), Table 1.1.
Note: (a) Repayment of previous borrowing is shown with a minus sign and borrowing with a plus sign.

goods in dollars, UK goods in sterling) the relative price of domestic to foreign goods may be defined as:

$$\frac{e\,P_D}{P_F} \qquad (4.1)$$

where (1) e = the exchange rate expressing domestic currency in terms of foreign currency
(2) P_D = the price of domestic goods in terms of domestic currency
(3) P_F = the price of foreign goods in terms of foreign currency.

Relative prices can change either because of: (i) changes in the exchange rate; or (ii) countries experiencing different rates of inflation. To illustrate, suppose the price of a UK car is £6,000 (P_D) while that of a similar US car is $12,000 ($P_F$). At an exchange rate of £1=$2 ($e$) the relative price of UK to US cars expressed in dollars is:

$$\frac{\$2 \times 6,000}{\$12,000} = \frac{\$12,000}{\$12,000} = 1$$

If both prices remain unchanged and the exchange rate falls, the price of UK goods relative to US goods will fall. Conversely, if the domestic price of UK goods rises with no change in the exchange rate, the relative price of UK goods will rise i.e. UK goods become less competitive. In the above example, if the price of a UK car rises to £8,000 the relative price of UK to US cars will rise to 1.33

$$\text{i.e. } \frac{\$2 \times 8,000}{\$12,000}$$

Under a system of fixed exchange rates changes in relative prices depend on different rates of inflation being experienced by countries. If a country experiences a lower rate of inflation than other countries home produced goods will become cheaper relative to imports, and vice versa.

Third, the level of a country's imports can partly be explained by tastes, etc. For example, British people consume more tea than residents of other European countries. The level of a country's imports will be affected by other non-price influences such as the quality, design, reliability, delivery time of the imported goods. Lastly, the foreign trade policies adopted by a country also influence its level of imports (e.g. the imposition of tariffs and import restrictions).

4.4 The determination of the level of exports

It should be evident that exports are determined by the same type of factors that influence imports since one country's imports are another country's exports. First, the income variable relevant to exports is income in the rest of the world. If world income rises then, ceteris paribus, the demand for a country's exports will increase. Second, the demand for a country's exports will depend on the price of its goods relative to those produced by competitors abroad. Thus the more competitive British goods are (i.e. the lower the relative price as defined in 4.1) the greater the demand for British exports. Third, in addition to income and relative prices, foreign tastes, non-price influences, and foreign trade policies influence the level of exports in a similar manner to the way in which they affect imports.

4.5 The determination of capital movements

The determinants of capital movements are far more complex to analyse. The main influences include: (i) expectations of exchange rate changes; (ii) nominal interest-rate differentials between countries; and (iii) differences in the expected rate of return on real investment opportunities in different countries. We will illustrate each of these influences in turn. Note that in the following discussion we are ignoring the effect of past activities, such as previous borrowings, which require repayment of debt in the current period.

First, exchange rate changes impose capital gains and losses. Take, for example, a resident of the US holding a UK bank deposit of £1,000. If the exchange rate is £1=$2.4 his dollar equivalent is $2,400, but, if the exchange rate falls to £1=$2.0 then his dollar equivalent is only $2,000. He would therefore lose $400 by holding sterling over a period during which devaluation occurred. Conversely if the exchange rate rises to say £1=$3 he would make a capital gain of $600. Hence one of the most important determinants of short-term capital movements is expected exchange rate changes. Expected devaluation will lead to a capital outflow and expected appreciation a capital inflow. Second, funds may be transferred from one country to another due to changes in the rate of return that can be earned in different financial centres. Thus if the rate of interest is higher in London than in New York, there will be short-term capital flows into London. Third, an increase in the expected rate of profit on real capital investment overseas relative to that at home will lead to more investment overseas (i.e. capital outflow). Other specific factors also play a part; for example, the strength of sterling is to some extent attributable to its use as a petrocurrency.

In concluding our discussion of the main determinants of imports, exports and capital movements it is useful to recall the conditions (other than exchange rate changes) which adversely affect a country's balance of payment position. With regard to the current account the following influences tend to raise a country's imports and reduce its exports: (i) a rise in domestic aggregate demand; (ii) a faster rate of inflation than abroad; and (iii) a fall in world income i.e. a recession abroad. On the capital account adverse movements are likely to occur when: (i) the exchange rate is expected to fall; (ii) interest rates at home are lower than those abroad; and (iii) the expected rate of profit on investment is higher overseas than at home.

4.6 Exchange rate regimes

4.6.1 *Foreign exchange market*
As we have seen the exchange rate is the relative price of different currencies. As far as the UK is concerned the exchange rate is quoted in terms of the number of units of foreign currency per £ (e.g. £1[1] = $2.4 or £1 = 10.5 French francs). The alternative method of quotation used by all other foreign countries is the number of units of domestic currency per unit of foreign currency e.g. price of the $ is £0.42

$$(\text{i.e. } \frac{1}{2.4})$$

or the franc £0.10

$$(\text{i.e. } \frac{1}{10.5}).$$

1. Note because of recent substantial fluctuations in exchange rates these rates are not necessarily representative of current actual market rates.

In the following discussion we will always use the UK method of quotation.

In the absence of government intervention the exchange rate is determined by the demand for and supply of that currency. Equilibrium in the foreign exchange market will occur when the quantity of the currency demanded equals that supplied. It is therefore necessary to look at the factors determining demand and supply.

As examined in section 4.2.1 the demand for domestic currency (i.e. £s) arises from: (i) UK exports, and (ii) flows of foreign investment into the UK. In other words the demand for domestic currency by foreigners corresponds to credit items in the balance of payments on both the current and capital accounts. In section 4.4 we examined the determinants of exports and we will now discuss in more detail the relationship between exports and the exchange rate using the concept of relative prices developed in section 4.3. We will take the example used earlier of a car costing £6,000 in the UK and a similar car in the US costing $12,000. If the exchange rate is £1 = $2 the relative price of UK to US cars is 1. If the exchange rate were reduced to £1 = $1.50 (in technical terms, depreciated or was devalued) the relative price would fall to 0.75

$$(i.e. \frac{\$1.5 \times 6,000}{\$12,000}).$$

British cars would thereby become more competitive i.e. cheaper relative to US cars. The same principles would apply to all exports to the US so that provided more British goods were purchased as the foreign currency price fell, due to exchange rate depreciation (i.e. the elasticity of demand for such goods was greater than zero) more £s would be demanded. In other words the demand curve for £s would slope downwards as is depicted in Figure 4.1.

Similarly the supply of domestic currency (i.e. £s) on the foreign exchange market corresponds to debit items in the balance of payments accounts and results from:(i) imports into the UK, and (ii) capital flows from the UK to the rest of the world. Exchange rate changes alter the supply of £s on the foreign exchange market in the oposite direction to that for demand. As we have seen earlier if the exchange rate falls (i.e. depreciates or is devalued) British goods become more competitive and imports will consequently decrease. In the example quoted above the US car would sell in the UK for £6,000.

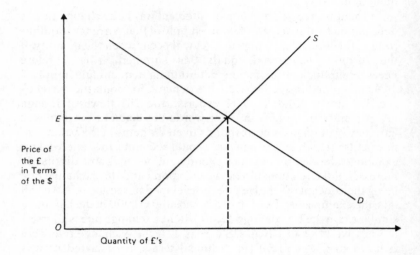

Figure 4.1. The determination of the equilibrium exchange rate

$$(\text{i.e. } \frac{\$12,000}{2})$$

before devaluation but for £8,000

$$(\text{i.e. } \frac{\$12,000}{1.5})$$

after the fall in the exchange rate. Thus the home currency price of imported foreign goods rises as the price of the £ falls. The supply of £s placed on the market depends on the quantity of imports purchased by UK residents multiplied by their sterling price i.e. total expenditure on imports by UK residents. Such expenditure will decrease in aggregate following the sterling price rise due to devaluation provided the elasticity of demand for such goods is greater than one. If the elasticity of demand for such goods is less than one total expenditure on them (i.e. price x quantity) will rise. Subject to the proviso that the elasticity of demand is more than one the supply curve of £s with respect to the exchange rate will slope upwards to the right i.e. the lower the exchange rate the smaller the total expenditure on imports into the UK and the smaller the supply of sterling placed on the market.

Equilibrium occurs where the quantity demanded equals that supplied and this is demonstrated in Figure 4.1 where the demand and supply curves intersect. This presentation assumes that there are no changes in any of the other variables which affect the demand for and supply of domestic currency in the foreign exchange market e..g. incomes, tastes, rates of interest, etc. At rate *OE* (see Figure 4.1) the demand for £s equal the supply of £s so that the market for £s is cleared. A change in any one of the factors held constant under the ceteris paribus assumption will shift the demand and/or supply curve for £s. For example an increase in the rate of interest will shift the demand curve to the right (i.e. net capital inflow will increase or net capital outflow decrease) thus causing the exchange rate to rise i.e. appreciate.

Under free and stable market conditions there will be a tendency for the exchange rate to fall when the supply of domestic currency exceeds the demand for it on the foreign exchange market, and vice versa (see Figure 4.1). The question arises as to what happens if the elasticity of demand for imports is less than one so that the supply curve has a negative slope. In fact the foreign exchange market will be stable (i.e. the market exchange rate will move towards the equilibrium exchange rate) provided the sum of the elasticity of demand for imports and exports is greater than unity. This so-called Marshall/Lerner condition is demonstrated in Figure 4.2 on the assumption that the elasticity of demand for UK exports is greater than zero but that for imports is less than unity and also assuming infinite elasticities of supply for both imports and exports. Despite the negative slope for the supply of £s there is excess demand for £s when the exchange rate is below the equilibrium rate (*OE*) and excess supply when the exchange rate is above equilibrium level. In both cases the market exchange rate will move back towards the equilibrium rate as indicated by the arrows in Figure 4.2.

If however the Marshall/Lerner condition is not satisfied the market will be unstable. This is demonstrated in Figure 4.3. The same assumptions as before are made but this time the sum of the two elasticities is less than unity.

At an exchange rate below *OE* there is excess supply (i.e. supply is greater than demand) so that the exchange rate will fall i.e. move further away from the equilibrium. Conversely if the exchange rate is above *OE* there is excess demand so that the market exchange rate will increase i.e. move further away from the equilibrium rate.

Most empirical studies of foreign trade suggest that the elasticity conditions are satisfied at least in the long run so that either Figure

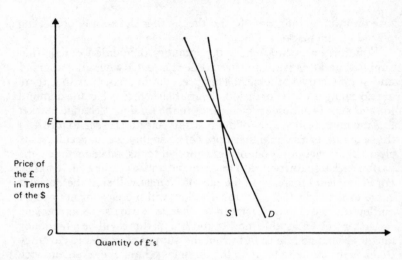

Figure 4.2. The stability of the exchange rate

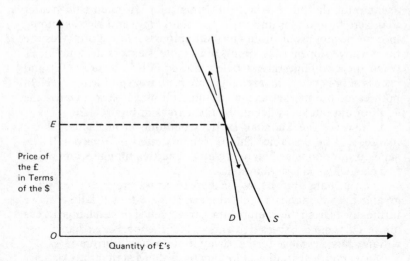

Figure 4.3. Instability of the exchange rate

4.1 or 4.2 is a reasonable representation of the real world. For the rest of this chapter we shall assume that the situation depicted in Figure 4.1 prevails.

4.6.2 *Fixed exchange rates*
A fixed exchange rate is a rate fixed at a certain level by the government and can only be altered by a government decision to change the rate. This does not mean that the exchange rate fixed by the authorities will never differ from that which would have been determined by the free market forces of demand and supply. Thus in order to maintain the exchange rate at the prescribed level the authorities must intervene in the market. In practice fixed exchange rates are normally maintained within bands rather than at a precise level so that intervention will take place whenever the exchange rate moves outside that band. For example, in the case where there is excess supply of sterling, at the fixed rate, the authorities would have to purchase the excess supply in order to prevent the exchange rate from falling. This is shown in Figure 4.4.

The central parity is *Oa* and *Oc* and *Ob* the upper and lower intervention points respectively. The gap *bc* represents the bands within which the exchange rate is to be maintained. In the absence of government intervention the equilibrium exchange rate would be *Od*. Thus the authorities must purchase sterling equal at least to *EF* (i.e. the excess supply at the lower intervention point) to keep sterling with the agreed bands. Conversely if the free market equilibrium exchange rates were to rise above *Oc* the authorities would have to sell sterling on the foreign exchange market. It should be remembered from section 4.2.4 that such intervention in the foreign exchange market will be matched by corresponding changes in official reserves i.e. ceteris paribus, sales of sterling lead to increases in reserves, whereas purchases lead to decreases in reserves. In additon, as we have seen in Chapter 3 section 3.3 such intervention influences the public sector borrowing requirement via BPF in equation (3.1). For example purchase of sterling to support the pound on the foreign exchange market provides a source of funds for the authorities to finance public sector expenditure.

4.6.3 *Freely floating exchange rates*
Under a system of freely (pure or clean) floating/flexible exchange rates the central monetary authorities do not intervene in the foreign exchange market. The exchange rate is determined by the market forces of demand and supply for domestic currency. The rate adjusts to clear the foreign exchange market (i.e. balance

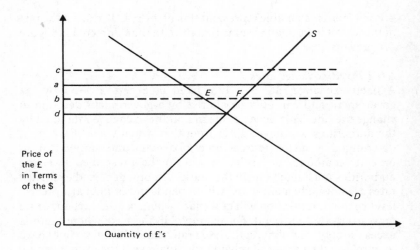

Figure 4.4. Intervention to maintain a fixed exchange rate

on current account plus net capital flow equals zero). In other words payments of domestic currency on: (i) imports, property income and transfers abroad (i.e. debit items on the current account) plus (ii) investment and lending abroad (i.e. capital outflow) equal receipts of domestic currency from: (iii) exports, property income and transfers from abroad (i.e. credit items on the current account) plus (iv) investment and borrowing from abroad (i.e. capital inflow). The balance for official financing will therefore be zero as payments of foreign currencies abroad equal receipts of foreign currencies from abroad.

4.6.4 *Managed float*
Finally, a situation somewhere between fixed and pure floating exchange rates may prevail where a government intervenes, in varying degrees, in order to influence the level of the exchange rate by buying and selling foreign currencies. This is often referred to as a system of managed or dirty floating exchange rates. What matters is the degree of government intervention. Intervention may be limited to smoothing out day-to-day fluctuations in the exchange rate partly attributable to speculative capital flows. In this case official purchases and sales of foreign currency will be roughly equal over time and the position will closely approximate to a system of pure floating exchange rates. On the other hand there may be fairly heavy

intervention by the authorities to manage the exchange rate in which case the position will be a fairly close approximation to a system of fixed exchange rates. The UK operated under a system of fixed exchange rates up to 1972 when it adopted a managed floating exchange rate.

4.7 Main theories of the balance of payments

Although we will leave the discussion of policy measures to remedy balance of payments disequilibria (deficits or surpluses) to subsequent chapters (e.g. Chapter 10) it is useful at this stage to summarise the main theories of the balance of payments.

4.7.1 *Elasticities approach*

The elasticities approach examines the conditions under which devaluation of the exchange rate will be successful in remedying a balance of payments deficit on the current account. As such it concentrates on the response of exports and imports to relative price changes following devaluation. We have previously discussed how, ceteris paribus, devaluation raises the home currency price of imports and lowers the foreign currency price of exports. For the current account balance to improve, the change in the demand for imports and exports must be sufficient to overcome the loss of foreign currency due to the lowering of the foreign currency price of exports. As we have seen earlier the necessary condition (known as the Marshall/Lerner condition) for devaluation to improve the balance of payments on the current account and cause a net reduction in the excess supply of domestic currency (see Figure 4.2) is that the sum of the elasticity of demand for imports and exports should exceed unity. We have also discussed in previous sections how the demand for and supply of domestic currency will change following devaluation. In that analysis we assumed an infinite elasticity of supply for exports so that domestic output of exported goods can be increased to meet increased demand for them. This can be illustrated using the model of income determination developed in Chapter 1. An increase in net exports (i.e. a rise in exports and fall in imports) will increase aggregate demand. This is demonstrated in Figure 4.5.

Equilibrium occurs initially at Y_1. After devaluation the aggregate demand curve shifts upwards from AD_1 to AD_2 where $(X - Im)_2$ is greater than $(X - Im)_1$. The normal multiplier expansion occurs so that national income increases to Y_2. If full capacity output (i.e. maximum output capable of being produced by the economy) is less than Y_2 then there will be excess demand so that inflation will occur. Therefore unless there are unemployed resources devaluation on its

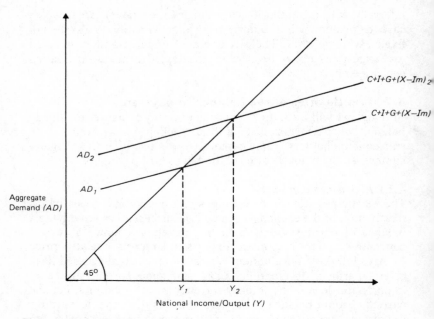

Figure 4.5. An increase in net exports

own will be sufficient to result in an improvement in the balance of payments. This leads us to a consideration of the absorption approach to the balance of payments.

4.7.2 *Absorption approach*
The absorption approach also examines the way in which government policy intervention can improve the balance of payments on current account. In Chapter 1 we saw how national income (Y) measures the aggregate expenditure made by domestic residents and foreigners on home produced goods and its division between private consumption (C), government spending (G), investment (I), exports (X) and spending on imported goods and services (Im).

$$Y = C + G + I + X - Im \qquad (4.2)$$

The sum of $C + G + I$ represents total domestic expenditure on all goods both home produced and imported. Insight into the true nature of the balance of payments is gained by re-arranging identity

(4.2) so that the current account of the balance of payments (i.e. $X\text{-}Im$) is equal by definition to output (Y) minus domestic expenditure or absorption (i.e. $C + G + I = A$):

$$Y - A = X - Im \qquad (4.3)$$

This shows that a balance of payments surplus (i.e. $X > Im$) occurs only when the flow of output is greater than the flow of absorption (i.e. $Y > A$). In other words the excess of output relative to absorption is sold abroad and generates a balance of payments surplus. Conversely a balance of payments deficit (i.e. $X < Im$) occurs only when absorption is greater than output (i.e. $A > Y$). The excess of domestic demand over production is obtained from abroad and results in a balance of payments deficit. Clearly for government intervention to improve the balance of payments it must produce:

(i) a reduction in absorption relative to output (known as expenditure reducing policies); or
(ii) an increase in output relative to absorption (termed expenditure switching policies); or
(iii) possibly some combination of (i) and (ii).

Relating these propositions to a devaluation, it is apparent that devaluation will only improve the current account of the balance of payment if:

(i) unemployment exists so that output can be increased relative to absorption; and/or
(ii) absorption is reduced relative to output (e.g. by government policy) to allow room for the extra output to be produced.

4.7.3 *Monetary approach*
The elasticities and absorption approach tend to ignore the role of money and stress the need for government intervention to remedy balance of payments disequilibria. In contrast the monetary approach views the balance of payments as essentially a monetary phenomenon with an automatic adjustment mechanism. It concentrates on the sum of the current and capital accounts (i.e. the balance for official settlement) rather than on just the current account.

In the monetary approach two key assumptions are made, namely that: (i) the demand for and supply of money are stable functions of a limited number of variables (see Chapter 3) and (ii) output and employment tend towards a situation of full employment in the long run. The relationship between the demand for and supply of money is regarded as the main determinant of balance of payments flows. Under a system of fixed exchange rates it is maintained that a balance of payments deficit occurs when the domestic monetary authorities create an excess supply of money. An excess supply of money will lead to a fall in interest rates which in turn causes a balance of payments deficit in two ways. First, a fall in interest rates leads to an increase in aggregate demand and hence a deterioration of the current account. Second, a fall in interest rates also leads to a capital outflow. Hence excess money balances will be disposed of through a balance of payments deficit. The converse argument applies when there is an excess demand for money by domestic units which will be satisfied via the consequent balance of payments surplus.

In order to outline the automatic adjustment mechanism held to exist we must also consider the relationship between the balance of payments and the domestic money supply. As we have seen under fixed exchange rates the central monetary authorities are committed to buy and sell foreign exchange for the home currency at a fixed price. In the case of a balance of payments surplus residents will sell foreign currency to the central bank for home currency. Ceteris paribus, a balance of payments surplus results in an increase in residents' holdings of home currency and therefore the domestic money supply. In this way residents obtain the additional money balances they require. Conversely, in the case of a balance of payments deficit the authorities will purchase sterling balances in order to prevent the exchange rate depreciating below the prescribed limit. Withdrawals of sterling balances from residents reduce the domestic money supply. Although it is possible for the authorities to attempt to neutralise these monetary effects by making offsetting policy changes it is argued that neutralisation is impossible or very difficult in the long run. This is certainly true of a deficit because the central authorities will eventually run out of reserves with which to purchase sterling. To sum up, a balance of payments surplus tends to increase the supply, or its rate of growth, and vice versa.

In the case of floating exchange rates, the monetary approach holds that movements in the exchange rate are determined by the rate of monetary expansion in one country relative to that in the rest of the world. For example, a faster rate of monetary expansion will lead, ceteris paribus, to a depreciation of the exchange rate for exactly the same reasons as an excess supply of money leads to a balance of payments deficit in a world of fixed exchange rates.

5 Inflation

5.1 Introduction

Inflation can be defined as a process of continually rising prices (i.e. the general price level) and is therefore equivalent to a continually falling value of money. The important aspects of this definition are the concepts continually and general. Inflation is not a once-and-for-all jump in prices (due, for example, to an increase in oil prices). It refers to rises in the average price level over a period of time. Similarly not all prices must rise, just the average level. For example, even though Britain has experienced a fast rate of inflation through the six years up to 1982 (see Chapter 6, Figure 6.4) the price of electronic calculators has actually fallen during this period.

Inflation can be classified in at least two ways: (i) with respect to speed and (ii) with respect to causation. First, with respect to speed it is useful to consider two types: (i) hyper-inflation and (ii) gradual inflation. There is no precise division between these but gradual inflation refers to the type of speeds experienced in the UK since 1945 (i.e. varying from virtually zero to near 30 per cent per annum). Hyper-inflation is characterised by extremely rapid rates of inflation. The German experience of 1922/23 is well known; the ratio of price levels at the end of the period to that at the beginning was 1.02×10^{10}! Even faster rises of price levels were experienced in Hungary in 1945/46 where the ratio of prices at the end of the period of hyper-inflation to those at the beginning was the staggering figure of 3.81×10^{27}. Second, classification of gradual inflation according to causation normally examines the two extreme positions: (i) the monetarist view and (ii) the sociological stance. We shall examine these two stances in sections 5.3 and 5.4 but first of all in section 5.2 we shall look at the problem of how to measure inflation.

5.2 Measurement of inflation

Since inflation refers to changes in the average level of prices, measurement involves consideration of movements in an index pertaining to the average level of prices. There is however a wide range of price indices which may be used for this purpose; for example, the index of retail prices, the index of wholesale prices of output, the index of consumer prices, and the implicit deflator for GDP (i.e. GDP valued at current prices/measured in constant prices). There is no single correct index but in view of the fairly widespread use of the index of retail prices we will describe how this index is constructed.

The Retail Price Index attempts to show movements in the average level of prices of goods and services bought by a typical household. The basis of constructing any index number is to define a certain time period as the base. This can be a specific day (as in the case of the Retail Price Index) or a month, or even a year. Values of the variable concerned (in this case prices) in subsequent periods are calculated as a ratio of the base. Thus, for example, if the price of potatoes was £1 per 56lb sack in the base year and subsequently rose to £2 the index would be

$$\frac{£2}{£1} \times 100 = 200.$$

The price index for a single commodity is more correctly called a price relative, with the term index being reserved for the average of the price relatives of a group of commodities. This of course immediately raises the problem of how to combine the price relatives into a single index. A simple average would be inappropriate since some of the commodities are more important in consumer's expenditure. The normal procedure is to derive an average in which the price relatives are weighted according to the share of the goods concerned in total expenditure. Consider the simple example of three commodities shown in Table 5.1.

A simple average of the three price relatives is

$$\frac{150 + 50 + 133}{3} = 111.$$

This gives a misleading picture since only a relatively small amount of expenditure is attached to commodity *B* i.e. it is relatively unimportant in the customer's budget. The weighted average would be calculated by:

$$(150 \times 0.3125) + (50 \times 0.0625) + (133 \times 0.6250) = 133.$$

This gives a more correct indication of the average price level in year 2 as a ratio to that ruling in year 1. A problem with the weights is that as expenditure patterns change 'weights' become out of date. The method of constructing the retail price index attempts to overcome this problem by changing the weights every year. The information on which these changes of weights are based is derived from family expenditure surveys.

The Retail Price Index is divided into a number of main groups (e.g. housing, clothing, food) which are themselves split into sections (e.g. food: fish, bread, meat, fruit, etc.). Price relatives are calculated for each commodity (e.g. bread) within a particular group (e.g. food) and are weighted according to the share of expenditure made on it in relation to the total expenditure made on that group (in precisely the same way as for the numerical example qouted in Table 5.1). The group index is then obtained from these relatives. Each group index is in turn weighted according to its relative importance to total household expenditure. Finally, the average of the weighted group indices is calculated to arrive at the 'all items index' or the Retail Price Index as it is more familiarly known. This index does not show directly the rate of inflation between any two years and to obtain this information a further calculation is necessary. Inflation is the

TABLE 5.1. Example of calculating an index number

	Price		Price relatives	Total expenditure on the goods		Relative importance
	Yr 1	Yr 2	Yr 2	in Yr 1		
A	£5.00	£7.50	150	£5,000	$\frac{5000}{16000} =$	0.3125
B	£4.00	£2.00	50	£1,000	$\frac{1000}{16000} =$	0.0625
C	£6.00	£8.00	133	£10,000	$\frac{10000}{16000} =$	0.6250
				£16,000		1.0000

percentage change in prices thus it is necessary to calculate the percentage change in the index. For example, if the index showed values of (i) 136 and (ii) exactly one year later 157 then the annual rate of inflation as measured by that index is

$$\frac{157 - 136}{136} \times 100 = 15.4 \text{ per cent.}$$

To sum up therefore, the Retail Price Index attempts to measure movements in the retail cost of selected goods and services bought by the average household. There are of course problems of how far this index attains its object e.g. it is very difficult to distinguish between price changes due to inflation and those due to an improvement in the quality of the goods themselves. Despite these difficulties it is one way of measuring changes in material living standards and it is used as the basis for wage and salary negotiations in the UK.

5.3 Inflation: the monetarist view
In Chapter 3, section 3.6.2 we discussed the quantity theory of money in which a continuous expansion of the money supply causes inflation. The monetarist view is that inflation is due to excessive monetary expansion and is best summed up by Friedman's dictum that 'Inflation is always and everywhere a monetary phenomenon in the sense that it is and can only be produced by a more rapid increase in the quantity of money than output'. It is also the view of monetarists that the money supply is under the control of the government or at least potentially so if it wishes to exercise that control. In fact there is a variety of reasons why the government may fudge the issue; one example is the unwillingness of the government to face up to the level of interest rates necessary for control of the money supply to be established. This chain of causation can be illustrated by the flow diagram shown in Figure 5.1.

The basic idea is that increases in the money supply lead to increases in aggregate demand via the channels discussed in Chapter 3. Excess demand causes both rising prices and rising money wage rates. These feed on each other and cause the familiar wage price spiral. Of course rises in aggregate demand can be caused by other factors but it is believed that only continuous increases in the rate of monetary expansion can lead to continuing inflation.

In the following sections we shall look at the interaction of excess demand and money wage rate increases using Phillips curve analysis.

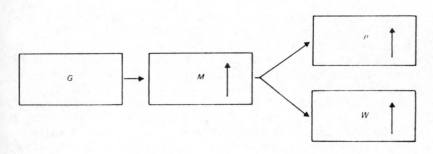

Figure 5.1. The chain of causation in the monetarist view of inflation

These concepts are particularly important since the prices of most industrial goods are administered (i.e. set by firms) and are therefore not particularly responsive to changes in aggregate demand. Empirical evidence suggests that such prices are however sensitive to cost changes. Wages are the most important element of cost and if wages respond to excess demand then so will prices indirectly via the changes in wage costs.

5.3.1. *The basic Phillips curve*
In general terms the analysis is concerned with the relationship between the proportionate rate of change of money wages and the level of excess demand for labour. The original study was an investigation carried out by A.W. Phillips into the statistical relationship between the level of unemployment (U) and the rate of change of money wage rates (W) in the UK over the period 1861 to 1957. Phillips found that the average relationship between these two variables was non-linear and followed the general shape shown in Figure 5.2.

At unemployment levels of approximately $5\frac{1}{2}$ per cent the rate of change of money wage rates was zero. With $2\frac{1}{2}$ per cent unemployment, the rate of increase of money wage rates was roughly 2 per cent which was approximately equal to the then average growth of productivity so that prices would remain constant.

The economic rationale for this relationship was provided subsequently by Lipsey. He argued that normal demand and supply analysis predicts that money wages will rise in response to excess demand for labour i.e. move back to their equilibrium level. Moreover he argued that the speed of adjustment will be faster the greater the amount of excess demand for labour i.e. the further away existing wage rates are from their equilibrium level. This is demonstrated in Figure 5.3.

The equilibrium wage rate is OW_1. If the actual wage rate is OW_2 there is excess demand for labour equal to AB which will cause money wage rates to rise to their equilibrium value OW_1. Similarly if the actual wage rate is OW_3 there is excess demand equal to CD again causing money wage rates to move upwards to OW_1 (the equilibrium level). Since CD is greater than AB the rise in money wage rates (i.e. towards their equilibrium level) will be faster from an initial wage rate of OW_3 than from OW_2.

The next step in the analysis is to consider how to measure excess demand for labour. One such measure is the number of unemployed. As excess demand for labour increases so unemployment will fall. A combination of: (i) the hypothesis that the rate of increase of money wage rates depends on excess demand for labour and (ii) that unemployment figures are a good proxy for excess demand for labour, produces the traditional Phillips curve shown in Figure 5.2.

It should also be noted that unemployment will not fall to zero because of various factors such as workers being unemployed whilst changing their jobs. The nature of registered unemployment is examined in Chapter 6, section 6.2.1.

5.3.2. *The augmented Phillips curve*
The basic flaw in the analysis so far is that it is conducted in terms of money wage rates. Workers will however be concerned with real wages i.e. the amount of goods they can purchase with their wage. Real wages decline if money wages are fixed and prices rise. Similarly employers will be concerned with the real cost of labour i.e. the cost of labour input relative to the value of output produced. Inflation will lower the real cost of labour with money wages fixed because the price of output rises. Thus both firms and workers will be concerned with the course of inflation during the period of the wage bargain. However because the wage bargain is struck for an advance period (e.g. one year from 1 January), it is not the actual known rate of inflation which matters but rather that which is expected to occur in the future period of the wage contract. Thus the agreed wage rate increase is likely to consist of two components:

(i) the increase in real wage rates attributable to excess demand for labour (proxied by the level of unemployment);
(ii) the expected rate of inflation.

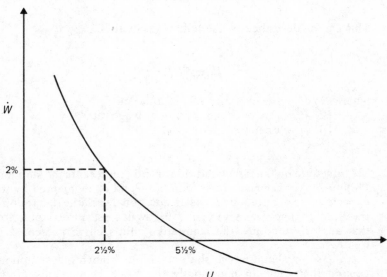

Figure 5.2. The basic Phillips curve

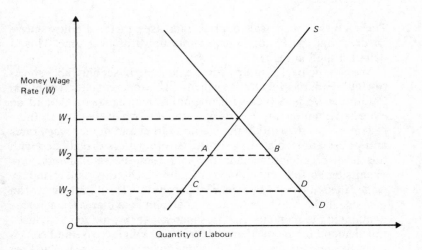

Figure 5.3. The determination of the equilibrium money wage rate

This can be described by the following equation:

$$\ddot{W} = f(U) + \dot{P}^e \qquad (5.1)$$

where (1) $\dot{P}^e$ = the expected rate of inflation
      (2) $\ddot{W}$ = rate of change of money wage rates
and   (3) U = unemployment

The first term on the right hand side of (5.1) represents the standard Phillips curve discussed in section 5.3.1 and is augmented by the expected rate of inflation ($\dot{P}^e$) as an additional variable determining the rate of change of money wages. It is now necessary to examine how this analysis modifies the standard Phillips curve presented in Figure 5.2.

To ease presentation we shall make the following assumptions (noting that they do not modify the basic conclusions of the analysis):

(1) the Phillips curves are linear;
(2) the growth of productivity is zero so that any change in money wages is ultimately matched by a corresponding change in prices.

The inclusion of expected price increases in the Phillips curve ensures that the Phillips curve shifts upwards over time. This is demonstrated in Figure 5.4.

We call the basic Phillips curve examined in section 5.3.1 short-run Phillips curves for reasons which will be apparent later. The initial Phillips curve is $SRPC_1$ with unemployment equal to Oa and an expected inflation rate of zero. At an unemployment level of Oa there is zero excess demand in the labour market and money wage rates and prices are stable. Suppose the government is dissatisfied with this level of unemployment and increases the rate of monetary expansion so that unemployment falls to Ob, this causes money wage rates to increase by 3 per cent per annum. The initial effect of an increase in the rate of monetary expansion is to increase aggregate demand in the economy. As firms increase their production to meet this demand for goods, demand for labour will increase and consequently unemployment will fall. Money wage rates increase by 3 per cent per annum due to the increased demand for labour. In turn the supply of labour will respond to the increased demand because, having recently experienced a period of stability (i.e. $\ddot{W} = \dot{P} = O$),

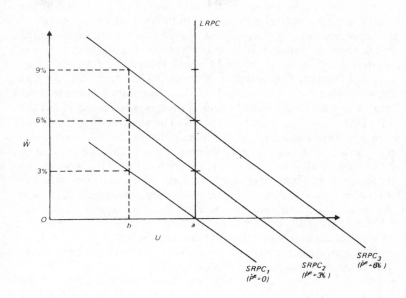

Figure 5.4. The augmented Phillips curve

workers interpret the increase in their money wages as an increase in their real wages. The rise of money wages feeds into firms' costs and causes prices to rise eventually by 3 per cent. Note that we are assuming that such wage increases cannot be financed by squeezing profits. Once individuals begin to expect future price increases they will take their expectations into consideration when negotiating wage agreements. Consequently money wage rates will have to rise by 6 per cent to achieve the rise of 3 per cent in real wages required to maintain the level of unemployment at *Ob*. This would require a further increase in the rate of monetary expansion to finance the rise in prices. In terms of Figure 5.4 the short run Phillips curve would shift upwards from $SRPC_1$ to $SRPC_2$ as individuals revise upwards their expectations of future rates of inflation. Again as money wage rates rise by 6 per cent this will feed into prices bringing about expectations of price increases of 6 per cent so that money wage rates must rise by 9 per cent to achieve the 3 per cent increase in real wages necessary to maintain unemployment at *Ob*. In contrast suppose the government was alarmed at the 3 per cent rise in inflation generated by reducing unemployment to *Ob* and refused to increase further the rate of monetary expansion. What then happens? The rising price level lowers the real value of the money supply—remember it was an initial increase in the nominal money supply that brought about the reduction in unemployment and increase in inflation. Unemployment will rise due to rising rates of interest and reduced demand for real goods i.e. via the transmission mechanism discussed in Chapter 3, section 3.6. In fact unemployment will rise precisely to *Oa* with inflation equal to 3 per cent. A similar result would occur if the government accepted the inflation rate of 6 per cent but refused to increase further the rate of monetary expansion. In that case unemployment would return to *Oa* but with a rate of inflation of 6 per cent. These points are marked on Figure 5.4 and if joined up produce a vertical line. This is known as the long-run Phillips curve (*LRPC* in Figure 5.4). *Oa* is described as the natural rate of unemployment, the level at which it is held depends on the structural characteristics of the labour market e.g. mobility of labour, market imperfections, etc. In other words the natural rate is independent of the rate of inflation.

This concept of the natural rate of unemployment can be linked to the notion of the capacity of the economy developed in Chapter 1, section 1.4. Unemployment is by definition equal to the total labour supply minus the level of employment. Thus specification of a unique level of unemployment (i.e. the natural rate of unemployment) also specifies a unique level of employment. This level of employment (full in an economic sense) will in turn be associated with a level of (full in an economic sense) will in turn be associated with a level of output which we call the capacity output of the economy. Thus as output rises above capacity output, unemployment falls below the natural rate. We can therefore specify the capacity output of the economy either in terms of national income or unemployment.

The policy implications of this analysis are important. Unemployment can only be maintained at a level below the natural rate at the cost of accepting accelerating rates of inflation i.e. 3, 6, 9, per cent, etc., in our example. Eventually such a cost would prove unacceptable to any government. This implies that there is no trade off (i.e. compromise) between unemployment and inflation in the long run. Lower unemployment now (i.e. below the natural rate) can only be achieved at the cost of accepting higher inflation later. An increase in the rate of monetary expansion initially causes unemployment to fall because the resulting inflation is not perfectly anticipated. Once expectations adjust so that actual and expected rates of inflation are again equal unemployment returns to its natural rate. The faster expectations adjust, the shorter the period of time unemployment will remain below the natural rate as a result of an increase in the rate of monetary expansion.

The policy prediction of this analysis requires some qualification. If expectations of future inflation were slow to develop then the movement upwards of the Phillips curve would also be slow. In this case there may exist a practical policy option to lower unemployment now and accept rising rates of inflation in the far distant future. Thus the speed with which expectations of future inflation respond to changes in the current rate of inflation is important. In the analysis we have assumed that expectations of future inflation rise when actual inflation rates increase. In other words expectations of future inflation depend on actual rates of inflation experienced in the past. However using such an approach means that it is open to argue that changes in expectations only develop after a long time. A fairly short time period is envisaged by those monetarists who believe that expectations of future inflation do depend on current and past experience of inflation. Typically the argument is that the initial response to a change in the rate of monetary expansion occurs mainly in output after a lag of some six to nine months. Some six to nine months later prices start to rise due to the increase in output. This causes output to return towards its previous (i.e. natural) level. Thus after a period of twenty-four months or so the main effect of the monetary expansion is on prices not output. This sort of time period leaves little practical scope for a policy designed to reduce unemployment below the natural rate. Other monetarist go further. Why should agents wait to see prices rise before expecting inflation? Students of economics would know that monetary expansion leads to rising rates of inflation so it is reasonable to assume that they would adjust their expectations immediately any sustained change in the rate of monetary expansion was perceived. This hypothesis of expectations formation is called the 'Rational Expectations Hypothesis'[1] and puts forward the view that expectations are formed in accordance with the predictions of the relevant economic theory, in this case the augmented Phillips curve analysis. The rational expectations hypothesis implies that adjustment of expectations to changed monetary conditions would be very quick though actual wages may respond more slowly because of existing contractual arrangements. In this case there would be no real scope for policy designed to lower unemployment below the natural level. It should be noted that even if firms and individuals themselves lacked the economic expertise and information to form rational forecasts,

---

1. The rational expectations hypothesis is discussed in more detail in Chapter 7, section 7.6.

they could obtain the relevant information from forecasting agencies and union advisers.

5.3.3 *Concluding remarks*

To sum up the monetarist view of inflation contained in the causal chain of Figure 5.1: an increased rate of monetary expansion will create excess demand for labour pulling unemployment below the natural rate. This causes money wage rates to rise raising firms' production costs and provoking price increases. At the same time expectations of further price increases are created causing the familiar wage/price spiral. The adjustment process (i.e. the process of the short-run Phillips curve shifting upwards) can and often does cause both unemployment and the rate of inflation to increase at the same time. Reference to Figures 6.3 and 6.4 in Chapter 6 shows that (particularly since 1974) this has been the case in the UK. This phenomenon arises because of (i) the role of expectations in the inflationary process and also (ii) the catching-up process as workers endeavour to obtain compensation for past losses in real wages due to unexpected increases in the rate of inflation. As a result current inflation may be the consequence not of current excess demand but rather that which occurred in the past. In which case comparison of rates of inflation with contemporaneous excess demand will reveal very little relationship between the two variables. Finally in this connection, if the short-run Phillips curve shifts above the position given by the long-run equilibrium rate of inflation (i.e. where the actual rate equals the expected rate of inflation) it is possible to experience temporary increases in unemployment above the natural rate, even though inflation is accelerating due to the lagged response to previous excess demand. The process may be short circuited if expectations are formed rationally inasmuch as expectations of future price increases will occur at the time of the increase in the rate of monetary expansion without the need for unemployment to fall below the natural rate.

5.4 Inflation: the sociological view

At the other extreme there is the sociological view of inflation. This encompasses the view generally described as cost push inflation. The basic argument is that wage increases are at the heart of the inflationary process. Wage increases are regarded as being largely exogenous i.e. independent of the state of the demand for and supply of labour in the labour market. They arise from sociological factors. Because wages are the most important component of cost, rises in wage rates that are not offset by growth of productivity lead to rises in

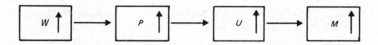

Figure 5.5. The chain of causation in the sociological view of inflation

prices and possibly lower profit margins. This rise in prices has two consequences. First, expectations of further inflation will feed into the wage bargaining process in precisely the same manner as analysed for the monetarist view of inflation. Second, in the absence of a change of government policy unemployment will rise because the rise in prices reduces the real value of the money supply. Protagonists of this approach argue that governments have, in the past, expanded the money supply to validate the rise in prices. Thus the chain of causation can be depicted in the flow diagram shown in Figure 5.5.

The familiar wage spiral would occur because trade unions will respond to the price increases by attempting to push up money wage rates to compensate for the increase in prices. It is important to note that in this view increases in the money supply are the response to and not the cause of inflation.

The critical difference between this approach and the monetarist approach is the view that wage increases are exogenous, i.e. occur independently of demand and supply conditions in the labour market. Validity of the sociological approach depends on the ability of trade unions to negotiate higher wage rates even given the existence of high levels of unemployment. Monetarists agree that trade unions will negotiate higher wages if they believe that the government will respond by increasing the money supply to prevent rising levels of unemployment. What monetarists dispute is the ability and willingness of trade unions to negotiate wage increases over and above the growth in productivity if they believed that the government would not respond by increasing the money supply since in this case their actions would cause unemployment amongst their members.

We now move on to consider some of the reasons why trade

unions may negotiate for wage increases in excess of the growth of productivity i.e. why they are militant. There is a wide divergence of views on the social pressures which lead to wage increases and we will attempt to indicate some of them. First, the price increase due to the wage increase negotiated by one trade union only directly affects its members to the extent that they buy the products of the industry in which they work. Thus union members may feel that they can raise their wages at the expense of the workers in other industries without retaliation by these other workers or at least without retaliation to a sufficient extent to offset completely their own gain. Second, the various unions may have ideas about a 'just' level of wages within their industry but aggregation of all such desired wage levels exceeds the capacity of the economy to produce the required quantity of goods. In other words perceived 'fair' wage structures are inconsistent with the capacity of the economy. Inconsistency can also arise in another way. Suppose one union feels that its wage rates should be 10 per cent above those of a second union but the second union believes that the two sets of wage rates should be equal. This will lead to conflict and 'leapfrogging' as each union tries to reach its desired position. Third, unions may believe that the existing division of shares of national output between labour and capital is unjust and that to attain a more just society wages should increase at the expense of profits. This view is unlikely to be held by firms so that wage demands will cause price increases. Indeed some writers suggest that class conflict is inevitable in a capitalist society and consequently argue that inflation is the result of a struggle for incompatible shares of national income. Fourth, there is the argument that increasing wage demands reflect a decline in the general moral climate so that union leaders no longer take a responsible attitude in wage negotiations. Finally, there is an argument based on the slower rate of economic growth achieved in the 1970s. Workers accustomed to the previous higher rates of growth of real income and consumption try at least to maintain their living standards by demanding increased money wages.

The common strand amongst these arguments is that the increases in money wages above the growth of productivity feed into prices. However in order to make the step from wage claims to wages paid it is necessary to look at reasons why firms accede to such wage claims. Generally arguments are made that power in wage negotiations has moved away from employers in favour of employees. One reason for this is that increased welfare benefits have enabled strikers to exist for longer periods without wages. Conversely employers have become more vulnerable as the productive process has become more capital intensive so that some small numbers of workers can dislocate whole production processes. Again growth of foreign competition has meant in the event of disruption of production, customers can easily obtain supplies from foreign competitors. Consequently it is argued that it is less costly for a firm to accede to the request for wage increases than to resist and face strike action.

Our discussion of the sociological view of inflation has been rather shorter than that of the monetary view. This does not mean that we regard it as less important but is due merely to the fact that less formal analysis is involved.

5.5 International aspects of inflation

5.5.1 *Fixed exchange rates*

So far we have discussed inflation within the context of a closed economy. However in a regime of fixed exchange rates, such as the Bretton Woods system (see Chapter 14, section 14.4) which existed from the late 1940s to 1972, inflationary experience in one country is vitally affected by experience in other countries. Three main economic channels of this interdependence can be distinguished: (i) changes in the prices of imported goods; (ii) the foreign trade multiplier; and (iii) monetary movements. First, one country's exports are another country's imports. Thus price rises in one country will lead to rises in the prices of its exports and consequently rising prices of other countries' imports. To the extent that the elasticity of demand for these imported goods is less than perfect (i.e. less than infinite) this will cause rises in the average price level of the importing countries. Furthermore home-produced goods will be substituted for higher-priced imported goods. This raises domestic aggregate demand and will therefore tend to raise the domestic general price level. Second, the foreign trade multiplier provides another channel whereby inflation in one country spreads to other countries. Any increase in aggregate demand in one country will lead to an increase in its imports provided the marginal propensity to import is greater than zero. As its imports increase so other countries' exports rise. This will lead to a 'multiplied' increase in output in other countries. If output is already near the capacity of these economies (i.e. unemployment is near the natural rate) this increase in demand is likely to lead to inflation. Third, if some countries are experiencing lower than average rates of inflation their goods will become more competitive. This will cause exports to increase and imports to decrease, i.e. net exports to increase. Rising net exports will lead to balance of payments surpluses for the countries concerned and these will, in turn, cause an expansion of their money supplies in line with the process examined in Chapter 4. Conversely the money supplies of those countries experiencing deficits will decrease. Consequently changes in the rate of monetary expansion in the various countries due to balance of payments deficits/surpluses will tend to lead to equalisation of rates of inflation among countries. One non-economic factor influencing the international transmission of inflation also needs to be discussed, i.e. demonstration effects. Groups of workers may look at wages earned by corresponding workers in different countries. These divergences in wages will tend to be taken into consideration in their own wage negotiations. Hence upward pressure on wages in one country will lead to upward pressure on wages in other countries through these 'demonstration' effects.

For all these reasons, inflationary pressures initiated in one country will be transmitted to other countries provided exchange rates are fixed.

5.5.2 *Floating exchange rates*
In the case of pure floating exchange rates, the economic link between inflation in one country and that in the rest of the world is broken. Differences in the rates of inflation will be reflected in movements in the exchange rate. Hence countries experiencing faster rates of inflation will also experience depreciating exchange rates. The converse would apply for countries experiencing lower rates of inflation than average i.e. their exchange rates would appreciate. Therefore inflation in countries, which have adopted pure floating exchange rates, is purely due to to domestic factors, though of course wage increases may reflect international factors due to demonstration effects. In the case of a managed float, the link between a country's rate of inflation and that in the rest of the world is still maintained to the extent that the authorities intervene in the foreign exchange markets.

5.5.3 *Inflation rates since 1960*
Figure 5.6 shows the rates of inflation experienced by five industrial countries during the period 1960-82. The main feature revealed is that, while the levels of inflation experienced by the individual countries may have differed, the general pattern has been remarkably similar over the period concerned. Monetarists have argued that the start of the inflationary pressures experienced in the Western World occurred in the early 1960s when the United States

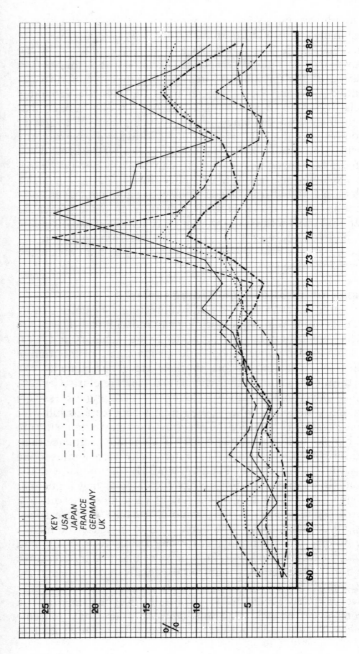

Figure 5.6. Inflation rates, 1960–82
Source: International Monetary Fund (1982), *International Financial Statistics: Yearbook & August 1983*
Note: Percentage change, over corresponding period of previous year, of consumer prices (calculated from indexes).

began to adopt expansionary policy measures. The acceleration of inflation in the late 1960s, they have argued, was the consequence of the financing of the Vietnam War via monetary expansion by the U.S.A. and that under the system of fixed exchange rates (that existed up to 1972-3) the inflationary pressure initiated in America was transmitted to other Western economies through the economic channels discussed in section 5.5.1. Figure 5.6 also reveals that although there is a tendency for the development of a greater variation between the inflation rates of the individual countries, the similarity of the pattern of their rates continues after the breakdown of the fixed exchange rate regime. This can be explained by the fact that the exchange rate regime in existence since 1972 has not been a pure float, but rather a managed float with significant degrees of intervention by the various national authorities. In consequence the international transmission of inflation, through the channels noted earlier, has still operated to produce some conformity among the individual inflation rates though to a lesser degree than during the fixed exchange rate system.

5.6 Cause of inflation: concluding remarks

We have presented two extreme and competing views of inflation. Monetarists argue that while sociological and political factors are indirectly important because they influence the monetary and fiscal policies pursued by governments, the prime cause of inflation is excessive monetary expansion. In their view, governments can control the money supply if they choose to do so. Monetarists believe that since governments cause inflation by pursuing excessively expansionary monetary policies, they must accept responsibility for inflation. Possible reasons for the excessive monetary expansion are varied. For example, governments may be reluctant to finance their expenditure by either raising (i) tax rates or (ii) interest rates to the necessary levels because such policies would be unpopular with the electorate. In contrast adherents of the sociological view argue that inflation is caused primarily by exogenous wage increases due to a variety of social pressures. Furthermore, because of these social factors, governments have little choice but to increase the money supply to prevent unemployment from rising to socially and politically unacceptable levels. In both views inflationary pressures will be transmitted between countries especially in the case of fixed exchange rates.

However many economists, especially Keynesians, take a compromise or eclectic position between these two extreme viewpoints. They would argue that both the monetarist and sociological viewpoints contain some truth. Consequently from this compromise view inflation can be caused by both excessive monetary expansion and sociological pressures. In fact an assessment of the controversy which commands a faily wide degree of acceptance especially in America is that in the long run persistent inflation is not possible without an excessive rate of monetary expansion. However in the short run inflation can be caused by a wide range of factors operating both from the demand and from the supply side of the economy especially wage costs in the latter case.

Part II
MACROECONOMIC POLICY

6 Objectives of Macroeconomic Policy

6.1 Introduction to macroeconomic policy

The theoretical models examined in Chapters 1, 3-5 provide the foundation for the discussion of economic policy in this and subsequent chapters. Macroeconomic policy is concerned with the attempts of policy makers to influence the behaviour of broad economic aggregates in order to improve the performance of the economy.

The main macroeconomic objectives of policy in advanced industrial countries are generally accepted to be the attainment of: (i) a high and stable level of employment; (ii) a stable general price level; (iii) a growing level of real income (i.e. economic growth); (iv) balance of payments equilibrium; and (v) certain distributional aims. The underlying nature of these targets is examined in more detail in sections 6.2-6.6 below.

The question arises as to how the government can achieve these objectives. In a democratic society they are not under the sole control of the government. For example, the level of employment depends on the decisions not only of the goverment (e.g. for employment in the public sector) but also of private firms as to how many workers they wish to employ. Policy makers therefore have to operate on other variables in order to try and attain their targets. These variables are called instrumental variables. A distinction is sometimes made between actual or primary instruments and nominal or intermediate insruments. The authorities can directly change the former, but it is changes in the latter instruments which lead ultimately to changes in the target variables. For example, the authorities may change a tax rate (i.e. primary instrument) but it is the resulting change in total tax payments (i.e. an intermediate instrument), which affects expenditure, output and employment. The chain of action is shown in Figure 6.1.

Policy instruments can be classified in various ways. For example, one method is according to which government agency is responsible for initiating changes in them. If this classification were adopted it

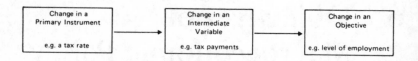

Figure 6.1. Instrumental and target variables

would mean that, for the UK (i) fiscal policy would cover activities whose responsibility lay within the Treasury (e.g. a tax change); and (ii) monetary policy would refer to those activities under the Bank of England (e.g. a change in minimum lending rate). One of the main weaknesses of such a classification is that decisions taken on fiscal matters often have monetary implications (e.g. the size of the public sector borrowing requirement). For the purposes of this book we will therefore define policy measures according to the nature of the instrument involved. Fiscal policy is defined as any measure that alters the level, timing, or composition of government expenditure and/or the level, timing or structure of tax payments. Monetary policy encompasses measures taken to alter: the supply of money and/or credit (e.g. a change in banks' reserve requirements); interest rates (e.g. a change in minimum lending rate); hire purchase conditions; etc. In Chapters 8 and 9 we will examine the importance of, and interdependence between, fiscal and monetary policy. Other important instruments available to the policy maker discussed in subsequent chapters include: expenditure switching policies (Chapter 10), prices and incomes policy (Chapter 11) and supply management policies (Chapter 13).

Since it is not possible to influence the policy objectives directly a considerable degree of knowledge is required about how the instruments affect the intermediate variables and finally the main objectives. The technical framework within which stabilisation policy is conducted is discussed in Chapter 7.

6.2 Full employment
Since the Second World War one of the main policy targets of the UK government has been the 'the maintenance of a high and stable level of employment' (1944 White Paper on Employment Policy, Cmd 6527: HMSO). There is wide disagreement over what precisely constitutes an acceptable/desirable level of unemployment. In a dynamic economy unemployment will always exist because: (i) individuals

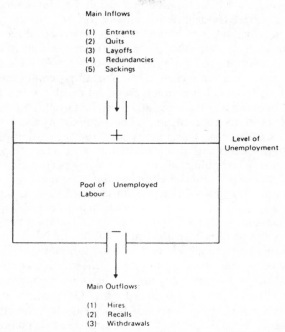

Figure 6.2. The main flows into and out of a pool of unemployed labour

will be changing jobs within an industry and will remain unemployed during the time they are searching for new employment; and (ii) some industries will be declining due to underlying changes in demand and supply. There is therefore great difficulty in specifying a precise level of unemployment consistent with the theoretical concept of full employment.

6.2.1 *Nature and measurement of unemployment*
Unemployment can be analysed in terms of flows into (i.e. those which increase unemployment) and out of (i.e. those which decrease unemployment) a pool of unemployed labour (Figure 6.2).

An individual may join the unemployment pool due to one or other of five main reasons. First, the person concerned may be a new entrant to the labour force looking for a job (e.g. school leaver) or someone returning to the work force (e.g. a woman having raise a family). Second, a person may quit his or her existing job and search for new employment. Where the person remains unemployed for a relatively short time this is often referred to as search or frictional unemployment. Third, a worker may be laid off for a period of time due to a temporary decline in demand for the firm's product or, a temporary interruption in the supply of materials essential for production. A specific example arising from a change in demand is seasonal unemployment. Fourth, a person may be made redundant due to a permanent change in demand or supply conditions for his or her firm's product. Where unemployment results from shifts in the relative demand for, or supply of, labour in particular industries it is sometimes referred to as structural unemployment. Examples of this, in the UK, include jobs lost in the textile and shipbuilding industries and also those lost with the introduction of the micro chip and other labour saving technological changes. Fifth, a person may be sacked or fired from a job and therefore become unemployed.

There are three main outflows from the pool. First, an unemployed person may find a temporary or permanent job. Second, a person who has been temporarily laid off may be recalled to his or her job. Third, an unemployed person may withdraw from the labour force either temporarily or permanently (e.g. due to retirement).

Whether or not unemployment increases or decreases over time depends upon the extent to which inflows are counterbalanced by outflows from the unemployment pool. Only where inflows are perfectly matched by outflows will the level of unemployment remain unchanged. It should be noted that if workers search more carefully for a new job and consequently remain unemployed for a longer time measured unemployment in the pool will rise even though the rate at which people leave jobs remains unchanged.

Unemployment can also be analysed according to the type of unemployment. Traditionally three main types or categories have been identified namely: frictional, structural and demand deficient (i.e. Keynesian) unemployment. As noted above frictional unemployment exists because, having left one job, it takes time for a person to search for and find a new job. Structural unemployment occurs, as the name implies, because of structural changes that take place in the economy. Due to such changes particular industries and regions will contract, while others expand. In the sectors experiencing contraction an excess supply of labour will be reflected in more individuals looking for jobs than there are job opportunities available. In contrast, in the expanding sectors new job opportunities will outstrip the supply of individuals looking for jobs i.e. an excess demand for labour will prevail. The extent and duration of structural unemployment will consequently depend on both the occupational and geographical mobility of labour. Lastly, as discussed in Chapter 1 Keynesian unemployment (also referred to as cyclical unemployment) arises from a state of deficient aggregate demand. It is worth noting that in practice it is sometimes difficult to distinguish between various types of unemployment.

Clearly each type of unemployment requires different remedial policies. Frictional unemployment could, for example, be reduced by policies which improve the provision of information concerning job vacancies. Structural unemployment could be reduced by policies designed to improve the occupational mobility of labour (e.g. retraining programmes) and geographical mobility of labour (e.g. financial assistance to help cover the costs of moving from one area to another). The microeconomic policy measures noted above attempt to reduce frictional and structural unemployment by improving the structure of the labour market. In contrast the remedy for Keynesian unemployment involves macroeconomic policies that increase the level of aggregate demand in the economy.

Figure 6.3 shows the behaviour of registered unemployment in the UK over that last thirty-three years. The graph reveals significant increases in the level of unemployment since the mid-1960s. One reason advanced for this rise is the increase in social welfare benefits and redundancy payments which allows workers to take a longer time to search for the 'right' job. Other reasons put forward include changes in the structure of the UK economy and more recently depressed demand due to anti-inflation policies. It is worth noting that changes in the percentage unemployed are not entirely determined by the factors summarised in Figure 6.2. Changes in the size of the working population also influence these figures. For example, with no change in the number unemployed a fall in the total working population would raise the percentage unemployed.

The extent to which published unemployment figures in a particular country reflects the true nature of unemployment depends upon how unemployment is measured. In the UK unemployment is measured by the number of people who register as being unemployed and seeking employment at local employment exchanges.[1] The main purposes of registration by workers are: (i) to receive unemployment benefit and (ii) to obtain new employment. In one respect the UK statistics tend to underestimate the true extent of unemployment as they exclude those unemployed individuals who want a job but who may not register as being unemployed because they are not entitled to unemployment

1. In October 1982 a new system of measurement was introduced—unemployment is now measured by the number of unemployed people *claiming* benefit at Unemployment Offices.

benefit. Examples of this category include school leavers and women wishing to return to work after raising a family. The extent of this type of so-called hidden unemployment is likely to increase when the chances of finding a job are poor (e.g. during a recession). On the other hand UK statistics include unemployed workers who are not actively seeking a job (e.g. those near retirement). Furthermore they include unemployed workers in industries which are subject to periodic fluctuations in the level of employment. In this case a worker is not 'economically' (as opposed to socially) unemployed until such time as his enforced period of idleness exceeds the customary level for that industry. Registered unemployment figures also include those individuals who register as being unemployed but who work on their own account i.e. one component of the so-called black economy.[1] Estimates of the importance of the total black economy vary from a low of somewhere near $2\frac{1}{2}$ per cent of total GNP to a high of up to 15 per cent. The Inland Revenue has stated that it believes the figure to be in the region of 5-$7\frac{1}{2}$ per cent of GNP.

Clearly therefore unemployment figures are unreliable indicators of the true extent of unemployment. Another indicator of unemployment sometimes used is figures of job vacancies published by the government. These indicate, perhaps imperfectly, the state of the total demand for labour in the economy (i.e. via firms, the government, etc.).

6.2.2 *Costs of unemployment*
The simple approach of analysing unemployment in flow terms needs to be supplemented by three considerations when discussing the costs of unemployment. Here it is important to take into account: (i) the length of time a person remains unemployed; (ii) the breakdown of unemployment figures between particular groups, which may be identified, within the labour force (i.e. according to age, sex, qualifications, etc.); and (iii) regional variations in the rate of unemployment. These factors may be, and often are interrelated. For example, the duration of unemployment may be related to the types of job available in a particular region and such considerations as the age, qualifications and race of the person concerned (e.g. high unemployment among young unskilled coloured workers in Liverpool). It is important to remember that the aggregate unemployment rate for an economy may conceal marked variations between particular regions and groups within the labour force.

---

1. The term 'black economy' is used to describe that section of the output of the economy which is not declared for tax purposes.

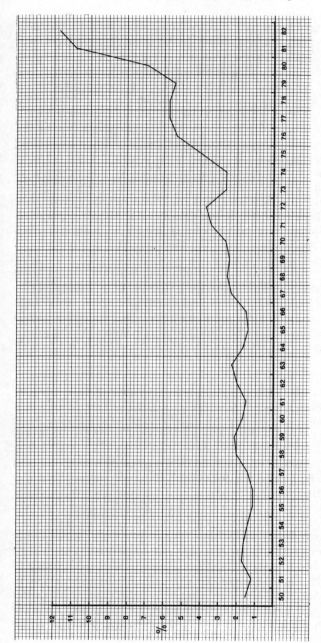

Figure 6.3. Unemployment in the UK, 1950–82
Source: Central Statistical Office (1983), *Economic Trends: Annual Supplement & August 1983* (London: HMSO).
Note: Unemployment rates graphed are the numbers unemployed (excluding school leavers and adult students registered for temporary employment during a current vacation) expressed as a percentage of the appropriate mid-year estimates of total employees (employed and unemployed).

The costs associated with unemployment include those borne by an individual and society as a whole. An unemployed person will suffer loss of income (the extent of which depends on the amount of benefits which can and are claimed) and probably also some social distress e.g. insecurity, family tensions, etc. Both costs are likely to depend upon and be positively related to the length of time the person remains unemployed. Although a cost like social distress is almost impossible to quantify it is likely to be very important to the individual concerned and should not be ignored. Furthermore unemployment statistics fail to indicate accurately the cost borne by individuals. First, no indication is given of the number of people in the family who depend on the unemployed person. Second, some costs are borne by those who are still employed but who experience a reduction in hours worked. To the extent that the total output of an economy is below its potential level if full employment prevailed society as a whole also loses. The cost incurred is in respect of foregone output. For example, it has been estimated that for the US economy the cost of a 1 per cent increase in the rate of unemployment, in the short run, is a 3 per cent fall in the level of real output. Apart from the economic cost there is the social cost of high unemployment leading to social and political tensions within a country. It is not far-fetched to link increases in crime and the growth of extremist political parties to unemployment rising above tolerable levels.

6.3 Price stability
As we have seen earlier in Chapter 5 inflation can be defined as a process of continually rising prices (i.e. the aggregate or general price level). Although prices will on average rise, as inflation proceeds over time, they will not change at the same rate. Changes in relative prices will occur as demand and supply conditions for individual goods and services change. Indeed the price of certain goods and services may even fall e.g. the price of electronic calculators over the last ten years.

The maintenance of a relatively stable price level is one of the main policy goals pursued by Western governments. In practice though it is extremely difficult to define, in any precise manner, what constitutes an acceptable or tolerable rate of inflation. This will be influenced by changing economic, political and historical circumstances. Figure 6.4 shows the rate of inflation experienced in the UK over the last thirty-three years. The graph reveals that after the period of inflation (1951—3) associated with the Korean War the UK experienced a relatively low and steady inflation rate up to

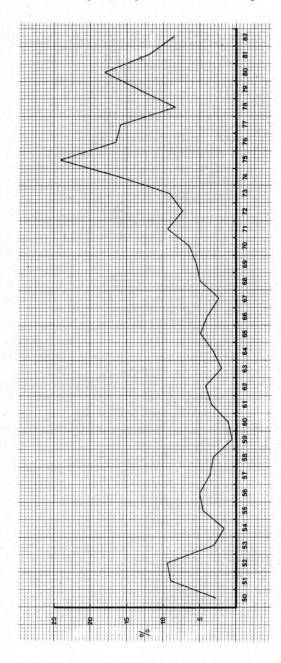

Figure 6.4. Inflation in the UK, 1950–82
Source: Central Statistical Office (1983), *Economic Trends: Annual Supplement & August 1983* (London: HMSO).
Note: General index of retail prices (percentage increase on year earlier).

to the mid-1960s. From the mid-1960s the rate of inflation accelerated reaching a peak in 1975. Similar patterns of inflation up to the early 1970s have been experienced by other major Western industrial countries (see Figure 5.6).

6.3.1 *Costs of inflation*

The costs of inflation depend critically upon whether inflation is perfectly or imperfectly anticipated. For example, in an economy with money wages growing at 10 per cent (per annum) and prices at 6 per cent, real wages would grow at 4 per cent (per annum). Provided: (i) these were equilibrium rates of growth; and (ii) there was no change in these rates, workers and employers would have little concern about inflation. Similarly if owners of financial assets (e.g. bonds, bank deposits) received a return above 6 per cent (e.g. 8 per cent leaving them a 2 per cent real return) which they regarded as adequate inflation would cause them no concern.[1] The sole cost incurred would be the loss of the purchasing power of the notes and coins they (i.e. the public) carry in their pockets.Contrast this with a situation in which the rate of inflation suddenly rose unexpectedly from 6 to 10 per cent. Workers would incur zero growth in their real wages and holders of financial securities would see the real return on their assets turn into a loss of 2 per cent (per annum). In other words distributional costs would result and in this example workers and lenders would lose out to profit earners and borrowers respectively. To put it more formally, in an economy with a perfectly anticipated rate of inflation the expected inflation rate can be correctly taken into account in economic transactions thereby avoiding arbitrary changes in the distribution of wealth and income.

In the real world however inflation is not perfectly anticipated. There are those who gain from and those who lose from inflation. The main areas of concern are the relationships between: (i) tax payers and the government; (ii) borrowers and lenders; and (iii) workers in strong trade unions and those in weak unions.

In the UK a progressive tax system is in operation (i.e. the rate of tax payment increases as the tax payer's income increases) so that inflation changes the real value of tax payments in two ways. First inflation erodes the real value of tax allowances (i.e. those allowed before an individual becomes liable to pay tax). Second, by increasing nominal incomes inflation results in individuals being moved into higher income brackets where they must pay higher

1. Note that for ease of exposition we are ignoring the fact that interest payments may be subject to tax.

marginal rates of tax. Finally, liability for taxes on capital gains on assets is measured in nominal terms so that tax is paid if the value of assets sold has increased in money terms, whether or not this is matched by a change in the real value of assets. Therefore inflation causes the real value of tax payments, made by the private sector to the government, to increase. This distributional cost could be avoided if the government altered the level of allowances and income brackets for taxation purposes in line with inflation. This procedure is called indexation and is discussed in Chapter 12.

The second main area of growth is the relationship between borrowers and lenders. The important distinction here is between nominal and real interest rates. The rate of interest paid by the borrower is called the nominal interest rate. If the expected rate of inflation is deducted from the nominal rate we obtain the real rate of interest. The problem is that the nominal rate of interest only adjusts slowly to changes in the rate of inflation so that if the rate of inflation is rising the borrower benefits and the lender is penalised. This can easily be seen since in recent years the real rate of return has often been negative i.e. the rate of inflation has been greater than the nominal interest rate.

Finally, we come to the third main distributional effect. In general when average earnings rise in line with inflation, earnings in some industries will rise more quickly and some less quickly. These changes are often unconnected, in the short run, with changes in demand and supply conditions but are attributable to the different relative bargaining strengths of the various trade unions involved.

While the main costs of inflation occur when it is imperfectly anticipated, there are certain costs involved even when inflation is perfectly anticipated. Economic units hold a certain amount of money in the form of currency (i.e. notes and coins). This money is held for transaction purposes and because money provides a range of services (e.g. convenience) to the holder of it. No interest is paid on currency so that a positive rate of inflation generates a negative rate of return on cash balances by reducing the real value of money held in this form. It is clear therefore that economic units will tend to economise on their holdings of cash balances. Unless inflation starts to disrupt the payments system (e.g. during hyper-inflations) the costs involved (e.g. visiting the bank more frequently to cash smaller cheques) are not likely to be large. Finally, the costs of inflation also include the time spent and real resources used in changing the prices on goods in shops, parking meters, vending machines, etc.

6.4 Economic growth

6.4.1 *Nature and measurement of economic growth*
In additon to full employment and price stability the governments of advanced industrial countries have also been committed to attempting to achieve rapid and sustained economic growth of real GNP. Such an increase in the quantity of output and services produced can result from two main sources: (i) an increase in the utilisation of existing resources (i.e. an increased utilisation of existing capacity); and (ii) an increase in actual productive potential (i.e. an increase in a country's capacity to produce goods). Strictly speaking economic growth refers to the latter of these two sources. In an economy suffering heavy unemployment production can be increased by reducing unemployment and utilising spare capacity (i.e. (i) above). On the other hand production can be increased by the invention and introduction of new machinery which increases labour productivity and therefore the capacity of the economy (i.e. (ii) above). While these two sources of an increase in real GNP should be distinguished when discussing a country's rate of growth they rarely are in practice.

Economic growth is desired by governments to achieve political aims such as international prestige and military power and also to increase the living standards of the inhabitants of a country. However two important considerations must be taken into account before it is possible to use real GNP as a measure of living standards. First, what is important is real income per head of the population. If GNP in real terms increases by 4 per cent but at the same time population increases by 1 per cent then the per capita growth rate is only 3 per cent. Second, whether or not an increase in GNP improves living standards and the quality of life partly depends on its composition. For example, the standard of living is not likely to increase to the same degree if increased military spending, rather than expenditure on consumer goods, private or public (e.g. hospital or education provision) accounts for the rise in GNP. Defence expenditure is necessary for national security rather than for providing increased consumption for the inhabitants of a country. Furthermore as we noted in Chapter 1, section 1.2.3 international comparisons of GNP are fraught with difficulty because of differences in the methods of preparing accounts. It is therefore important whilst making international comparisons of real GNP per capita to ensure that the same definitions and methods have been used to calculate GNP and that any differences in the composition of GNP are taken into account. Finally, it should be remembered that growth of real GNP per head gives no indication of how such increases are distributed among the various sectors of the economy (e.g. between the rich and poor).

Figure 6.5 shows the rate of economic growth achieved in the UK over the last thirty-three years. Reference to the graph reveals that up to the end of the 1960s the UK economy tended to fluctuate fairly regularly between periods of fairly rapid growth and relatively mild recession. In general GDP increased quite sharply in boom periods (e.g. 1959-60, 1963-4) and increased at less than the average rate in times of recession (e.g. 1956-8, 1961-2). Since the 1970s this regular pattern has tended to break down and in certain years economic growth has been significantly negative e.g. 1980 and 1981. Over the entire period 1950-82 economic growth has been somewhat irregular. Finally, it should be noted that UK growth performance has been low compared to that achieved in many Western industrial countries (e.g. Japan, West Germany, France, etc.).

6.4.2 Costs of economic growth

One of the main causes of growth is investment which increases the quantity and quality of a country's capital stock and raises its productive potential. If an economy's resources are fully employed additional investment will entail the sacrifice of present consumption (living standards) to achieve faster growth and extra consumption in the future. The opportunity cost involved depends on society's rate of time preference. This concept refers to the degree to which society is prepared to sacrifice a given amount of present consumption for extra consumption in the future.

In addition to this opportunity cost certain social and environmental costs may be incurred in achieving economic growth which are not adequately reflected in GNP figures. These costs may include increased pollution, traffic congestion, noise, urban sprawl and other external diseconomies. Although it is very difficult to quantify such costs an increase in the output of these 'bads' is likely to affect welfare adversely. Mishan, for example, in *The Costs of Economic Growth* (1967) has been vociferous in bringing people's attention to these costs arguing that growth may cause a decrease in an individual's range of choice and welfare. This can happen when certain goods are withdrawn from production and when amenities are adversely affected by growth (e.g. erosion of the countryside).

A further economic cost of economic growth involves the question of the depletion of natural resources. The current debate over sources of energy is just one example. This topic is nevertheless the subject of considerable controversy since some economists argue that the price mechanism will overcome this problem. For example, increasing oil shortages will lead to price increases which in turn will lead to: (i) oil economy; and (ii) the development of alternative sources of energy. In contrast another school argues that a major energy crisis is looming in the future.

Apart from these costs there is also the problem of the distribution of the benefits of economic growth both between nations (developed and developing) and individuals within the same nation. Nevertheless despite the increasing recognition of these economic, environmental and social costs growth is still likely to remain one of the main objectives of macroeconomic policy makers.

6.5 Balance of payments equilibrium

In this section on the main targets of macroeconomic policy we will examine the objective of maintaining balance of payments equilibrium. This is an important goal since failure to attain a satisfactory balance of payments position may act as a constraint on a country's ability to achieve the other main policy targets.

Figure 6.6 shows the current UK account surplus/deficit as a percentage of GDP over the period 1950-82. During the 1950s and 1960s the balance of payments tended to move with changes in the level of economic activity. Periods of rapid expansion were generally associated with balance of payments deficits and vice versa. Following devaluation in 1967 (and also domestic deflation and rapid growth of world trade), the balance of payments moved into surplus between 1969 and 1972. The market deterioration in the balance of payments which occurred between 1973 and 1976 largely reflects the effects of the quadrupling of oil prices in 1973 and the subsequent world recession. As we have already examined the nature and measurement of the balance of payments in Chapter 4 we will move on to examine the costs of balance of payments disequilibrium.

6.5.1 *Costs of balance of payments disequilibrium*

As discussed in Chapter 4 it is possible for a country under a system of fixed exchange rates, at least in the short run, to experience balance of payments disequilibria (deficits or surpluses). If a country achieves a balance of payments surplus it can add to its foreign exchange reserves and/or repay official government debt. There is, however, an opportunity cost involved in achieving continuous balance of payments surpluses since a country is foregoing consumption or investment in return for the acquisition of foreign reserves. A country experiencing a deficit on its balance of

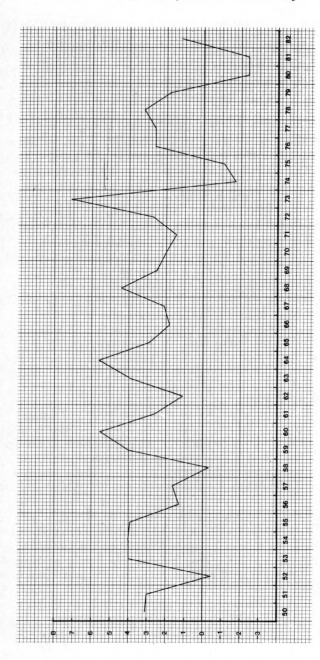

Figure 6.5. Economic growth in the UK, 1950–82
Source: Central Statistical Office (1983), *Economic Trends: Annual Supplement & August 1983* (London: HMSO)
Note: GDP at factor cost (1975 prices), average estimate from expenditure, income and output data (percentage increase on year earlier).

payments must run down its reserves and/or incur debts by borrowing from abroad, to pay for the deficit. The level of a country's foreign exchange reserves (and the extent to which other governments, foreign monetary authorities or private financial institutions are prepared to lend funds to a deficit country) provides a limit to the time a country can experience a balance of payments deficit.

However the nature of the balance of payments target is more precise than just general balance of payment equilibrium. In the long run it is necessary for a developed nation to achieve a balance on the current account. Such a country is unable to finance persistent current account deficits by continuous borrowing via the capital account. There are at least three reasons why such a policy is not feasible or desirable in the long run. First, persistent borrowing requires rising interest rates to attract the necessary funds from abroad and consequently increasing levels of total interest payments. Second, high interest rates will retard investment and subsequently the economic growth which is necessary to repay the debt. Third, lending nations are unlikely to be so generous as to continue to increase their lending without requiring some control over the economic policy followed by the borrowing country.

Adoption of floating exchange rates removes the balance of payments as a major policy constraint but, as we have examined in Chapter 4, does not completely insulate an economy from the outside world.

6.6 Distributional aims

Every government is concerned with the distribution of income and wealth both between individuals and regions within an economy. Traditionally socialist governments have been concerned with the distribution of income and wealth between rich and poor members of society. Their general aim is to ensure a more equitable distribution (defined in practical terms as a redistribution of income and wealth from the rich to the poor) in order to achieve a more just and humane society. On the other hand conservative governments have generally been more concerned with rewarding those members of society who undertake risk and show initiative whilst at the same time not losing sight of the objective of alleviating poverty. Most policies have distributional effects that must be taken into consideration. To take just one example, more complicated tax systems are likely to bear more heavily on small businesses than large undertakings who will already possess sophisticated financial accounting systems.

During recent years the problem of regional imbalances has come

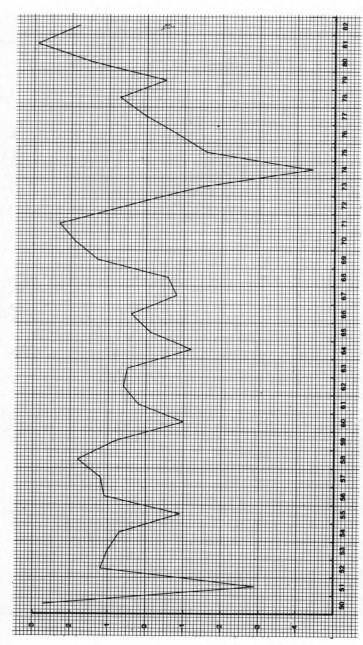

Figure 6.6. UK current account Surplus(+) / Deficit(-) as a percentage of GDP (1950–82)
Source: Central Statistical Office (1983) *Economic Trends: Annual Supplement & August 1983* (London: HMSO).

increasingly to the forefront. It is widely recognised that labour is not perfectly mobile so that changes in the structure of industries within regions lead to unemployment. This is evident in the United Kingdom where Scotland, Wales, Northern England and Northern Ireland have experienced higher levels of unemployment than other regions. Government policy has therefore attempted to restore the balance by favouring these regions though the success of such policies is open to considerable dispute.

Macroeconomic policy also influences the allocation of resources. Thus a commitment to a large public sector necessitates taxes on the private sector so as to allocate resources (i.e. land, labour and capital) to the production of goods required by the public sector.

Distribution aims are the subject of a considerable degree of controversy but at the very least policy makers must take into consideration the distribution effects of macroeconomic policies adopted.

6.7 Potential conflicts between aims

So far we have discussed each aim in isolation. Unfortunately for the policy maker the issue is not so simple since attainment of these aims may involve conflicts. This make it difficult to achieve all aims simultaneously. For example, a policy decision might be made to maintain a fixed exchange rate and attempt to correct a balance of payments deficit by reducing imports by domestic deflation. In this case there is a potential conflict between full employment and balance of payments equilibrium for a country adhering to a fixed exchange rate.

A second example of a potential conflict is between full employment and price stability. As we saw in Chapter 5, section 5.3.2 a level of unemployment below the natural rate can only be maintained at the expense of accelerating inflation. Thus if the specified target of full employment is lower than the natural rate there is a potential clash between the two aims of price stability and full employment. In fact this problem is more severe because the Phillips curve analysis examined in Chapter 5 predicts that the only way inflation can be reduced is to allow unemployment to rise temporarily above the natural rate.

There are many such examples of potential conflicts between objectives and it is the job of the policy maker to allocate priorities to the various objectives. It is largely the function of the politicians to establish priorities between conflicting goals and this inevitably involves their personal value judgements and preferences. Considerable disagreement may result over the desirability of particular choices. Different political parties may list the same basic objectives yet attach different priorities to individual targets. For example, the main goal of a particular administration might be to reduce the rate of inflation to X per cent, while keeping the level of unemployment to below Y per cent, subject to a satisfactory (however defined) balance of payment position.

In contrast another political party may desire to reduce inflation to $\frac{1}{2}X$ per cent whilst permitting unemployment to rise above Y per cent. Furthermore a change in political and/or economic circumstances may result in declared objectives being changed, even during one political party's term of office. It is very difficult therefore to provide a single criteria for policy evaluation. The role of the economist is to give advice on the feasibility and desirability of economic policies designed to attain the ultimate targets. He will also be interested in the targets and the costs of failing to attain any target though of course the ultimate responsibility in policy making lies with the politician.

TABLE 6.1 Average value and variability of main policy targets in the UK, 1950–82

Target	^5M = Arithmetic mean ^5S = Standard deviation	1950–9	1960–9	1970–9	1980–2
[1]Unemployment	M	1.5	1.9	4.1	9.8
	S	0.3	0.4	1.3	2.1
[2]Inflation	M	4.3	3.5	12.6	12.8
	S	2.7	1.3	5.3	3.9
[3]Economic	M	2.4	3.2	2.1	− 1.2
growth	S	1.7	1.5	2.3	1.7
[4]Balance of	M	0.7	− 0.1	−0.4	2.1
payments	S	1.5	0.8	1.8	0.6

Source: Central Statistical Office (1983), *Economic Trends: Annual Supplement* (London: HMSO).
Notes: (1) Percentage unemployed (excluding school leavers and adult students registered for temporary employment during a current vacation).
(2) General Index of Retail Prices: percentage increase on a year earlier.
(3) Average estimate of GDP (factor cost) at 1975 prices: percentage increase on a year earlier.
(4) Current account surplus (+)/deficit (−) as a percentage of GDP at factor cost.
(5) Students unfamiliar with these two measures should consult any elementary statistical methods text.

6.8 Concluding remarks

In this chapter we have examined the objectives of economic policy and some of the constraints faced in trying to achieve them. As a guide to the sucess of the UK authorities in achieving their declared objectives Table 6.1 shows the average value and variability of the main policy targets over the last three decades. Reference to this table and Figures 6.3–6.6 (which show the behaviour of the target variables over the period concerned) casts doubt on the success of UK governments in attaining these objectives. Indeed the disappointing experience of the 1970s has continued into the present decade. In the next chapter we examine the problems of using stabilisation policy to achieve these aims.

7 Problems of Stabilisation Policy

7.1 Introduction

In Chapter 6 we discussed the main policy goals pursued by governments of advanced industrial countries. In this chapter we will outline the nature of stabilisation policies and the technical framework within which stabilisation policy is conducted. This involves a discussion of some of the problems and constraints faced by the policy maker and provides a framework in which to place the analysis contained in subsequent chapters. We begin by discussing the nature of stabilisation policies.

7.2 Nature of stabilisation policies

Stabilisation or demand management policies[1] are designed to control aggregate demand so as to achieve the objectives discussed in Chapter 6. The two main policies which can be used to control aggregate demand are: (i) fiscal policy i.e. varying government expenditure and/or taxes; and (ii) monetary policy i.e. changing the supply of money, interest rates, or the supply of credit to finance expenditure.

It is desirable to indicate the general nature of these policies. First, demand management policies can be used to try to achieve full employment and avoid inflation. It is important however to realise that if the analysis of the natural rate of unemployment, examined in Chapter 5, section 5.3.2, is correct the full employment target is not some measure derived for political purposes but that consistent with the natural rate of unemployment. If the natural rate is too high to be politically acceptable, then supply side policies should be used to lower the natural rate. These policies are discussed in Chapter 13. Second,

1. Traditionally economists have regarded stabilisation policies as being demand management policies. More recently some economists have advocated the use of supply management policies to stabilise the economy. Such policies are discussed in Chapter 13.

demand management policies can be used to achieve balance of payments targets.

We deal with domestic issues first, abstracting from the practical difficulties of carrying out stabilisation policies discussed later in this chapter (sections 7.3-7.6). If national income is less than the full employment level expansionary fiscal (i.e. increases in government expenditure and/or reductions in taxes) or monetary policies (i.e. increases in the quantity of money, supply of credit, or reductions in interest rates) can be implemented in order to increase aggregate demand. Conversely, if aggregate demand exceeds the full employment output of the economy so that inflation occurs, contractionary monetary and fiscal policies need to be implemented. The precise nature of these is discussed in Chapters 8 (fiscal policy) and 9 (monetary policy).

The role for demand management policies in achieving domestic objectives is demonstrated in Figure 7.1 using the 45° diagram developed in Chapter 1.

Initial equilibrium occurs at Y_1 where aggregate demand AD_1 $(C+I+G+X-Im)$ is equal to output. This is less than the full employment level of output denoted by Yc. By implementing

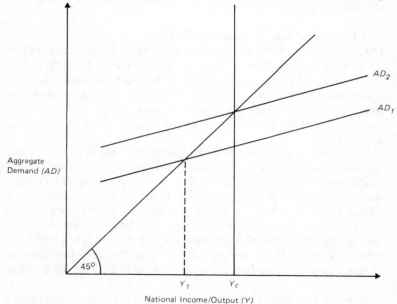

Figure 7.1. The role for demand management policies in achieving domestic objectives

expansionary fiscal or monetary policies the government can increase aggregate demand i.e. in terms of Figure 7.1 induce the aggregate demand curve to shift upwards to AD_2, eliminating unemployment. The analysis for situations of excess demand is precisely the reverse of that described above.

With regard to balance of payments objectives, it should be noted that in the context of the terminology developed in Chapter 4, section 4.7.2, contractionary fiscal and monetary policies are known as expenditure reducing policies since they reduce domestic expenditure or absorption. As income falls imports of goods and services decrease so that the current account of the balance of payments improves. These results are demonstrated in Figure 7.2. The top panel shows the standard 45° line diagram and the lower panel represents the current account of the balance of payments. Exports are treated as exogenous i.e. independent of the level of national income, whereas imports increase as domestic national income increases.

The initial equilibrium level of income is Y_1. Reference to panel 2 shows that, at this level of income, imports are greater than exports so

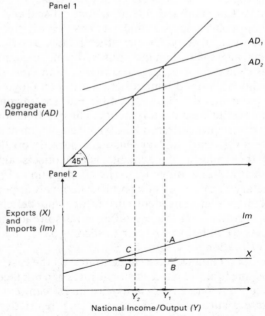

Figure 7.2. The effect of restrictive demand management policies

that there is a deficit on the current account of the balance of payments equal to *AB*. Restrictive demand management policies will cause the aggregate demand curve to move downwards to AD_2 which, as stated earlier, reduces both the level of output (i.e. to Y_2) and the balance of payments deficit on current account (i.e. to *CD*). Clearly if pushed hard enough restrictive monetary and fiscal policies could completely eliminate the deficit. The problem arises if the level of national income compatible with a zero balance on the current account is less than the full employment or capacity level of national income. This would mean that the deficit on the balance of payments (current account) would be eliminated at the cost of unemployment. The appropriate measure in this case would be to adopt policies to alter the position of the export and import functions in Figure 7.2. Such policies known as expenditure switching policies are dealt with in Chapter 10.

Expansionary monetary and fiscal policies will have the reverse effect on the current account of the balance of payments. An increase in aggregate demand will cause national income to rise. Consequently total imports will also increase causing deterioration in the current account of the balance of payments.

Finally, it is worth noting that contractionary fiscal and monetary policies have opposite effects on interest rates. A restrictive monetary policy raises interest rates. On the other hand a restrictive fiscal policy lowers aggregate demand thus reducing income and the transactions demand for money, and therefore interest rates. One way out of the potential dilemma between full employment and a balance of payments deficit is to combine an expansionary fiscal policy with a restrictive monetary policy. The combination of these two policies can, in principle, produce (i) full employment and (ii) an interest rate sufficiently high to ensure a surplus on the capital account of the balance of payments which offsets any current account deficit at full employment. The combination of policies is called monetary/fiscal policy mix and is deceptively appealing. The main problem is that consistent current account deficits require continuous borrowing on the capital account so that total debt is increasing. As we noted in Chapter 6, section 6.5.1. this is not an equilibrium situation.

So far in this section we have concentrated on the case where the exchange regime is one of fixed exchange rates or a managed float so that balance of payments deficits/surpluses can exist. If the exchange rate regime is one of pure floating, restrictive demand management policies will lead to an appreciation of the exchange rate instead of an improvement in the balance of payments.

Having discussed the nature of stabilisation policies we now move on to discuss the main problems and constraints faced by the policy maker.

7.3 Theoretical and empirical controversies

Economic policy is designed against the background of a theoretical model. Any student who has studied marcroeconomics will be aware that the 'true' model is a subject of considerable controversy. To illustrate this point we will take just one example concerning the specification of the consumption function. While there is general agreement among economists that consumption depends upon income, there is no such agreement over which concept of income is appropriate (i.e. is it current, permanent, or some other concept of income?). In Chapter 1, section 1.3.1. we discussed the Keynesian view that consumption expenditure depends upon current disposable income. In contrast some economists (e.g. Milton Friedman) have argued that consumption is related to permanent rather than current income. The concept of permanent income refers to a household's future expected income stream (i.e. its normal or long-run income). If an individual believes that a specific income change is only temporary, it will have only a small effect on his permanent income and consequently a small effect on his consumption. An economist who believes that consumption is a function of permanent income is likely to be more sceptical about the usefulness of a tax change for stabilisation purposes than one who believes that consumption depends upon current disposable income. In the former view expenditure would only be altered to the extent that a tax change influenced people's assessment of their long-run income. In contrast, if consumption depends on current disposable income then a tax change will alter current consumption and consequently fiscal policy will be a potentially more powerful instrument for stabilisation purposes. Such controversies are not uncommon given the current state of economic knowledge; further examples include the New Cambridge view of the use of import controls (discussed in Chapter 10) and the role of monetary policy and the monetarist debate.

Despite the large number of empirical studies carried out on the behavioural relationships a considerable degree of uncertainty remains over the precise values of the parameters of models used to analyse the economy. This uncertainty influences the way in which policy instruments are used in order to achieve certain declared objectives. It is not sufficient that the policy maker knows the general direction of the effect of any change in a policy instrument on the target variables. He must also know how much the target variables respond to a change in an instrument. For example, if government expenditure is increased by £100 million in real terms, the policy maker needs to predict accurately by how much and over what time period the target variables will change. Such precise econometric evidence is hard to come by in the real world and in practice we have a variety of estimates of the size and timing of policy multipliers which, in many instances, do not agree. These differences are also reflected in, rather than resolved by, the existing generation of macroeconomic models of the UK economy (surveyed in Chapter 15 section 15.4). For the UK economy it is generally believed that the government expenditure mutliplier, in the short run, is between $1\frac{1}{2}$ and 2. This means that an increase in government expenditure of £100 million will lead ultimately (after two years) to a rise in national income of approximately £175 million. Due to these differences of opinion regarding both economic theory and econometric estimation of various economic relationships the conduct of policy remains a highly controversial area. Policy is then constrained by the current state of economic knowledge.

7.4 Lags in the effects of policy

Any policy change operates with a lag i.e. a period of time before it is effective. It is customary to divide lags into two broad components. First, the inside lag which is the time taken for an authority to initiate a policy change. Second, the outside lag which is the time taken for that policy change to influence the target variables.

The inside lag can be subdivided into a recognition or detection lag, a decision lag, and an administration lag. It takes time to collect, process and analyse statistical data on economic variables (see section 7.5). As a result of this time lapse there will be a gap between the time when planned policy changes are needed and when the authorities realise that action is required. This is the recognition or detection lag. Furthermore the policy maker in analysing data must decide whether the disturbance affecting the economy is only temporary and relatively minor or more permanent so that policy changes are required to bring the economy back to its target value. This is a major problem in itself as the government may be reluctant to initiate the change (e.g. the case of devaluation in 1967). Having decided that action is needed it takes further time to implement the decision to change policy (i.e. an administration lag). Overall the length of the inside lag will not be constant but will depend on a number of factors including, for example, the administrative procedures involved in obtaining approval for a planned policy change. In America the administrative lag associated with monetary policy is shorter than that for fiscal policy changes. While monetary policy actions can be initiated fairly rapidly, fiscal policy changes require the consent of Congress and are slower to implement. In America it took more than a year between the recommendation for the cut in income tax which occurred at the beginning of 1964 and the legislation which provided for the cut. In contrast the distinction between the implementation lag associated with fiscal and monetary policy changes is less pronounced in the UK. Indirect taxes can be varied, via what is known as the regulator, by up to 10 per cent between budgets without having to obtain the approval of Parliament. On the other hand income tax changes are generally made to operate with effect from the beginning of the financial year. Finally, it is worth pointing out that the inside lag will normally be a discrete lag in that nothing at all will happen until the policy change is initiated. There will be a definite, though not necessarily a fixed, time lapse between the recognition of the need for a policy change and when the policy change is implemented. If, on the other hand, a package of policy changes is introduced the inside lag may be spread out over a period of time (i.e. distributed).

Once the administrative decision has been taken we pass on to the outside lag. The outside lag can also be subdivided into two components. First, the time taken to influence the intermediate policy variables (e.g. the time between a tax rate change and its influence on aggregate demand). Second, the time lag between the change in the intermediate policy variables and the target or ultimate policy variables (e.g. the time gap between a change in aggregate demand and the level of employment).

It should be noted that unlike the inside lag, the outside lag is a distributed lag as the effects of a policy change will be spread over a period of time. To illustrate why this is the case consider the effect of a tax reduction. It will take some time for consumers to adjust their pattern of consumption and their response to a rise in disposable income is likely to continue over several periods. Similarly firms' investment decisions will not be altered immediately when the rate of interest changes following a change in monetary policy.

Like the inside lag the length of time associated with the outside lag is unlikely to be constant. The time lag involved would be likely to vary depending on such factors as whether fiscal or monetary policy changes are initiated; the state of the economy at the time of the policy changes; and the way expectations are formed (as this will influence the way the private sector responds to the policy changes introduced).

Given that lags exist it is possible for stabilisation policy to be destabilising. This is especially true if the disturbance affecting the economy is temporary or is part of a normal cyclical movement (as

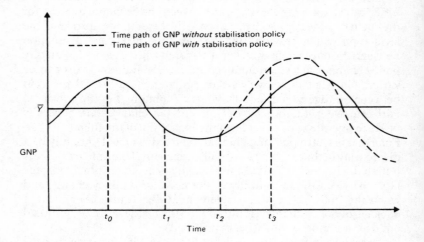

Figure 7.3. Stabilisation policy and instability

shown in Figure 7.3). Consider Figure 7.3 where Y represents both the mean and the target level of income and which is assumed, for ease of exposition, to be constant (i.e. there is no economic growth).

At time t_1 the government after recognising that GNP has fallen below the target level of Y initiates an expansionary policy (i.e. the discrete inside lag). There then follows a further time lag (i.e. the distributed outside lag) before the policy change starts to affect the economy at time t_2 and thereafter. At time t_3 the authorities recognise that income has risen above the target level and commence a contractionary policy which again only begins to affect the economy after a period of time has elapsed. It can be seen that, in this example, due to lags stabilisation policy has actually made the fluctuations more severe i.e. destabilised the economy.

This possibility arises because of the lags discussed above so that by the time policy changes affect the target variables the underlying state of the economy may have changed making the measures adopted inappropriate. One way to overcome this problem would be to allow for these lags by taking policy decisions earlier e.g. at time t_0. This requires the authorities to forecast accurately the time path of the economy and it is to this question that we now turn.

7.5 Forecasting
How successful policy turns out to be will depend, in part, on

forecasts of the future course of the economy. Forecasts are essential to the policy maker as they provide a frame of reference in order that the authorities can allow for lags in the response of the economy to planned policy changes. However as uncertainty over the accuracy of the forecasts is likely to increase as the forecasting period lengthens, the speed at which policy works is, as discussed above, an important consideration. Forecasting is dependent upon two main inputs. First, there are various sources of information available to the forecaster. Second, there is the theoretical framework and empirical evidence on which the forecasting model is based.

We will examine first the range of information that may be available to the forecaster. Both the recent history and the latest statistical data on certain key economic variables give an indication of the current state of the economy and its likely future course. Such information includes data on unemployment, prices, investment, exports, imports, the volume of production, etc. This data takes time to collect, process and analyse so that the current state of the variables is not known for certain. For example, in the UK when the Treasury makes its forecast in February, prior to the April budget, the most recent detailed national account statistics available are those for the third quarter of the previous year. In consequence there is a need to obtain whatever monthly statistics are available on the key variables in order to assess as accurately as possible the current state of the economy. It should also be noted that official statistics are often subsequently amended and revised so that the forecaster has no easy task. Due to these imperfections the forecaster needs to begin by forecasting or assessing the present state of the economy before he can forecast its most likely future course.

In addition to that noted above, information can also be collected from a number of other sources. Two examples taken from the UK economy will suffice. First, the government publishes annually a White Paper on public expenditure in which it sets out its plans for both central and local authority spending and fixed investment by the public corporations. Second, forecasts of private investment can be obtained from the sample surveys carried out by the Confederation of British Industry (CBI) and the Department of Trade and Industry. These surveys enquire into the investment intentions of firms within certain sectors of the private sector. For example, after making an assumption about the time required for construction, forecasts of housing investment can be obtained by combining data on the future intentions of private house builders with data on housing starts. These two examples illustrate that the forecaster has at his disposal a range of information.

The second main input into short-term forecasting concerns the role of the model used: An econometric model is a list of equations describing economic relationships within an economy. Such equations are based on standard macroeconomic theory but in practice econometric models tend to be more disaggregated (i.e. possess more equations) than the models of standard macroeconomic textbooks. For example, in the UK the Treasury model of the economy consists of 500 or so equations. Estimates of the equations are derived from past empirical evidence and the performance of the model is monitored continuously so as to incorporate modifications and improvements whenever appropriate.

The model is used to provide forecasts of key variables such as total employment, consumer prices and the main components of final expenditure. Forecasts are made on a quarterly basis for a period of up to two years ahead on the assumption that there will be no change in any of the instrumental variables (i.e. that existing conditions continue). The model is used not only to provide projections of GDP and other key variables but is also used to quantify the effects of policy changes on these variables. In this way the government attempts to monitor the future progress of the economy and plan policy changes accordingly. In the UK similar forecasting models are used by the National Institute for Economic and Social Research, the London Business School and the Bank of England.

Kennedy (1982) has estimated that the average error (ignoring the sign) in Treasury forecasts between 1955 and 1981 was about 1.1 per cent of GDP.[1] Although an average error of this magnitude appears quite small it is important in relation to policy objectives and changes. Kennedy has estimated that '...it implies an average deviation of about 0.4% between the actual and desired unemployment rate, and is equivalent to an error between the appropriate rate of income tax and the actual rate of about 3p in the £'. Even a 1 per cent error is fairly substantial in terms of the absolute size of GDP. The size of the error further constrains the ability of the government to carry out a policy of fine tuning (see section 7.7). Finally, with regard to forecasting it should be noted that if lags are variable as well as long forecasting changes in the economy becomes more difficult.

1. Kennedy, M. C. (1982), 'The Economy as a Whole', in A. R. Prest and D. J. Coppock (eds), *The UK Economy: A Manual of Applied Economics,* 9th edition (London: Weidenfeld and Nicolson).

7.6 Expectations

In addition to the considerations we have discussed so far expectations play an important role in policy decision making. Decisions with an economy are normally taken with regard to expected rather than actual values of variables. There are two problems here. First, policy changes are themselves likely to influence expectations. For example, an announcement that the rate of monetary expansion is about to be increased may cause an increase in the expected rate of inflation. Such a change in expectations is in turn likely to influence the behaviour of economic units so that the effect of monetary expansion may be felt mainly in price rather than quantity changes. An extreme example of the view that stabilisation policy is ineffective has been put forward by economists who believe in rational expectations. In their view announced monetary and fiscal stabilisation policies will be ineffective because people dealing in markets will immediately take such policies into consideration when devising their own strategies. This of course would render stabilisation policies powerless to influence real income even in the short run. Such a strong conclusion merits further discussion.

The basic idea underlying the rational expectations hypothesis is that economic agents form their expectations in accordance with the relevant body of economic theory. For example, assume for the sake of argument that inflation is always caused by monetary expansion, then agents would forecast future rates of inflation in the light of current rates of monetary expansion. Consequently any government policy change which is perceived to lead an altered rate of monetary expansion would cause an immediate adjustment of expectations about future rates of inflation. For this reason some economists distinguish between the effects of anticipated and unanticipated monetary expansion. It is only in the case of unanticipated monetary expansion that real output would be increased. In terms of the augmented Phillips curve analysis examined in Chapter 5 section 5.3.2 (in particular Figure 5.4) the shift of the short run Phillips curve would be immediate in response to anticipated monetary expansion. This does not mean that unemployment would never deviate from the natural rate. Expectations of future inflation could be inaccurate. The rational expectations hypothesis does not hold that expectations will always be accurate only that they will be correct on average and that therefore there is little scope for policies designed to stabilise the economy.

Clearly several objections can be raised against this hypothesis.

First one of the more serious objections concerns the severe knowledge requirements necessary for the assumption that economic agents form their expectations according to the relevant body of economic theory. Economic agents must have knowledge of the 'true' economic model including the time path of responses of the economy to economic disturbances. There are of course many controversies about the 'true' economic model. It is possible to argue that agents can derive some information second hand from published forecasts and commentaries in the news media. In this case the problem becomes one of discerning which is the correct view when, as is often the case, forecasts differ. A second serious objection arises because in many cases agents are prevented from altering their behaviour in response to changed expectations due to the existence of contracts. These contracts may be explicit or implicit as in the case of wage agreements. In such circumstances economic policy retains the power to influence the level of output and employment.

Summing up this debate it is unlikely that the conditions necessary to render stabilisation policy completely powerless to influence real income in the short run will hold. Nevertheless the possibility that economic agents will anticipate the results of changes in economic policy does mean that the scope to influence real income is considerably reduced.

The second problem is essentially a practical one i.e. how to model expectations. This difficulty exists due to disagreement on how expectations are formed.

7.7 The conduct of policy

The difficulties of stabilisation policy discussed in sections 7.3–7.6 above are crucial to the debate on whether the authorities should pursue discretionary stabilisation policies or adopt certain rules in order to achieve their desired targets. Discretionary policy takes place where the strength of the policy is varied in a counter-cyclical way according to prevailing economic circumstances. It may be varied either only occasionally and in response to large changes in, for example, the level of unemployment (i.e. rough tuning), or frequently in response to small divergencies of employment from its target value (i.e. fine tuning). Alternatively the authorities may pursue some rule which may or may not be linked to prevailing economic circumstances. For example, the authorities might adopt a given fixed rate of monetary growth or might vary monetary growth according to some pre-specified rule depending upon the level of unemployment.

The rules vs. discretion controversy hinges critically not only on the problems of stabilisation policy discussed earlier but also on views of the inherent stability of the economy. If one regards the economy as being inherently stable and in addition believes that the problems facing the policy maker are large then stabilisation policy is clearly inappropriate. Conversely, if the economy is regarded as being inherently unstable, then it may well be better to attempt to offset such instabilities by counter-cyclical policy, despite the difficulties facing the policy maker.

Stability of the economy can come from two sources: first, where the behavioural relationships specifying the endogenous variables are functions of the long run rather than the current values of the other variables; and second, where automatic stabilisers exist. An example of the first factor is the idea that consumption depends on normal income (e.g. the permanent income hypothesis) as distinct from current income. To the extent that this is true, consumption and therefore aggregate demand will be slow to change following any disturbance. Similar cases could be made out for other components of aggregate demand such as investment and net exports. In addition there are likely to be costs of adjustment in respect of any changes by an economic agent and such costs are likely to be larger the quicker the adjustment.

Automatic stabilisers exist within an economy when there is a mechanism that automatically produces offsetting changes to current movements in GNP. The most important examples arise from the government's budget position. Thus if GNP falls, the average tax receipts by the government will tend to fall because of the progressive nature of income tax payments. At the same time unemployment and other means tested benefits will increase. These arrangements will prevent consumption from falling as low as it would otherwise have done and therefore act in a counter-cyclical manner. The important point to note is that such stabilisers operate automatically without a conscious policy change initiated by the government so that there is no recognition or administration lag involved (i.e. the inside lag is zero). However such stabilisers are two-edged weapons as they retard movements in the economy both to and away from target levels of GNP. That is, by reducing the size of the multiplier they reduce the extent of fluctuations due to autonomous disturbance to aggregate demand.

It now seems fairly widely accepted that the economy is 'far less unstable than early Keynesians pictured'.[1] Nevertheless this does

1. Modigliani, F. (1977), 'The Monetarist Controversy or, Should We Forsake Stabilisation Policies?' *American Economic Review,* Vol. 67 (March).

not mean that there is no role for stabilisation policy. Arguments justifying intervention can be made out on the grounds of either the time required for the economy to return to the natural rate of unemployment, or the existence of shocks to the economy.

Monetarists tend to argue, due either to (i) a lack of knowledge of how the economy operates, or (ii) from a basic political philosophy that governments are not to be trusted, that policy should be carried out according to rules. Conversely Keynesians tend to emphasise the inherent instability of the economy and the potential role for stabilisation policy.

7.8 Conclusion
The role of macroeconomic stabilisation policy remains one of controversy. Many governments have introduced targets for the rate of growth of the money supply and such targets preclude the use of monetary (or fiscal policy) for fine tuning, but not rough tuning since the targets can be changed. In Chapters 8 and 9 we will examine the interdependence of fiscal and monetary policy and analyse more fully the role of these policies.

8 Demand Management: Fiscal Policy

8.1 Introduction

In Chapter 1 we discussed how national income is measured and gained some insight into the importance of the government in the working of the economy. In this chapter we propose to look at the way the government may vary the level of its expenditure and revenue to influence the behaviour of the economy i.e. the role of fiscal policy. More formally fiscal policy may be defined as any measure that alters the level, timing, or composition of government spending, and/or the level, timing or structure of tax payments.

In recent years the role of government in the economy has become the subject of considerable controversy. This is concerned not so much with the role of the central government itself but the role of the public sector as a whole i.e. central government, local authorities, nationalised industries and other public corporations. Table 8.1 shows central government's and local authorities' current expenditure on final goods and services and gross domestic fixed capital formation by the entire public sector for the period 1972-82. In addition to final expenditure the general government (i.e. central government and local authorities) also pays out subsidies and makes various forms of transfer payments (e.g. unemployment benefits, social security and welfare payments and interest payments on government debt). In order to give some idea of the sums involved Table 8.2 presents general government current expenditure on subsidies and transfer payments of grants and debt interest for the period 1972-82.

The government has to raise a corresponding amount of finance to meet such levels of expenditure. This is done by way of (i) taxation and (ii) borrowing. The controversy centres on the extent to which the levels of public sector expenditure indicated in Tables 8.1 and 8.2 have been to the detriment of private expenditure in the economy.

Views concerning the role of fiscal policy have changed over

TABLE 8.1 Public sector final expenditure in the UK, 1972–82

(current prices: £ million)

	1972	1973	1974	1975	1976	1977	1978	1979	1980	1981	1982
Central government:											
(a) final current expenditure	6,931	7,815	10,033	13,364	15,949	17,614	19,808	22,961	29,474	33,170	36,675
(b) gross domestic fixed capital formation	641	773	956	1,243	1,389	1,274	1,268	1,537	1,728	1,814	2,134
Local authorities:											
(c) final current expenditure	4,744	5,557	6,595	9,592	10,792	11,648	13,263	15,400	18,945	21,368	23,407
(d) gross domestic fixed capital formation	2,091	2,888	3,420	3,741	4,021	3,531	3,338	3,608	3,800	2,827	2,326
Public corporations:											
(e) gross domestic fixed capital formation	1,774	2,073	2,859	3,920	4,695	4,779	4,943	5,624	6,651	6,899	7,221
Total	16,181	19,106	23,863	31,860	36,846	38,846	42,620	49,130	60,598	66,078	71,763
Total as a percentage[1] of total domestic expenditure at market prices	25	25	27	30	29	27	26	25	27	27	27

Source: Central Statistical Office (1983), National Income and Expenditure (Blue Book), (London: HMSO), Tables 1.1, 7.1, 8.1 and 6.3.
Note: Correct to nearest whole number.

the years. Prior to the Keynesian revolution the traditional roles assigned to fiscal policy within the confines of a balanced budget were (i) the determination of the distribution of income and (ii) the allocation of resources between the private and public sectors. For example, defence spending financed by taxation involves a reduction in private expenditure matched by a corresponding increase in government expenditure. Consequently by these means resources are allocated to the public sector away from the private sector

However as noted in Chapter 6, section 6.2, the UK government has been concerned since the 1940s to maintain a high and stable level of unemployment. The pursuit of this objective was conditioned by the experience of high levels of unemployment in the inter-war years and the widespread acceptance, by that time, of Keynes' (1936) General Theory of Employment, Interest and Money. The 1944 White Paper on Employment Policy (Cmd 6527: HMSO) recommended that policy proposals to meet this employment objective should be examined annually by Parliament in the debate on the budget. Since the mid-1940s the budget has been used to influence the overall level of aggregate demand and employment in the economy. More recently in the 1970s the view that fiscal policy is unable to achieve any long-run changes in employment (i.e. that crowding out occurs) has attracted many supporters.

8.2 The budget
Traditionally the government presents a budget once a year, normally in late March or early April. More recently, concern with the economy has led the governmnet to introduce so called 'mini-budgets' which alter the stance of government fiscal policy. These have been presented at various times throughout the year and to some extent have reduced the importance of the spring budget. Nevertheless their frequency has not been such as to undermine completely the importance of the traditional budget. In his budget speech the Chancellor of the Exchequer reviews the performance of the economy over the past year and outlines the likely course of the economy in the coming year. In addition the Chancellor explains how the government intends to raise its tax revenue in the coming year and presents measures the government plans to put into force (e.g. proposals for tax changes) to modify the future course of the economy. Those economic measures which require legislation are embodied in the Finance Bill (published shortly after Budget Day) and they become formally enacted into law by the Finance Act around July/August.

TABLE 8.2 General government current expenditure in the UK, 1972–82

	(excluding final expenditure on goods and services) (current prices: £ million)										
	1972	1973	1974	1975	1976	1977	1978	1979	1980	1981	1982
(a) Subsidies	1,153	1,443	3,004	3,690	3,476	3,307	3,661	4,446	5,303	5,785	5,452
(b) Current grants to personal sector	5,845	6,420	7,876	10,284	12,765	15,092	17,871	20,957	25,484	31,173	36,169
(c) Current grants paid abroad (net)	234	358	320	358	803	1,116	1,703	2,058	1,823	1,689	1,844
(d) Debt interest	2,286	2,738	3,607	4,211	5,394	6,367	7,207	8,961	11,363	13,218	14,265
Total	9,518	10,959	14,807	18,543	22,438	25,882	30,442	36,422	43,973	51,865	57,730
Total as a percentage[1] of GNP at market prices	15	15	17	17	18	18	18	19	19	21	21

Source: Central Statistical Office (1983), National Income and Expenditure (Blue Book), (London: HMSO), Tables 1.1 and 9.1.
Note: 1. Correct to nearest whole number.

8.2.1 *Preparation of the budget*

In preparing his budget the Chancellor receives advice from a number of important sources. These include the departments of Inland Revenue (concerned with direct tax receipts such as income tax) and Customs and Excise (concerned with indirect tax receipts such as duties on alcohol), the Bank of England and the Treasury. The Treasury is responsible for policy and prepares three main forecasts of the economy during a year. The most important of these in terms of policy is the February forecast available just before the budget. Forecasts of the major categories of expenditure in the economy (to the middle of next year) are published on Budget Day in the Financial Statement and Budget Report. This report, sometimes referred to as the 'red boook', also includes tables of revenue and expenditure for the central government and public sector (i.e. central government, local authorities and public corporations) and summarises the tax changes proposed in the budget.

8.2.2 *The government accounts*

Central government revenue and expenditure is recorded under two categories, namely the Consolidated Fund (or Exchequer) and the National Loans Fund. The Consolidated Fund deals with revenue (obtained mostly from taxation) and expenditure (mainly on supply services such as the National Health Service). In contrast the National Loans Fund (NLF) covers transactions in financial assets and liabilities. For example, the NLF account includes all transactions with respect to the national debt (see section 8.3) and most transactions concerned with central government lending. Table 8.3 is a summary of these accounts for the financial year 1980/81.

The combined balances of the two funds, plus any net receipts from other funds and accounts (e.g. National Insurance Fund) establish the Central Government Borrowing Requirement (CGBR).

The central government is only one component of the public sector and the most important accounts presented in the Financial Statement and Budget Report (red book) are those for the whole public sector. These accounts cover not only payments and receipts of the central government but also transactions of local authorities and public corporations (e.g. nationalised industries). A summary of the relationship between borrowing by the public sector as a whole (i.e. the public sector borrowing requirement) and borrowing by the three components of the public sector is shown in Table 8.4.

The central government borrowing includes borrowing to finance both its own account and its lending to local authorities and public

TABLE 8.3. UK central government: Consolidated and National Loans Funds
(financial year 1980/81, £ million)

Consolidated Fund:	
Total revenue	66,213
Total expenditure	76,170
(1) *Deficit*	−9,957
National Loans Fund:	
Total receipts	9,854
Total payments	13,411
(2) *Deficit*	−3,557
Total Deficit (1) + (2)	−13,514
Net receipts from other funds and accounts	639
Central government borrowing requirement	−12,875

Source: Central Statistical Office, *Financial Statistics July 1981*, (London: HMSO), Table 3.1.

TABLE 8.4. Components of the PSBR in the UK
(£ million, 1980/81)

Central government borrowing requirement	12,875
Local authorities' contribution	1,020
Public corporations' contribution	−703
Total PSBR	13,192

Source: Central Statistical Office, *Financial Statistics July 1981*, (London: HMSO), Table 2.3.

corporations. In order to avoid double counting direct borrowing from the central government is excluded (i.e. netted out) from the contributions to the total PSBR shown for local authorities and public corporations. An alternative presentation shown in Table 8.5 records only borrowing on own account for the three sectors.

Comparison of Tables 8.4 and 8.5 reveals that the central government lent £1,311 million and £2,379 million to the local authorities and public corporations respectively during the financial

TABLE 8.5. Components of the PSBR in the UK: own account
(£ million, 1980/81)

Central government borrowing requirement	9,185
Local authorities' borrowing requirement	2,331
Public corporations' borrowing requirement	1,676
Total PSBR	13,192

Source: Central Statistical Office, *Financial Statistics July 1981*, (London: HMSO), Table 2.5.

year 1980/81. The local authorities borrowing requirement of £2,331 million on own account (Table 8.5) was partly financed by direct borrowing of £1,311 million from the central government (mainly from the National Loans Funds) leaving a local authorities' contribution of £1,020 million (Table 8.4) to the total PSBR.

The authorities financed the PSBR of £13,192 million, for the financial year 1980/81, by borrowing: (i) £9,282 million from the non-bank private sector i.e. financial institutions other than the banks, industrial and commercial companies and the personal sector; (ii) £3,231 million from the banking sector; and (iii) £679 million from the overseas sector. Borrowing took a number of forms including notes and coin, government Gilt-Edged Securities, National Savings and direct borrowing.

Table 8.6 shows (i) the growth of the PSBR i.e. column A, (ii) the PSBR as a percentage of GDP i.e. column B, and (iii) changes in sources of finance i.e. columns C–E, over the period 1972–82. The table reveals a sharp rise in the PSBR as a percentage of GDP, from 1972 to 1975, and the way the percentage has fluctuated since 1975. It also shows the importance of the non-bank private sector as a source of funds for the PSBR. In fact in certain years (e.g. 1977) debt sales to the non-bank private sector have been greater than the PSBR and this has allowed net repayments of debt to be made (i.e. in 1977 to the overseas sector). The reader will recall from the discussion in Chapter 3, section 3.3.1 that a PSBR not fully financed by sales of debt will lead to a change in banks' reserve assets and ultimately to a change in the money supply. Fiscal and monetary policy are therefore highly interdependent.Fiscal policy decisions influence the size of the PSBR and monetary policy decisions determine how the PSBR is actually financed.

TABLE 8.6 Public Sector Borrowing Requirement in the UK, 1972–82
(£ million)

Year	A Total PSBR	B PSBR as a % of GDP[1]	C Non-bank private sector (%)[2]		D Monetary sector (%)[2]		E Overseas sector (%)[2]	
1972	2,039	3.2	1,478	(72)	−1,026	(−50)	1,587	(78)
1973	4,198	5.7	2,286	(54)	1,995	(48)	−83	(−2)
1974	6,365	7.6	4,160	(65)	701	(11)	1,504	(24)
1975	10,477	9.9	6,338	(60)	3,379	(32)	760	(7)
1976	9,144	7.3	6,172	(67)	345	(4)	2,627	(29)
1977	5,975	4.1	9,720	(163)	2,381	(40)	−6,126	(−103)
1978	8,335	5.0	7,183	(86)	−290	(−3)	1,442	(17)
1979	12,638	6.5	11,716	(93)	924	(7)	−2	–
1980	12,192	5.4	9,789	(80)	1,652	(14)	751	(6)
1981	10,620	4.2	9,189	(87)	−538	(−5)	1,969	(19)
1982	5,432	2.0	6,193	(114)	−2,265	(−42)	1,504	(28)

Source: Central Statistical Office (1983) National Income and Expenditure (Blue Book), (London: HMSO), Tables 1.1 and 13.13.
Notes: 1. GDP (expenditure based) at market prices.
   2. Correct to nearest whole number (due to rounding percentage figures may not exactly sum to 100).

TABLE 8.7. Composition of the National Debt, 31 March 1980
(nominal values: £ million)

Sterling National Debt		Percentage of total National Debt
a. Treasury Bills	4,608	4.8
b. *Other marketable securities:*		
Up to 5 years to maturity	24,233	
Over 5 years and up to 15 years	16,772	
Over 15 years and undated	29,980	
Total stocks	70,985	74.3
c. Non-marketable debt	16,026	16.8
Total sterling National Debt	91,619	
d. External foreign currency debt	3,949	4.1
Total National Debt	95,568	100

Source: Bank of England, *Quarterly Bulletin*, December 1980.

8.3 The National Debt

8.3.1 *Composition of the National Debt*

The National Debt comprises the sum total of outstanding debt of British central governments and broadly represents the total liabilities of the National Loans Fund. It therefore comprises the cumulative sum of central government borrowing requirements (i.e. it includes borrowing to finance its own account and its lending to the other members of the public sector). At the end of March 1980 the nominal value of the National Debt was £95,568 million. The different kinds of securities which make up the debt are shown in Table 8.7.

In Chapters 2 and 3 we examined the nature of the various types of financial securities issued by the government. Treasury Bills (item a) are short-term loans which mature (i.e. reach their repayment date) after a period of three months. This component is sometimes called the floating debt. Other marketable securities (item b) refer to Gilt-Edged Securities and represent borrowing undertaken on a longer-term basis. At the end of March 1980 marketable securities (i.e. Treasury Bills and Gilt-Edged Securities) accounted for just over three-quarters of the total National Debt. Although Gilt-Edged Securities can be sold through the stock exchange there is no guarantee that the market value of a bond will equal its nominal value. As discussed in Chapter 2, section 2.1 the price individuals are willing to pay for a bond varies inversely with the rate of interest. Non-marketable securities (item c) are so-called because their ownership can be transferred. They can only be held and redeemed by the original buyer. Examples include national savings certificates, premium bonds and national saving stamps. The final component of the National debt (item d) consists of external foreign currency debt (e.g. inter-government lending). As various forms of debt mature or in the case of non-marketable debt are redeemed, additional debt is issued to finance redemption and repayments.

8.3.2 *Distribution of the National Debt*

Table 8.8 shows how the National Debt was disributed among holders as at 31 March 1980.

Official holdings (1) of the Bank of England, government departments, the Northern Ireland Government, and the National Debt Commissioners constituted approximately 19 per cent of the total National Debt. Market holdings of sterling debt are identified for five broad sectors (2–6). Other public sector holdings (2) include those of the public corporations and local authorities. Official statistics on the holdings of banks (3) and other financial institutions (4) are presented separately. Together they owned approximately 43 per cent of sterling debt in market hands at 31 March 1980. Securities are held by the banking sector both as reserve assets and to provide additional liquidity in view of their marketability. Other financial institutions tend to have longer-term liabilities. To them government debt provides the means both to (i) hold reserves which are fairly liquid and (ii) match the terms of their liabilities with the maturity structure of government securities held. This latter motive is particularly relevant to the behaviour of pension funds and insurance companies. At 31 March 1980 the largest holder of debt within the category of other financial institutions was insurance companies, followed by private sector pension funds and building societies respectively. British government securities are also held by overseas holders (5) such as overseas firms and banks and international organisations like the International Monetary Fund. The final category of other holders (6) includes the sterling debt holdings of charities, individuals and industrial and commercial companies. Holdings by this sector accounted for approximately 25 per cent of the total National Debt and 33 per cent

TABLE 8.8. Distribution of the National Debt, 31 March 1980
(nominal values: £ million)

Sterling debt	Treasury Bills	Stocks	NMD	Total	Percentage of total National Debt	Percentage of sterling market holdings
1. Official holdings	2,327	10,688	5,146	18,161	19.0	—
Market holdings:						
2. Other public sector	104	93	207	404	0.4	0.5
3. Banking sector	1,226	2,946	99	4,271	4.5	5.8
4. Other financial institutions	41	36,180	84	36,305	38.0	49.4
5. Overseas holders	826	5,361	2,158	8,345	8.7	11.4
6. Other holders	84	15,717	8,332	24,133	25.3	32.9
7. Total market holdings of sterling National Debt	2,281	60,297	10,880	73,458	76.9	100
8. External foreign currency debt				3,949	4.1	
				95,568	100	100

Total National Debt = 1 + 7 + 8   Total National Debt

Source: Bank of England, *Quarterly Bulletin*, December 1980.

of sterling market debt at the end of March 1980.

8.3.3 *Burden of the National Debt*

Reference to Table 8.8 shows that approximately 87 per cent of the total National Debt is held by residents and only 13 per cent by non-residents. Out of this last figure only 4 per cent take the form of external foreign currency debt.

The question arises as to whether the National Debt imposes a burden on present or future generations of inhabitants of the country. We discuss the domestically held component of the National Debt first. To the extent that debt is held domestically, interest payments on the debt financed by taxation represent transfers between one section of the community (the tax payer) and another (the receiver of the interest). There is also a transfer between generations since borrowings are repaid by th government at a later date. These transfers impose no burden on the community since any 'undesirable' allocation of wealth implied by these transfers could be altered by taxation. Two caveats to this argument are applicable. First, to the extent that taxes have to be raised to a level higher than would otherwise be the case and higher taxes act as a discentive to initiative, such transfers do impose a burden. Second, the transfers require some administration to carry them out and therefore involve some real cost. The second type of burden is likely to be small and the first category controversial as it is far from certain that high tax levels act as a disincentive to initiative and risk taking. It is also necessary to consider the use to which the borrowings have been directed. If the government borrowed to add to the productive capacity of the economy (e.g. to finance investment in the nationalised industries) no burden is involved. In fact present and future generations benefit from the increased output. Expenditure directed to non-productive uses offers no such future benefits though it may be necessary for other non-economic reasons e.g. defence expenditure. Finally with regard to domestically held debt a large National Debt may create difficulties for the authorities in their operation of monetary policy. The larger the size of the National Debt the larger the quantity of debt periodically maturing which requires financing. This may make it necessary for the authorities to intervene in the market to ensure price stability of outstanding securities to maximise debt sales. This was certainly the view held by the authorities up to 1971 though since that date the authorities have been far less willing to intervene in the gilt-edged market. Nevertheless the large quantities of maturing debt must make monetary management more difficult for the authorities.

Externally held debt represents a different situation. Payments of interest and principals on maturity represent a transfer not between domestic residents but between residents and non-residents. There is therefore a loss of real resources to the residents of a country. Again however, notice must be taken of the uses made of the resources borrowed. If they are directed towards extending the productive capacity of the economy, the repayments (i.e. loss of real resources) will be matched by accumulation of real resources so no burden is involved. If on the other hand use of the resources is directed towards non-productive uses, no such benefits accrue and the debt is a burden.

There is therefore some truth in the widely held view that the National Debt represents a burden to the present and future inhabitants of a country. Nevertheless the extent of the burden seems quite small.

8.4 Instruments of fiscal policy

8.4.1 *Introduction*
An expansionary fiscal policy consists of either (i) an increase in government expenditure or (ii) a reduction in taxation. As we examined in Chapter 1, section 1.3 and Chapter 7, section 7.2 the general effect of these two policies is to increase aggregate demand. What is not so readily apparent however is that a balanced increase in government expenditure matched by an equivalent increase in taxation will also increase aggregate demand. Nevertheless it is true. Therefore in discussing the impact of a particular budget programme it is important to take into account that changes in taxation and spending have different multiplier effects on the level of economic activity. An increase in government expenditure will have a greater impact on the economy than a rise in tax payments of the same amount. A budget which changes government spending and tax receipts equally (e.g. both increase by £100 million so that the budget balance remains the same) will have an expansionary effect on the economy. While government spending will on the first instance increase national income by the entire £100 million, in the latter case some part of consumers' reduced disposable income will be matched by reduced saving so that not all the £100 million will be removed from the circular flow of income in the first round of income changes.

The balanced budget multiplier can be illustrated using a simple model of income determination for a closed economy. In this model we will assume that (i) tax payments (T) are independent of income (i.e. taxes are paid in a lump sum); consumption (C) depends positively upon disposable income $(Y_D = Y - T)$; (iii) investment is exogenously determined; and (iv) no foreign trade takes place. In chapter 1 we discussed how national income (Y) can be measured as the sum of the components of aggregate demand as shown in equation (8.1).

$$Y_0 = C_0 + G_0 + I_0 \qquad (8.1)$$

Consumption depends on disposable income:

$$C_0 = ß (Y_0 - T_0) \qquad (8.2)$$

where (1) ß = marginal propensity to consume. Substituting (8.2) into (8.1):

$$Y_0 = ß (Y_0 - T_0) + G_0 + I_0 \qquad (8.3)$$

where the subscript $_0$ indicates the initial values of the variables specified.

The balanced budget multiplier can be expressed in algebraic form. If the government increases its spending and tax by equal amounts (i.e. $\Delta G = \Delta T$) national income will increase. In equation (8.4) the subscript$_1$ indicates the new values of government spending, taxation and national income.

$$Y_1 = ß (Y_1 - T_1) + G_1 + I_0 \qquad (8.4)$$

Investment remains at its original level due to the assumption that it is exogenously determined. Subtracting equation (8.4) from (8.3) and factorising:

$$\Delta Y(1 - ß) = - ß\Delta T + \Delta G \qquad (8.5)$$

Dividing equation (8.5) by $1 - ß$:

$$\Delta Y = \frac{ß\Delta T}{1-ß} + \frac{\Delta G}{1-ß} \qquad (8.6)$$

Given that $\Delta T = \Delta G$ equation (8.6) can be rewritten:

$$\Delta Y = \frac{\text{\ss}\Delta G}{1-\text{\ss}} + \frac{\Delta G}{1-\text{\ss}} \tag{8.7}$$

Factorising and cancelling out:

$$\Delta Y = \Delta G \tag{8.8}$$

Equation (8.8) shows that in this model the increase in income is equal to the increase in government expenditure (i.e. balanced budget multiplier = 1. In other words given that the multiplier effect of a change in government expenditure

$$(\text{i.e.} \frac{-1}{1-\text{\ss}}),$$

is greater than that of an equal change in tax

$$(\text{i.e.} \frac{-\text{\ss}}{1-\text{\ss}}),$$

a balanced budget will have an expansionary effect on output and employment. An equal amount of spending stimulates economic activity more than taxation restricts it. Relaxing the rigidity of the assumptions, so that both (i) foreign trade and (ii) tax payments based on income, are incorporated into the model leaves the essential conclusion unaltered i.e. an increase in government expenditure matched by an equivalent increase in tax revenue will increase aggregate demand. In this more general case the size of the multiplier will be less than 1. Finally it is worth pointing out that the special case of the balanced budget multiplier is not accepted by all economists (see section 8.6 on crowding out).

We will now discuss the main instruments of fiscal policy i.e. government expenditure and taxation (both direct and indirect). Since not all public sector expenditure is under the direct control of the central authorities it is also necessary to examine the methods by which the central authorities try to control expenditure by local government and public corporations.

8.4.2 *Government expenditure*

As we have noted in Chapters 1 and 7 changes in government expenditure have a direct effect on aggregate demand and therefore output and employment. An increase in government expenditure will increase aggregate demand and reduce the level of unemployment. Conversely a reduction in government expenditure will reduce the level of aggregate demand and hence employment. Also as we noted in Chapter 7, section 7.2, such demand management policies can be used to regulate the balance of payments. If the government could control precisely the level of its expenditure it could stabilise national income at the desired target level.

In fact it is not easy to manipulate government expenditure in such a way to fine-tune the economy. One reason is that it is difficult to bring about changes in spending quickly. Many government expenditure programmes (e.g. road and hospital building) take a long time to plan and complete. Abandoning a project once it had been started would be extremely wasteful. Furthermore much of government expenditure consists of payment of salaries. Decreases in this component of government expenditure can only be achieved by reducing the quantity of labour employed by the government. Decisions to reduce the level of general government employment take time to implement. For these reasons it is difficult to alter (especially in a downward direction) the quantity of government expenditure quickly enough to stabilise the economy in the short run. Variations in government expenditure are undertaken in the context of a much longer time horizon than that envisaged for short-run stabilisation policies.

8.4.3 *Taxation*

Unlike government expenditure, tax rates can be varied quickly and have therefore been the main instrument of fiscal short-run stabilisation policies.

Taxes can be classified under two headings: (i) direct taxes and (ii) indirect taxes. Direct taxes are taxes paid to the appropriate revenue department by the economic unit assessed (e.g. income tax paid by individuals). Indirect taxes are mainly expenditure taxes and in this case the tax is paid by the manufacturer or provider of the service who in turn attempts to pass the tax on to his customers by making the necessary adjustments to the prices charged by him.

In the British tax system the main forms of direct taxation are income tax, national insurance contributions, corporation tax (on company profits) and various capital taxes. Given the complexity of the tax system the Chancellor has a number of options open to him. For example, he can alter the basic rate of income tax, income-tax thresholds and allowances, the rate of national insurance contributions, etc. In practice the Chancellor normally announces a package of tax changes on Budget Day due to the practical difficulties of operating direct tax changes on dates other than the beginning of the financial year.

The authorities can calculate the initial effect of direct tax changes. The Inland Revenue can estimate how different types of taxpayer (e.g. companies and individuals in different income groups) will be affected. Estimates can then be made of the subsequent effects of such changes on aggregate demand, employment, the balance of payments and prices. For example, the initial or first round effect of a rise in people's disposable income due to a reduction in income tax will be an increase in consumer spending. This increase will be followed by further rounds of spending leading to a multiplier effect on output and employment. In Chapter 1 we discussed the leakages that occur and which cut down the value of the multiplier. The initial change in consumer spending will be partly taken away in indirect taxes and increased import purchases. As incomes increase in subsequent rounds further leakeages result from increased direct tax payments and savings. For the UK it is generally believed that the income tax multiplier is approximately 1.5. The induced changes make it rather difficult to calculate accurately the effect of tax changes on tax revenue.

The Chancellor can also change indirect taxes. Indirect taxes are levied directly on expenditure and take the form of value added tax (VAT) and excise duties (e.g. duties paid on petrol, tobacco and alcohol). VAT is an ad valorem tax i.e it is levied at a specified percentage on the cost of goods. Excise duties are specific (i.e. fixed in money terms per unit purchased) and the rate must be periodically increased if tax revenue is to keep pace with inflation. In one important respect most indirect tax changes have an advantage over direct tax changes in that they affect consumer spending fairly quickly. For example, if the tax in petrol is changed the price of a gallon of petrol at filling stations will be altered within a matter of hours. Similarly a change in VAT alters shop prices immediately. In contrast it may take several months before people's take home pay and spending is affected following a change in the rate of income tax announced in the budget. The multiplier effects of indirect tax changes are complicated and difficult to estimate. Changing indirect taxes results in changes in relative prices and the composition of aggregate demand. To calculate the effect on government tax receipts and consumer spending requires an estimate of how quantities demanded change and the price elasticity of demand for the taxed goods.

In comparing direct and indirect taxation we have already noted the fact that indirect taxes can be varied so as to have a quicker affect on the economy. It is also argued that indirect taxes have a beneficial incentive effect since they leave the consumer more disposable income which he can decide whether to save (and pay no tax) or spend (and pay the tax). The last advantage claimed for indirect taxation is that it can be used to affect resource allocation by changing relative prices. Thus increasing the rate of the indirect tax on one commodity relative to other goods will promote the use of its substitutes.

In contrast the main disadvantage of indirect taxes is that they are regressive and bear more heavily on the poor. A tax is said to be proportional when a tax takes the same proportion of income irrespective of the size of income. A regressive tax is a tax that takes a higher proportion of income as income falls. In contrast a progressive tax takes a higher proportion of tax as income rises. A regressive tax offends against the principle of equity or justice. On the other hand direct taxes are normally progressive since the rate of tax increases as the level of income rises. Therefore direct taxes are more equitable. However direct taxes may offer a discentive to work especially if the rate of increase of tax rates as income rises is very steep, since at high incomes leisure may be preferred to work. Finally, changes in rates of indirect tax alter prices directly and may therefore provoke wage demands. The link between wage demands and changes in disposable income is, it is argued, less direct.

In terms of buoyancy of revenue there is little to choose between the two methods. A general increase in the rate of VAT will produce a significant and predictable increase in government revenue as will an increase in the standard rate of income tax.

Finally, in this section we briefly summarise the main tax changes introduced in the tax economy by Labour and Conservative governments during the 1970s. In addition to the changes surveyed below, tax rates and government expenditure levels were varied as part of the attempt by successive governments to stabilise the economy. The interested reader is referred to Kay and King (1980)— see list of texts recommended for further reading— for a full treatment of the nature of the present British tax system and how it has evolved.

The Conservative government in office from June 1970 to March 1974 introduced three major areas of tax reform in the April budget of 1973. First, in order to simplify the tax structure, the existing system of income tax and surtax was replaced by a unified system of personal taxation. This system forms the basis of the present direct tax structure. Second, purchase tax and selective employment tax were replaced by value added tax, applied then at a single rate of 10 per cent. Third, changes were introduced to the corporation-tax system whereby all profits (distributed and undistributed) became subject to the same corporation-tax rate.

The Labour government in office from March 1974 to May 1979 also has introduced a number of important changes to the tax system. These included the introduction of a Petroleum Revenue Tax (1974) and a Development Land Tax (1976). In 1975 the Labour government abolished estate duty and replaced it by a Capital Transfer Tax (donor-based) on transfers during a person's lifetime and on death. In 1977 two innovatory measures of particular interest were introduced. First, the government granted certain income tax concessions in return for TUC support for wage restraint (see Chapter 11, section 11.6). Second, an amendment to the 1977 Finance Act provided that personal allowances set against income tax liablity should be increased each year (in the main budget) in line with the rise in the Retail Price Index over the previous calendar year. This adjustment was to apply automatically unless the government sought and obtained the approval of Parliament to do otherwise (see Chapter 12, section 12.5). In April 1978, in an attempt to alleviate the poverty trap the Labour government introduced a new tax rate of 25 per cent on the first £750 of taxable income. Lastly under the 1979 Finance Act the system of child allowances was finally phased out and replaced by a system of child benefits of a fixed amount per child.

On returning to power in May 1979 the Conservative government changed the emphasis of policy from direct to indirect taxation by (i) reducing taxes on income (e.g. the basic rate of income tax was reduced from 33 per cent to 30 per cent) in an attempt to increase incentives and (ii) increasing VAT to its present rate of 15 per cent. In addition the present Conservative government has introduced public expenditure cuts. We now turn to discuss how cash limits and expenditure ceilings have been applied during the 1970s as an indirect instrument of control over the expenditure of local authorities and nationalised industries.

8.4.4 *Cash Limits*
As noted in Tables 8.4 and 8.5 much of the PSBR is outside the direct control of the central government since components are generated by

the local authorities and public corporations. Not all public expenditure is then under the direct control of central government. The central government has no formal powers of direct control over the current expenditure of the local authorities. Consequently as an indirect instrument of control, cash limits were first introduced in 1974-75 on certain central and local government building programmes. Subsequently in 1976 cash limits were linked to the rate support grant and supplementary grants paid to the local authorities. Approximately two-thirds of local authority current expenditure is financed by grants from the central government (mainly the rate support grant which is a block grant to individual local authorities for allocation, as they choose, between different services). The rate support grant is determined each year by central government in relation to estimated expenditure in the coming financial year after consultation with local authority representatives. Since 1976 cash limits have been applied on additional grants to cover pay and price increases subsequent to the annual rate support grant settlement. The amount of grant central government is prepared to pay to supplement revenue from other sources (namely rates and charges) is limited to a predetermined figure. In this way, given the relative importance of the rate support grant to local authority revenue, central government has indirectly sought to control local authority current expenditure. Cash limits were also introduced in 1976 on the capital expenditure of local authorities and nationalised industries. Control has taken a variety of forms. For example, central government can indirectly control capital expenditure by limiting the amount of capital expenditure that can be financed by borrowing (loan sanctions) or from government grants. The introduction of cash limits has allowed a form of indirect control over expenditure of local authorities and nationalised industries by imposing ceilings on such expenditure.

8.5 Measuring the stance of fiscal policy

As we have discussed governments attempt to influence aggregate demand and thereby stabilise the level of economic activity by budget manipulation. Therefore in planning policy some measure is needed to indicate the direction (i.e. restrictive or stimulative) and impact of a particular budget programme in the economy. We will consider two budget measures which attempt to indicate whether fiscal policy is expansionary or contractionary.

8.5.1 *Budget balance*
The first of these measures is the budget balance. The budget balance

(B) is the difference between revenue from all taxation and central government total expenditure.

$$B = {}^n\sum_{i=1} T_i - {}^n\sum_{i=1} G_i$$

(8.9)

where (1) $T_1 \ldots T_n$ and $G_1 \ldots G_n$ are different types of tax revenue and government expenditure respectively

(2) $\sum$ = Greek capital letter sigma, meaning the sum of.

When the budget balance is in deficit (i.e. revenue is less than expenditure) fiscal policy is considered to be expansionary, whereas a budget surplus (i.e. revenue is more than expenditure) is considered restrictive. One of the problems of using the actual budget balance to indicate the direction of policy is that its size will partly depend on the level of economic activity (i.e. the balance is endogenous to the level of GNP). The balance can change even when the government does nothing to alter its planned tax and spending programmes (i.e. in the absence of discretionary policy changes). The reason for this is that certain forms of government spending and tax revenue vary with the level of national income. Unplanned increases in spending on social security benefits will occur when unemployment is rising. Similarly, tax receipts from personal incomes and company profits will fall during a recession. Consequently tax revenue tends to fall and public expenditure to rise when unemployment increases. A change in the actual budget balance over time may be the result of: (i) planned or discretionary changes introduced at the time of the budget (e.g. a change in tax rates); and/or (ii) unplanned, non-discretionary or automatic changes, due to changes in the level of economic activity. Therefore the budget balance is an unreliable guide to the direction of fiscal policy.

8.5.2 *Full employment budget balance*
In order to try and distinguish discretionary policy from automatic fiscal policy changes the concept of the full employment budget balance has been developed. This is illustrated in (8.10).

$$B = {}^n\sum_{i=1} T_i (Y_{FE}) - {}^n\sum_{i=1} G_i (Y_{FE})$$

(8.10)

where (1) Y_{FE} = the level of national income at full employment
(2) $\sum_{i=1}^{n} T_i$ and $\sum_{i=1}^{n} G_i$
are total revenue from taxation and total government expenditure respectively.

Given a particular budget programme the concept measures what tax receipts and expenditure would be if the economy were at full employment. In so doing it attempts to separate the influence of the budget on the economy from that of the economy on the budget. A budget deficit at full employment indicates an expansionary policy, and vice versa. Planned fiscal changes will be reflected in a change in the full employment budget balance. A discretionary change that increases (reduces) the full employment budget deficit (surplus), either through increased spending or reduced taxation indicates an expansionary fiscal policy. In contrast a planned change that reduces (increases) the full employment budget deficit (surplus) by decreasing expenditure or increasing taxation indicates a contractionary policy stance. It is also possible for discretionary changes to leave the balance unchanged and still have a positive influence on the level of economic activity (see section 8.4.1 for a discussion of the so-called balanced budget multiplier).

One of the problems with this measure is that it is difficult in practice to calculate full employment budget deficits/surpluses. Various classes of expenditure are subject to different rates of taxation. For example, exports are free from tax whereas most of consumer expenditure is subject to VAT (currently at the standard rate of 15 per cent). Thus in building up estimates of government revenue it is necessary to project the totals of the various categories of aggregate demand. Not a particularly easy task!

Apart from problems involved in calculating the level of the full employment budget deficit/surplus there is also the problem of fiscal drag. This arises because changes in the full employment budget balance can occur in an economy experiencing economic growth. Even with unchanged spending and taxation (i.e. no discretionary changes introduced) the budget balance will change as the level of national income associated with full employment increases over time. With economic growth tax receipts tend to rise more than expenditure so that the full employment budget deficit (surplus) falls (rises). Automatic changes in the full employment budget balance will also occur in an economy experiencing inflation. This is because tax rates are related to nominal incomes which in times of inflation tend to rise faster than real incomes. These automatic changes in the full employment budget balance are commonly referred to as fiscal drag because they act as a drag on the expansion of the economy.

8.6 The crowding out debate

This debate is concerned with the problem of whether fiscal expansion actually leads to an increase in output and employment or whether it merely crowds out or replaces an equivalent amount of private expenditure leaving total output unchanged. While it is generally agreed that fiscal expansion will positively influence output and employment in the short run, some economists have argued that in the long run it will merely displace or crowd out some components of private expenditure so that real income remains unchanged. Complete crowding out will occur when private expenditure is reduced by the same amount that government expenditure is increased, so that the long-run fiscal multiplier is zero. A fiscal multiplier between 0 and 1 indicates the existence of partial crowding out (i.e. income rises by an amount less than the rise in government expenditure).

We will now examine the five main instances in which crowding out may occur. First, crowding out may arise as a direct result of the way in which fiscal expansion is financed. An increase in government expenditure financed by net open market sales of government debt will put upward pressure on interest rates. The rate of interest on new bond issues must increase to induce the public to lend the government more money. The rise in interest rates will in turn cause a reduction in the level of private investment expenditure undertaken in the economy as firms cancel investment projects they had planned to finance by borrowing before interest rates increased. Another way of looking at this finance effect is to argue that private securities will be replaced by government securities in portfolios. In other words increased sales of government bonds will lead to a significant reduction in the quantity of finance available to private firms as those people/institutions who lend funds to the government have less money to lend to others (or spend themselves). Second, crowding out may occur due to an expectations effect. If, for example, the private sector's confidence in the economic future were adversely affected by a budget deficit, private investment would be reduced as the business community lowered their estimates of the future returns from new investment projects. Third, crowding out may arise due to the effects of an increase in the general price level. An increase in government expenditure will cause a rise in the price level in the long run if sufficient unemployed resources are not available to produce the extra goods demanded. The rate of interest will rise as the private sector sells bonds to restore the real value of their nominal money holdings and cause a reduction in private investment. Fourth, crowding out may occur in an open economy operating a fixed exchange rate again due to a price effect. If prices rise following fiscal expansion exports will become less competitive with foreign produced goods, whereas imports will become more competitive with home produced goods. As discussed in Chapter 1 output and employment will fall as exports decrease and imports increase. Lastly, even in the case where an increase in government expenditure is financed by increasing taxes (i.e. balanced budget multiplier discussed in section 8.4.1) some partial crowding out of private expenditure will occur. As income rises the transactions demand for money will increase and with a fixed money supply cause interest rates to rise. This in turn will cause some reduction in the level of private investment undertaken in the economy. The value of the balanced budget multiplier will in consequence be less than one (i.e. partial crowding out will occur).

The issue of crowding out is the subject of considerable controversy. Unfortunately the empirical evidence from simulations of macroeconomic models is far from being clear cut. A summary of the evidence from several econometric models of the USA economy suggests a general consensus that sustained fiscal policy influences real income in the short run with a peak effect occurring after approximately two years. Most models estimate the government expenditure multiplier (with no accommodating monetary expansion) in the short run to be in the range 1.4-2.4. However agreement vanishes for simulations beyond two years. Some models estimate negative multipliers (i.e. over crowding out) in the long run while others show the value of the multiplier to be positive but considerably less than in the short run. Given the ambiguous nature of the empirical evidence the crowding out debate is likely to continue and remain a controversial area.

8.7 Fiscal policy: an assessment
The role of fiscal policy as an instrument to stabilise aggregate demand remains controversial. A fairly wide consensus exists that fiscal expansion is crowded out in the long run so that fiscal policy per se cannot influence the long-run level of employment in a country. Nevertheless this leaves open the question of whether fiscal policy can be used to stabilise aggregate demand and offset temporary swings in private expenditure. Also it should be remembered that fiscal policy can be used to influence either the

distribution of income or output. Thus, for example, fiscal policy could discriminate in favour of investment by granting firms financial assistance for investment purposes which is financed by taxes on consumption. In this way total aggregate demand remains unaltered but its distribution between consumption and investment changes. Of course these types of policy run up against the problems discussed in Chapter 7 as to how far governments can usefully manage an economy. In the next chapter we will examine the role of monetary policy as an instrument to stabilise aggregate demand.

9 Demand Management: Monetary Policy

9.1 Introduction

In Chapters 2 and 3 we discussed the importance of financial variables such as the quantity of money and interest rates in the determination of the level of economic activity. It is not surprising, therefore, that governments have attempted to control the monetary system by a wide range of policies including (i) direct credit controls, (ii) interest rate changes and (iii) changing the quantity of money.

As we saw in Chapter 3, sections 3.5-3.6, a reduction in the money supply increases the rate of interest which in turn reduces private investment and also perhaps consumption expenditure. The consequential decrease in aggregate demand produces a 'multiplied' contraction in national income. This direction of policy can be termed a restrictive monetary policy. Broadly speaking similar results would occur if the government operated a restrictive monetary policy by either increasing interest rates or imposing direct controls to restrict the quantity of credit available to finance expenditure. Conversely precisely opposite effects would be achieved if the government pursued an expansionary monetary policy by (i) increasing the money supply, (ii) reducing interest rates or (iii) removing any controls which impeded the flow of credit.

In section 9.2 we examine the advantages and disadvantages of these three targets of monetary policy and subsequently in section 9.3 the associated problem of obtaining a good indicator of the stance of monetary policy. In section 9.4 we discuss the main instruments of monetary policy used in the UK. Other aspects of monetary policy are discussed in sections 9.5 (monetary base control), 9.6 (new system of monetary control) and 9.7 (the role of monetary targets or rules). Finally, discussion of the system of competition and credit control is included as an Appendix A to this chapter.

9.2 Targets of monetary policy

One vital question for the authorities is whether they should attempt to control the level of interest rates or the money supply as the target of monetary policy. They cannot control both. The government budget constraint showing how the public sector borrowing requirement is financed was discussed in Chapter 3, section 3.3.1 and is reproduced here for convenience.

$$PSBR = OMO + NMD + BPF + \Delta H \qquad (9.1)$$

where as before (i) $PSBR$ = the Public Sector Borrowing Requirement
(ii) OMO = sales of bonds in the open market
(iii) NMD = sales of non-marketable debt
(iv) BPF = finance available from a balance of payments deficit
(v) ΔH = change in banks' reserve assets.

We begin by assuming floating exchange rates so that BPF equals zero. If the rate of interest is fixed by the authorities OMO and NMD are determined by the market, i.e. given the rate of interest the private sector decides the quantity of bonds and non-marketable debit it will purchase. This means that ΔH is the residual method of financing the PSBR. In other words ΔH and the money supply become endogenous. In contrast if a money supply target is prescribed, a value for ΔH which is consistent with that money supply target is also prescribed. The rate of interest must therefore be varied until the prescribed quantity of bonds and non-marketable debt is sold to finance the PSBR. In this case the money supply is under the control of the authorities but not the rate of interest.

The decision as to which variable (i.e. the money supply or the rate of interest) is to be controlled depends on the question, 'Control of which variable will lead to greater stability of the economy?' In a world of perfect certainty the precise relationship between (i) the quantity of money and the level of national income and (ii) the rate of interest and private expenditure would be both known and fixed. In this case it would not matter which target was controlled since control of one would imply control of the other. Thus if the money supply was fixed the rate of interest would also be fixed at a known value as would the level of private expenditure. In the real world, however, both relationships are (i) imperfectly known and (ii) subject to variability. The choice between the money supply and the rate of interest as a target depends on the relative variability of the two relationships i.e. that between (i) money and national income (velocity of circulation) and (ii) interest rates and private expenditure. If the relationship between money and national income is subject to wide unpredictable variations and that between private expenditure and interest rates is more stable and predictable, it is better to control interest rates and allow the quantity of money to assume any value consistent with the interest rate target. Conversely in the opposite case the money supply target is to be preferred. In this instance the relationship between money and income is known to be more stable than that between interest rates and private expenditure so it is obvious that the more sensible policy is to control the money supply allowing interest rates to assume any value consistent with the money supply target. The relative stability of the two relationships is the subject of controversy. Monetarists believe that the velocity of circulation is stable and that therefore the appropriate target is control of the money supply. Keynesians tend to be less certain of this and tend to advocate control of interest rates as the appropriate target of monetary policy. In the extreme case, some Keynesians argue that control of the money supply is irrelevant. It should also be noted that control of the money supply is difficult if not impossible if exchange rates are not free to fluctuate. This problem was discussed in Chapter 4, section 4.7.3 and can be easily reiterated here by referring back to identity (9.1). Fixed exchange rates imply that the value assumed by *BPF* will be other than zero and this will make control of the money supply difficult. Similar difficulties wil be experienced by any country which attempts to control interest rates given fixed exchange rates. If, for example, domestic interest rates are higher than those in the rest of the world, inflows of capital from abroad will take place. These capital inflows will set up pressure directed towards a reduction in domestic interest rates towards those ruling in the rest of the world. Consequently under a regime of fixed exchange rates it is difficult for a country to pursue an independent monetary policy, whether the target variable be interest rates or the quantity of money. The third possible target noted earlier was the control of the flow of credit or lending. Individuals borrow to finance expenditure and therefore it is argued that, by limiting the amount of credit available, private expenditure can also be limited. The total volume of credit will be automatically influenced if either a money supply or interest rate target is followed but credit can also be controlled by the imposition of direct controls. As we discuss in section 9.4, the problem with this type of controls is that they distort the market mechanism.

9.3 The choice of an indicator

An indicator should indicate quickly and accurately the thrust (direction and magnitude) of monetary policy. The choice of an indicator is closely linked to the target of monetary policy. For example, if the money supply is the desired target then the money supply itself is one possible indicator of the thrust of monetary policy. The desirable properties of an indicator are that it should (i) possess a high degree of correlation with the target variable, (ii) be the subject of accurate and reliable statistics which are quickly available to the authorities and (iii) be under the control of he authorities. If the money supply is the target variable, then use of money supply statistics as an indicator will give an accurate picture of the thrust of monetary policy. However money supply figures are usually only available with a lag after the date to which they refer. Another possible indicator is data on the monetary base. In contrast to statistics on the money supply figures for the base are continually available especially if the definition of the base is restricted to banks' deposits at the central bank. However in the UK, the definition up to spring 1981 was not restricted to banks' deposits at the Bank of England. Furthermore as we noted in Chapter 3, section 3.3.2 the banks have considerable power to obtain extra reserve assets either by attracting a larger share of a given total or alternatively actually creating such reserves assets. This means that the monetary base would not have been a good indicator of the thrust of UK monetary policy in the period up to spring 1981.

Another indicator available to the authorities is a representative rate of interest. The problem with this indicator is that the authorities control the nominal rate of interest whereas the variable relevant to expenditure decisions is what people perceive to be the real rate (i.e. the nominal rate minus the expected rate of inflation). For example if the nominal rate of interest is 15 per cent but the inflation rate during the next year is 14 per cent then the real cost of borrowing funds for one year is only 1 per cent. Consequently a high nominal rate of interest could be consistent with either a tight or relaxed monetary policy; it all depends on what rates of inflation are expected during the period of the loan.

The final indicator to be considered is domestic credit expansion. As we have seen in an open economy with either fixed or managed floating exchange rates, the money supply is influenced by the state of the balance of payments. Consequently a better indicator of the thrust of domestic monetary influences would be an indicator which purged the money supply figures of the influence of the balance of payments. Such an indicator is termed Domestic Credit Expansion

(DCE) and can be roughly defined as the PSBR minus sales of bonds to sectors other than banks plus bank lending to the private sector. It therefore approximately represents credit extended by the banks to the private and public sectors. A precise definition of domestic credit expansion and the link between it and the money supply is discussed in the appendix to Chapter 3.

9.4 The instruments of monetary policy

9.4.1 *Introduction*
The instruments or techniques of monetary policy can be usefully classified into two categories:

    (i) market operations
    (ii) the imposition of portfolio constraints.

Market operations can be distinguished from category (ii) types of monetary policy because no additional constraints are placed on banks' portfolios. The Bank of England influences the behaviour of the banks by either varying interest rates or by its dealings in securities leaving the banks free to respond to these market forces within the framework of existing reserve requirements. Imposition of portfolio constraints involves the introduction of additional constraints on the banks' acquisition of assets and liabilities; i.e. they constrain banks' portfolios directly. Before going on to examine these techniques in more detail we wish to look at the role of fiscal policy in this connection.

Fiscal policy determines the size of the PSBR and consequently has a strong impact on monetary policy. For example, an expansionary fiscal policy will cause an increase in the PSBR which will in turn lead to either (i) an increase in sales of bonds or other government debt (i.e. *NMD* or *OMO* in identity 9.1) and therefore higher interest rates or (ii) an expansion of the money supply because of the changes in banks' holdings of reserve assets (ΔH in identity 9.1). Therefore one way of obtaining a relaxation in monetary policy would be to reduce the PSBR by a contractionary fiscal policy leaving the overall thrust of macroeconomic policy unchanged.

9.4.2 *Market operations*
Market operations consist of either varying (i) interest rates or (ii) debt management policies. The government can influence short-term rates of interest through the Bank of England's operations in the money market. For example, if short-term rates of interest are increased the effect will spread to long-term rates of interest as

investors on the margin move funds from the long-term market to gain advantage of increased returns on short-term lending. This will decrease the supply of long-term funds. At the same time marginal borrowers of short-term funds will try to borrow on a longer-term basis due to the increased short-term interest rates. The net effect of these movements will be to cause long-term interest rates to move upwards in sympathy with short-term rates. It should be noted that this link between short- and long-term interest rates depends on arbitrage and is therefore incompatible with the extreme form of the preferred market habitat view of the term structure of interest rates discussed in Chapter 3, section 3.5. The authorities can also influence interest rates by intervention in the market for Gilt-Edged Securities. Debt management can be widely defined to include all transactions by the authorities in government debt. It therefore includes all sales of bonds, Treasury Bills and non-marketable debt shown in identity (9.1). As we have noted in principle the authorities can either fix the quantity of money or the rate of interest. If they choose to determine the quantity of money they will have to sell a specific quantity of bonds to constrain ΔH to a particular value. This would require bonds to be sold by a 'tender' system similar to that followed for Treasury Bills (see Chapter 2, section 2.3.4) with the Bank of England accepting tenders at successively lower prices until the prescribed quantity of bonds was sold. In fact this system has not been followed in the UK and the authorities have been more concerned to act on interest rates. Nevertheless their interest rate policy is determined against the background of the size of the PSBR and the volume of debt to be sold. In practice then debt management policy has been a compromise between price (interest rate) and quantity (money supply) operation.

We now turn to examine the strategy followed by the Bank of England to maximise bond sales. Over the years this strategy has changed considerably. Throughout the 1960s the Bank of England intervened in the gilt-edged market, buying and selling bonds in order to ensure stability of their prices. The reason for this intervention was the belief that the gilt-edged market was essentially unstable. It was believed that a fall in bond prices (rise in the rate of interest) would lead to fears of further price falls and hence bond sales as bond holders attempted to avoid capital losses. It was believed that without such intervention bond prices would fluctuate widely making it difficult for the authorities to sell large quantities of bonds. This particular view of the market has been modified in recent years. In addition, with greater emphasis being placed on the control of the money supply, the authorities have been much less willing to buy and sell securities just to stabilise the prices of Gilt-Edged Securities. As a general rule the Bank is not prepared to buy automatically stock with more than one year to maturity though it has retained the right to do so.

One reason for holding Gilt-Edged Securities is speculation in the hope of making capital gains as interest rates fall (i.e. bond prices rise). Consequently the authorities' strategy has been to raise interest rates sharply when necessary and subsequently gradually reduce them. The attraction of fairly certain capital gains makes Gilt-Edged Securities very attractive to hold and stimulates their sales. This procedure has been dubbed 'The Noble Duke of York' tactics by *The Financial Times*. Additional aids to sell bonds have recently been adopted by the Bank of England. First, since March 1977 stocks have been sold in the form of partly-paid stocks. This procedure requires purchasers to pay only part of the full price to the Bank of England at the time of purchase with a commitment to pay subsequent instalments at predetermined later dates. This tactic enables the authorities to smooth out receipts of funds over time. Second, variable interest stocks have been issued whereby their rate of interest adjusts to changes in the average Treasury Bill discount rate. Third, convertible stocks have been issued. The initial issue is a short-term stock but the purchaser is offered the option to convert into long-term stock at specified rates of interest at a fixed date(s) in the future. It should be noted that the holder will only exercise his option to convert when it is attractive for him to do so i.e. when market long-term rates of interest have fallen below the rate offered in the option. Therefore to the extent that conversions into long-term stock do take place, it is expensive for the authorities. Fourth, in 1981, index-linked bonds were introduced but their sale has been restricted to pension funds and insurance companies.* Up to 1981, the strain of market operations designed to reduce the growth of the money supply has been almost entirely borne by the Gilt-Edged Securities market. Treasury Bills formed part of the specified reserve assets so dealings in Treasury Bills had no real effect on the money supply. Tactics for the sale of non-marketable debt were not very aggressive, one exception being sales of 'indexed' national savings certificates to old-age pensioners, so-called 'Granny Bonds'. Indexed securities are securities whose value increases in line with inflation (the whole question of indexation is discussed in Chapter 12). It is sufficient at this stage to note that these bonds have proved attractive to buyers and in fact the age qualification was progressively lowered and finally eliminated in the summer of 1981.

9.4.3 *Imposition of portfolio constraints*

Two types of portfolio constraint have been used by the Bank of England: (i) those which change reserve requirements; and (ii) those which inflict interest rate penalties on banks. Variations in reserve requirements alter the maximum level of bank deposits consistent with a given quantity of reserves. For example, an increase in the required reserve ratio will, provided banks collectively are unable to acquire extra reserves, force banks to reduce their deposits either by selling securities they hold (i.e. investments) or recalling (or not renewing maturing) loans. Conversely a reduction in the prescribed reserve ratio would allow banks to expand deposits by increasing their holdings of securities or loans and advances made. This process was discussed in Chapter 3, section 3.3.1. In fact this instrument (i.e. varying reserve ratios) has rarely been used in the UK. However, the policy of calling up special deposits has similar effects. A special deposit is a deposit lodged at the Bank of England but which does not count as a reserve asset along with the other deposits held there by banks. Hence the effect of a call for special deposits by the Bank of England is essentially to transfer banks' assets from reserve to non-reserve assets as the banks make the necessary payments to the Bank of England. Therefore precisely the same effect will follow from a call up of special deposits as would follow from an increase in the required reserve asset ratio. Repayment of a special deposit would have the same effect as a reduction in the required reserve asset ratio.

It must be stressed that the effectiveness of both these instruments depends on whether banks can attract extra reserve assets in response to increases in the required reserve asset ratio and/or a call up of special deposits. Clearly a single bank can attempt to obtain the extra reserve assets by bidding for them in the relevant financial markets. However if the total stock of reserve assets is under the control of the authorities, then banks in aggregate will be unable to acquire the extra reserve assets necessary to validate the existing level of deposits.[1] In this case the only possible response is for bank deposits to be decreased. In Britain up to spring 1981, as we have seen in Chapter 3, section 3.3.2, reserve assets were definitely not under the control of the authorities. The banks could acquire extra reserve assets so that control of bank deposits by either variation in

---

1. Even if the authorities could control the total amount of reserve assets, banks might be able to bid for more of these assets if they were also held by institutions (e.g. foreign institutions) not bound by a particular country's reserve ratio rules.

reserve ratios or by way of special deposits was unlikely to be reliable as an instrument designed to control the level of bank deposits.

Perhaps for these reasons the system of Special Supplementary Deposits (colloquially known as 'The Corset' in financial circles) was introduced in 1973. The basis of this scheme was that a rate of growth of interest bearing eligible liabilities (IBELS) was prescribed by the Bank of England. IBELS can roughly be defined as interest bearing deposits—for a precise definition see the appendix to Chapter 3. If the growth of IBELS at any bank exceeded the prescribed rate, deposits had to be made at the Bank of England by the bank concerned. The vital point was that these deposits earned no interest whereas the bank was paying interest to its customers on their corresponding deposits. Consequently the bank would incur a loss. This penalty was strengthened because the rate of supplementary deposit increased proportionately to the gap between the actual growth rate of IBELS and that prescribed within the scheme. The maximum rate of the supplementary deposit was 50 per cent of IBELS in excess of that permitted by the prescribed growth rate. Whenever introduced this scheme certainly controlled the growth of IBELS. However it is arguable that it was more of a window dressing exercise than a system of real control. Some sections of the financial system remained outside the sphere of control and some lending may have been diverted to uncontrolled sources. One particular example of this is that whenever the scheme was introduced, bank acceptances of bills of exchange increased. This suggests that the flow of credit was diverted to other sources.

In the past banks' portfolios have been influenced by the imposition of direct controls on the quantity of certain assets, especially loans and advances. Such controls have usually been both quantitative and qualitative. The qualitative aspect took the form of requests to ensure adequate lending in certain directions (e.g. to finance exports) and restrained lending in other directions not considered essential, a typical example being lending to finance speculative property development. The implied assumption behind qualitative controls is that of market failure. It is argued that imposition of such controls will improve the allocation of bank lending between various activities. Quantitative controls impose ceilings on bank lending. Because interest rates are not raised sufficiently to reduce bank lending to the required levels, credit is rationed by the banks leaving excess demand at the ruling rates of interest.

At a lower level the same effects could be achieved by 'moral suasion' whereby the central bank persuades the banks to restrict lending or grant preferences to certain types of borrowers without resort-

ing to formal requests. Lending controls have also been applied to
hire purchase companies. The traditional method of controlling the
activities of these institutions is to vary (i) the initial deposit to be
paid by the buyer and (ii) the duration of the loan. For example a restrictive policy would take the form of (i) increasing the percentage of
the deposit (i.e. the portion of the total cost to be paid by the buyer)
and/or (ii) shortening the maximum period of time for repayment of
the loan.

The objections to direct controls are twofold. First, they distort the
market mechanism. The rationale behind allocation of funds by the
market mechanism is that prospective borrowers with potential projects offering the highest returns will be willing to pay the highest interest rates to obtain funds. In this way the market mechanism will allocate scarce funds to those projects offering the highest rates of return. Imposition of direct (i.e. non-price) controls means there will be
excess demand for funds at the existing level of interest rates. Credit
will therefore be rationed and some would-be borrowers will be unable to obtain funds. There is no mechanism to ensure that those who
are able to obtain the rationed supply of funds are those with the best
investment opportunities. There is therefore an implied assumption
that credit rationing means that funds are not allocated to the areas
where highest returns can be earned. The second objection is that the
longer the controls are in operation the greater the scope for evasion
by borowing through uncontrolled channels; the development of the
inter-company money market (mentioned in Chapter 2, section
2.8.2) is just one example of such a development. It is therefore
doubtful if total credit is affected especially in the long run.

Direct controls have also been applied on movements of international capital. As we have seen international flows of capital tend to
make independent monetary policies difficult under a regime of
fixed exchange rates. One way of reducing such difficulties was to
impose restrictions on the freedom of individuals to concert foreign
currencies into domestic currencies. Such restrictions can be applied
either to inward or outward flows of capital; or for that matter to both
simultaneously. Such restrictions could also be justified in times of
floating exchange rates to prevent undesired movements of the exchange rate. Clearly such controls are open to similar objections to
those discussed in the context of domestic direct controls. Imposition of controls over international capital movements is likely to lead
to misallocation of resources between countries. There is also the
temptation to avoid the controls. Nevertheless such controls have
been widely used by a wide range of countries, thus implying that
various governments have believed that the balance of payments (or

exchange rate) gain due to such controls is worth the costs involved. As far as the UK is concerned restrictions on convertibility of sterling were abandoned in the autumn of 1979.

9.4.4 *Concluding remarks*

We have discussed the instruments of monetary policy used by the British authorities over the past twenty years or so. Direct controls on lending were extensively used throughout the 1960s but have been only sparingly used since. After 1973 Special Supplementary Deposits were widely used before being finally given up in 1980. As control of the money supply came more to the forefront of government macroeconomic policy, fiscal policy has been used more and more for monetary puroses, i.e. to control the size of the PSBR. In addition interest rate policy has been directed towards controlling the money supply. As we have seen higher interest rates can reduce the rate of growth of the money supply in two ways: (i) by increasing sales of bonds; and (ii) by reducing the demand for bank loans. Nevertheless throughout the summer of 1980 there was widespread criticism of the methods of controlling the money supply. The then existing system with its far from controllable reserve asset base proved difficult to control by any method. One possible way out is control via a new definition of the monetary base. We now turn to this topic.

9.5 Monetary base control

The unsatisfactory nature of the present system of monetary control in the UK has provided impetus to discussions concerning the possibility of introducing a system of controlling the monetary base. The rationale underlying the adoption of a system of monetary base control can be seen by recalling the fact that banks are required to maintain a ratio of specified reserve assets against deposits. If the specified reserve assets were completely under the control of the Bank of England, the banks' ability to create deposits would be restricted   to the supply of reserve assets available to them. Consequently the money supply would be under the control of the authorities through their control of the quantity of reserve assets or monetary base as it is often called.

Clearly introduction of such a system would require a redefinition of assets which could be included in the 'base'. Typically such assets would be restricted to (i) banks' deposits at the Bank of England and (ii) notes and coins in circulation. The only scope for banks as a whole to attract reserve assets would then be to attract additional deposits of notes and coins from their customers. This would require banks to persuade their customers either to make greater use of cheques for payment purposes or to economise on their cash holdings. Both these avenues seem to be limited in their potential. There would be no scope at all for banks to create reserves assets as happened under the UK system up to 1981.

The monetary base would be controlled by open market operations. This can be seen by referring to the government budget constraint i.e.

$$PSBR = OMO + NMD + BPF + \Delta H \qquad (9.1)$$

Assuming a pure floating exchange rate regime so that $BPF = 0$ and re-arranging (9.1)

$$\Delta H = PSBR - OMO - NMD \qquad (9.2)$$

This clearly brings out the essential feature of monetary base control that, given the size of the PSBR, OMO and NMD must be varied to ensure changes in the base (ΔH) which are consistent with the target value for the money supply.

The advantages claimed for the introduction of such a system are three in number. First, the base, as defined above, would be under the control of authorities. This would permit control of the money supply without recourse to direct controls. Second, the base as defined above excludes Treasury Bills. This would permit the authorities to deal in a wider range of securities. At present if the authorities wish to alter the size of the reserve asset base, they must either sell more long-term bonds (Gilt-Edged Securities) or persuade people to take up more non-marketable debt. This has meant that the gilt-edged market has taken most of the strain of restrictive monetary policies in recent years. Re-definition of the base to exclude Treasury Bills would enable the authorities to conduct open market operations in Treasury Bills as well as Gilt-Edged Securities, thus spreading the range of markets involved in monetary policy. Moreover the interest cost of financing the government debt might be reduced. More high interest debt could be sold short term than permitted by the existing system. Such debt could be refinanced at lower cost as interest rates fell. Third, the monetary base would provide up-to-date information on the state of monetary policy. The Bank of England has information on a day to day basis both of bank deposits held at the Bank of England and notes and coins in circulation. However such benefits would be obtained at a cost. One disadvantage is that interest rates would be subjugated to money supply control and could fluctuate quite widely if base control were rigorously applied. Second, there is a problem regarding the timing of the relationship between deposits and the base. For example, should the relationship be (i) an average so that the average level of bank deposits over a specific period is constrained to the average base of that period, (ii) applied on a day to day basis so that each day the level of deposits is constrained to the base, (iii) applied on a particular day such as the last day of the month, (iv) applied so that bank deposits throughout one month are constrained to base assets held at the end of the previous month (lead accounting), or (v) the base requirement is determined by the level of deposits at the end of the previous month (lagged accounting)? Method (ii) would be extremely rigorous and would be likely to lead to quite large fluctuations in interest rates. A third problem would arise in respect of the discount houses. Lending of last resort would have to be less automatic and clearly the present position of the discount houses as dealers in reserve assets would be prejudiced. Finally, reserve ratios are specified in terms of a minimum. If control were to be exercised the banks would hold reserve assets over and above the minimum level. In fact the quantity of excess reserves held as a safety margin would tend to increase the more rigorously the monetary base were controlled. This would mean that there would be no automatic fixed link between the base and the money supply. This would impose a severe problem for the authorities during the period immediately after the introduction of base control. They would have no previous experience to guide them over the question as to the extent of recent reserve assets likely to be held by banks. Consequently figures of the monetary base would be difficult to interpret.

To sum up on the question of monetary base control, there is nothing magical about such a system. It will not automatically solve all difficulties for monetary policy. Any control of the money supply is likely to lead to higher interest rates. The advantage of a system of base control is simply that, if the object is to control the money supply, it does offer a system which can achieve that end more easily than the system of monetary control in operation up to 1981. It is also true that dealing with a wider range of securities would ease the task of debt management.

In March 1980, the authorities issued a consultation paper (Cmnd 7858) with a view to entering into discussions with financial institutions over a new system of monetary control.

9.6 New system of monetary control
On 12 March 1981, the Bank of England issued a paper entitled 'Monetary Control: Next Steps', outlining proposed changes to the system of monetary control. After further discussions with the banks

the new arrangements for monetary control were set out in a further paper dated 5 August 1981 entitled 'Monetary Control-Provisions'.

The main provisions of the new scheme are that:

(1) the Special Deposits Scheme remains in place;

(2) the Supplementary Special Deposit Scheme (The Corset) is terminated;

(3) all banks and licensed deposit holders are required to hold non-operational non-interest bearing deposits at the Bank of England. These balances are set at a level of $\frac{1}{2}$ per cent of an institution's eligible liabilities and are reviewed twice a year in relation to its average eligible liabilities in the previous six months. The term non-operational refers to the fact that the banks are unable to use these balances in the course of their normal business. The funds are in effect frozen and provide a substantial part of the Bank of England's resources;

(4) in additon to the non-operational funds the banks will maintain balances (again non-interest bearing) at the Bank of England for their normal business operations. The quantity of funds so maintained will be purely at the discretion of the banks concerned. No legal ratios are imposed.

(5) the reserve asset ratio of 10 per cent ($12\frac{1}{2}$ per cent until 2 January 1981) is abolished.

This summarises the framework within which monetary policy will be conducted. Similarly changes of emphasis have taken place in the Bank of England's tactics in the money markets. Prior to 1981, the strategy followed was to over-issue Treasury Bills so that the discount market was short of funds. This shortage could then be relieved by the Bank of England at interest rates of its own choosing. Consequently the supply of base or high-powered money was infinitely elastic at the chosen rate of interest. This is shown in Figure 9.1 with the supply of high-powered money being represented by the line S^R and the chosen rate of interest by r^*.

Since the autumn of 1980, the Bank of England has placed greater emphasis on operations in quantities of bills in its money market management rather than the rate of interest as hitherto. Subsequently early in 1981 the Bank intimated that it will keep short-term interest rates within an unpublished band. Market factors will determine interest rates within the band but at the limits set by the authorities the supply of high-powered money will again become infinitely elastic. This situation can be represented by a slight adjustment to Figure 9.1. Within the interest band denoted in

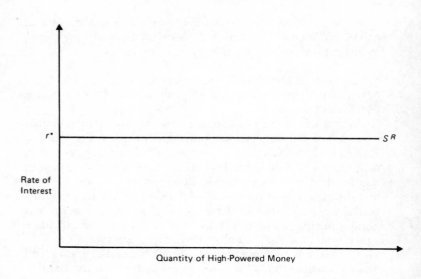

Figure 9.1. The supply of high-powered money with interest rate control

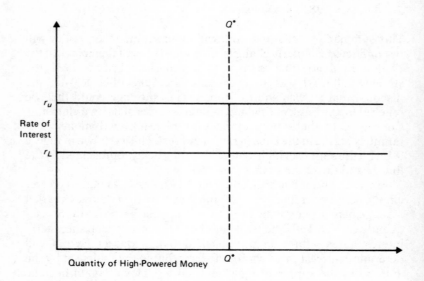

Figure 9.2. Interest rate fluctuations with monetary-base control

Figure 9.2 the quantity of high-powered money is that set by the authorities i.e. Q^*. At the limits the supply curve returns to the shape depicted in Figure 9.1 i.e the dotted sections of $Q^* Q^*$ are inoperative.

It is now necessary to examine the relationship of this scheme to a system of base control. A pure system of base control could be represented by all the lines $Q^* Q^*$ in Figure 9.2. It is clear therefore that the degree of approximation of the new system of monetary control to base control depends on the width of the interest rate bands. If they are wide the system will approximate base control but if they are extremely narrow the system will approximate interest rate control. The most that can be said at present is that the system is consistent with the introduction of monetary base control. This statement is not invalidated by the fact that no precise cash/reserve ratio is imposed on the banks. If open market operations push banks' balances at the Bank of England below the desired level, the banks will contract the scale of their activities in just the same way as if they were legally compelled to hold a specific quantity of such balances relative to the level of their deposits. Clearly therefore the new system allows the Bank of England to control the level of bank deposits using the voluntary cash ratio as a fulcrum against which pressure can be exerted. In fact experience of operation of this new system suggests that it has approximated a system of interest rate control rather than one of monetary base control.

9.7 Monetary targets

In many countries, monetary policy has taken the form of announcing targets for the rate of monetary growth during the subsequent year and often for future years. This type of policy is called a monetary rule and we discussed in Chapter 7, section 7.7 the general nature of the rules versus discretion controversy. Those who favour the adoption of a monetary rule, as against discretionary monetary policy, base their preference on one or more of the following arguments. First, because of the length and variability of the time lags associated with monetary policy, many economists argue that the target of growth of the money supply should not be varied in a discretionary manner to fine-tune the economy. They contend that in the current state of economic knowledge the consequences of varying the rate of monetary growth in a discretionary manner cannot be predicted with sufficient accuracy to permit successful fine-tuning. Indeed it is feared that discretionary policy could turn out to be destabilising. Second, some economists argue that the economy is inherently stable if not disturbed by erratic monetary growth and that by following a monetary rule and avoiding sharp swings in policy the authorities can remove an important potential source of instability. Third, as we discussed in Chapter 5, section 5.3.2, some economists argue that monetary policy can only be used to peg the level of unemployment in the short run. Further if unemployment is pegged below the natural rate accelerating inflation will occur. Finally, those economists who believe in rational expectations deny that discretionary monetary expansion can reduce unemployment even in the short run.

The precise target for the rate of monetary growth depends on the existing state of the economy. The long-run rule should be a rate of growth of money supply equal to the trend growth of real income multiplied by the income elasticity of demand for money. For example if the trend growth of real income is expected to be 4 per cent and the income elasticity of the demand for money is 1.5 the target rate of growth of the money supply should be 6 per cent. In this way it is argued that money will have neither inflationary nor deflationary effects but will provide for long-run price stability. In fact it is claimed that it will provide an additional automatic stabiliser. If real income grows at a rate less than its trend value, operation of a fixed monetary rule will ensure that monetary conditions have an expansionary effect because the rate of growth of the money supply exceeds that of real income. The converse applies if the rate of growth of real income temporarily rises above its trend value. If, however the rate of monetary expansion has exceeded the rate envisaged in the long-run rule, it makes little sense to reduce it immediately to the fixed long-run growth rate. A rapid reduction in the rate of growth of money supply would lead to a rapid increase in unemployment. Those who favour monetary rules (i.e. monetarists), tend to argue for a gradual reduction in the actual rate of growth of

TABLE 9.1 Target rates of monetary growth in the UK, 1976/77−1983/84

Financial year	Target rate of growth of sterling M3: percentage per annum
1976/77	9 to 13
1977/78	9 to 13
1978/79	8 to 12
1979/80	7 to 11
1980/81	7 to 11
1981/82	8 to 12
1982/83	8 to 12
1983/84	7 to 11

TABLE 9.2 Percentage growth rates of sterling M3
(percentage growth over corresponding quarter of the previous year)

1964	1	7.4	1972	1	16.1	1980	1	10.4
	2	6.7		2	21.9		2	16.4
	3	7.1		3	23.8		3	17.2
	4	5.6		4	24.5		4	19.7
1965	1	5.9	1973	1	25.1	1981	1	18.0
	2	6.7		2	23.1		2	16.6
	3	6.2		3	27.2		3	16.3
	4	7.6		4	26.3		4	13.2
1966	1	9.0	1974	1	23.5	1982	1	14.1
	2	6.7		2	18.5		2	12.0
	3	6.4		3	12.0		3	9.4
	4	3.4		4	10.2		4	9.8
1967	1	3.1	1975	1	8.5			
	2	4.7		2	9.6			
	3	6.9		3	10.8			
	4	9.5		4	6.6			
1968	1	8.9	1976	1	7.0			
	2	9.4		2	8.1			
	3	7.0		3	9.2			
	4	6.9		4	9.5			
1969	1	6.4	1977	1	7.6			
	2	2.1		2	8.0			
	3	2.1		3	6.6			
	4	2.4		4	10.0			
1970	1	1.7	1978	1	15.5			
	2	6.9		2	15.1			
	3	8.3		3	15.1			
	4	9.5		4	15.0			
1971	1	12.7	1979	1	11.4			
	2	10.9		2	12.7			
	3	11.0		3	13.1			
	4	15.9		4	11.4			

Source: Bank of England
Note: The percentage growth rates for 1982, quarters 1–3, allow for the change in definition made from the old banking sector to the new monetary sector.

one or two percentages points per year. It is argued that this method of adjustment to the desired long-run position will avoid an excessive rise in unemployment in the period of transition.

This is the procedure adopted by UK governments. Monetary targets were first introduced in 1976 when it was aimed to contain the rate of growth of the money supply (defined for this purpose as sterling M3) to the range 9 to 13 per cent. The use of monetary targets was confirmed by the Conservative government on attaining power and target rates of monetary growth showed progressive reductions and are shown in Table 9.1.

Comparison with the figures contained in Table 9.2 (the relevant figure for the whole financial year is that pertaining to quarter 1— thus 1977 quarter 1 shows the turn-out for the financial year 1976/77) reveals that taking the financial year as a whole for the period up to March 1983 the target was (i) attained four times (1976/77, 1978/79, 1979/80 and 1982/83, the actual out-turn for the latter year was 10.3 per cent) and (ii) missed three times (1977/78, 1980/81 and 1981/82).

Finally it should be noted that the adoption of a monetary rule acts as a constraint on the whole spectrum of macroeconomic policies followed by the government. It necessitates the adoption of pure floating exchange rates. In addition reference to the government budget constraint shows that adoption of a monetary rule prescribes a rate of growth of the reserve base and hence specifies that the level of interest rates must be consistent with the required volume of bond sales given the PSBR.

Concluding remarks

Up to 1981, monetary policy in the UK has been primarily an interest rate policy. This is true even when the object was to control the quantity of money rather than its price. No doubt this has been due in part to the virtual imposssibility of effecting any sort of control via the reserve base as defined prior to 1981.

In order to provide some assessment of UK monetary policy in recent years we show in Table 9.2 the rate of growth of sterling M3 over the period 1964-82. The figures are quarterly based and show the annual rate of growth between one quarter and the corresponding quarter of the previous year. It is noticeable that both the rate of growth of the money supply and its variability have tended to increase over the period. With variations in the annual rate of growth of at least 4 per cent between some quarters it is difficult to resist the conclusion that some successful adherence to a monetary rule would have produced better policy outcomes.

---

* The restriction limiting purchase of index linked gilt-edged securities to insurance companies and pension funds was removed in the 1982 Budget. These are now available to all would-be purchasers.

APPENDIX A

Competition and Credit Control

A9.1 Introduction

Competition and Credit Control (CCC) was introduced in 1971 and in order to assess this new monetary system it is necessary to describe the system in operation prior to 1971.

A9.2 System prior to 1971

Prior to the introduction of CCC, the London Clearing Banks operated a 'cartel' or price agreement whereby each bank agreed to pay interest on deposits at a rate of 2 per cent less than bank rate. There was therefore no price competition at all between banks to attract deposits. These banks also operated a similar but less precise agreement on the charges they raised on loans. There were further agreements between the London Clearing Banks and the discount houses by which the banks agreed: (i) not to tender directly for Treasury Bills; (ii) to charge a minimum interest rate of $1\frac{5}{8}$ per cent below bank rate on call money lent to the discount houses.

Not only were the banks not competing amongst themselves but also they were not required to disclose the true or actual profits they earned. On the other hand the clearing banks also suffered in some respects since they were the only banks required to maintain fixed reserve asset ratios. In addition monetary policy was conducted mainly by means of lending requests and these tended to bear more heavily on the clearing banks. Nevertheless these forms of discrimination were to some extent evaded since the clearing banks also operated through non-clearing subsidiary banks. This lack of competition extended to the discount houses who submitted a joint tender for Treasury Bills at a single rate of discount which they agreed amongst themselves.

Finally, as we have discussed earlier the authorities believed the gilt-edged market to be inherently unstable and intervened heavily in the market by buying and selling government stock to stabilise their prices. This prevented control of the money supply. By 1971 there was general dissatisfaction with the system. Controls on lending had been in operation fairly consistently since 1965 and there was a widespread belief that these controls had led to a misallocation of resources in at least three ways. First, efficient banks were prevented from expanding their lending at the expense of the less efficient banks. Second, competition was directed to service competition (e.g. excessive number of branches) which tended to raise costs. Third, credit was not being rationed by the price mechanism and was not therefore being directed towards areas where the highest returns would be earned. In fact credit rationing ensured that there was an excess demand for credit at the ruling rates of interest. This lack of competition had been adversely commented upon by both the National Board for Prices and Incomes (1967) and the Monopolies Commission in 1968. The clearing banks felt the system unfairly discriminated against them. The Bank of England was dissatisfied with the system since a large section of the financial system operated outside the controls. There was therefore general agreement that change was desirable.

A9.3 Changes introduced in 1971
The aim of the new system was to permit all banks to compete equally and to be subject to the same controls. Various restraints to competition were abolished. Thus both the clearing banks cartel and the discount houses syndicated bid for Treasury Bills were disbanded. A common reserve asset ratio of $12\frac{1}{2}$ per cent was applied to all banks (this is the same reserve ratio discussed in Chapter 2, section 2.4.2). All banks were required to submit special deposits when called upon by the Bank of England. The Bank of England gave up the imposition of quantitative lending controls but retained the right to issue qualitative requests to direct lending in certain directions. The Bank of England also had the right to impose a maximum interest rate which the banks could pay on deposits. This right has been exercised (e.g. September 1973 to January 1975) in order to protect the Building Societies and their borrowers. Finally automatic intervention by the authorities within the gilt-edged market to stabilise bond prices was also terminated.

A9.4 Subsequent amendments
In 1972 bank rate was abolished and minimum lending rate was introduced. Minimum Lending Rate was a market based rate inasmuch as it was linked by a fixed formula to the average Treasury Bill discount rate in the previous tender. In 1978 the market formula was given up and Minimum Lending Rate became an administered rate.

A more fundamental change occurred in 1973 with the

introduction of special supplementary deposits (see section 9.4.3). This system imposed constraints on the growth of interest bearing deposits for each bank and therefore was designed to prevent competition between banks to attract deposits. Some commentators regard the introduction of special supplementary deposits as the end of Competition and Credit Control.

A9.5 An assessment

Any assessment of this system must consider the two aspects i.e. (i) competition and (ii) control. Competition amongst banks certainly increased and this is perhaps evidenced by their desire to cut costs with the subsequent rationalisation of their branch network. Nevertheless demand from the industrial sector was slack during the period immediately after the introduction of CCC and so the banks directed a significant proportion of their lending towards property development which seemed to offer higher returns. At the same time there was little evidence of supervision or prudential control so that lending was not always soundly based. Ultimately of course the property boom collapsed causing severe problems for the banks involved and led to a greater emphasis on prudential controls. The interesting question which remains to be answered is how far the property boom was attributable to the introduction of CCC.

Reference to Table 9.2 shows that the introduction of CCC just preceded the extremely fast rates of monetary growth experienced throughout 1973 and 1974. Again the question arises of how far can this be attributed to the introduction of CCC. This is not an easy question to answer but certain indications can be observed. First, the authorities themselves seem to have had only a hazy idea about how control would be operated. It seems that credit was to be rationed by its price (i.e. the rate of interest) but it is far from clear that the authorities were ever prepared to allow interest rates to rise to a level high enough to choke off the demand for credit. Second, the banks were left with excess reserve assets given the new definitions and the then existing levels of their deposits. Third, as we have noted in the main body of this chapter the definition of reserve assets adopted ensured that the quantity of reserve assets held by the banks was certainly not under the control of the authorities. It is sometimes argued that the massive increase in the money supply was due to the 'pent up' demand for the bank credit frustrated between 1965 and 1971 by the continuous imposition of controls on bank lending. Whether this is so or not is debatable but it does seem fairly certain that the introduction of CCC in 1971 was at least partly responsible for the lack of control of the authorities over the growth of the money supply in the period 1972/73.

10 Expenditure Switching Policies

10.1 Aims of switching policies

In Chapters 9 and 10 we examined the role of fiscal and monetary policy as instruments to stabilise the level of economic activity; while in Chapter 7, section 7.2 we discussed how contractionary fiscal and monetary policies can be used to remedy a balance of payments deficit on the current account. On their own expenditure reducing policies only eliminate a balance of payments deficit at the cost of increased unemployment. In this chapter we turn our attention to expenditure switching policies which provide the authorities with an additional policy instrument to solve a balance of payments deficit without having to abandon the goal of full employment.

We begin our discussion of expenditure switching policies by summarising the analysis contained in Chapter 4, sections 4.3–4.4. It will be recalled that the main determinants of the demand for imports are: (i) domestic aggregate income; (ii) the price of imported goods relative to those of home produced substitutes

$$\text{(i.e. } e\frac{P_D}{P_F} \text{)}$$

where e is the exchange rate expressing domestic currency in terms of foreign currency. P_D is the price of domestic goods in terms of domestic currency, and P_F is the price of foreign goods in terms of foreign currency); and (iii) other factors (e.g. the foreign trade policies adopted by a country). In a similar manner the main determinants of the demand for exports are: (i) income in the rest of the world; (ii) the price of a country's exported goods relative to those produced by its competitors abroad; and (iii) other factors.

Expenditure switching policies attempt either: (i) to switch the expenditure of domestic firms and households away from foreign goods towards domestically produced goods thereby reducing

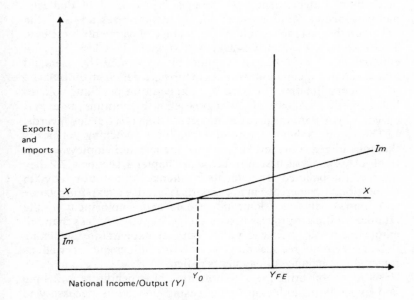

Figure 10.1. Import and export functions

imports; or (ii) to switch the expenditure of foreign firms and households away from goods produced by competitors abroad towards domestically produced goods thereby increasing exports. These aims can be achieved, for example, by reducing the exchange rate (e) so that relative prices

$$(e\frac{P_D}{P_F})$$

of British goods decrease. A second method is to impose controls directed to reducing the quantity of imports given the level of income. A third choice open to the authorities is to give some assistance to stimulate exports. These three methods of expenditure switching policies are discussed in sections 10.2, 10.3 and 10.4 respectively.

The potential scope for expenditure switching policies is demonstrated in Figure 10.1.

In line with our earlier comments we assume that imports (Im) increase as domestic national income increases, and exports (X) are determined independently of changes in the level of domestic national income. As domestic national income rises above Y_o the deficit on the current account of the balance of payments increases. The problem the authorities face is that when Y_o is less than full employment (Y_{FE}), output cannot be expanded by demand management policies alone without incurring a deficit on the balance of payments. In terms of Figure 10.1 expenditure switching policies help remedy a balance of payments deficit by shifting the export curve (XX) upwards and/or the import function ($Im\,Im$) downwards.

The second salient feature of expenditure switching policies is that they increase the level of national income and employment. In terms of the analysis first introduced in Chapter 4, section 4.7.2 they improve the balance of payments by increasing output relative to absorption. Any increase in net exports (i.e. a rise in exports relative to imports) will raise domestic income and employment by the familiar multiplier process discussed in Chapter 1. At less than full employment (i.e. below capacity output) expenditure switching policies help to reduce the level of unemployment as well as remedying a balance of payments deficit.

As a general principle a combination of expenditure switching and expenditure reducing or increasing policies is necessary to achieve a zero balance on the current account of the balance of payments and full employment. This is just one example of the general rule that a government needs at least as many policy instruments as it has targets. In this case there are two targets (i.e. balance of payments equilibrium and full employment) so two instruments (i.e. expenditure switching and expenditure reducing or increasing policies) are needed. This analysis is illustrated in Figure 10.2.

Initially at the equilibrium level of income of Y_1 there is a current account deficit equal to AB. At the full employment level of income (Y_{FE}) the deficit would be still larger (i.e. equal to CD). In theory (i.e. ignoring the practical problems of stabilisation policy discussed in Chapter 7, sections 7.3-7.6) the authorities could restore balance of payments equilibrium and cause national income to return to full employment by an appropriate combination of expenditure switching and expenditure increasing (or reducing) policies. In the sections that follow we discuss the main types of expenditure switching policies open to the authorities starting with exchange rate policies.

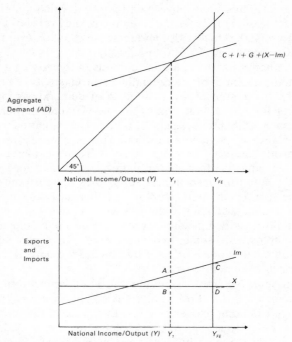

Figure 10.2. The need for equality of targets and instruments

10.2 Exchange rate policies

Under fixed exchange rates a country could attempt to remedy a balance of payments deficit by devaluing its currency. Devaluation changes the relative price of home to foreign produced goods. More specifically it increases the home currency price of imports and lowers the foreign currency price of exports. By making domestic goods relatively more attractive domestic demand is switched away from foreign imports towards domestically produced goods and foreign demand is switched towards domestically produced exports. This process has been discussed in Chapter 4, sections 4.3-4.4, but it is worthwhile recapitulating the basis of the argument. Suppose a specified commodity costs £1,000 to produce in the UK. If the exchange rate is $2 = £1, then it will sell in the USA for $2,000 (ignoring other costs). On the other hand if the exchange rate is $1.5 = £1 it will sell in the USA for $1,500. Conversely goods produced in the USA at a cost of $3,000 will sell in the UK for £1,500 if the exchange rate is $2 = £1, but for £2,000 if the exchange rate is $1.5 = £1. Thus as we have stated above devaluation of the £ (i.e. from $2 to $1.5) reduces the foreign currency price of UK exports (i.e. from $2,000 to $1,500) and increases the home currency price of UK imports from £1,500 to £2,000).

Whether or not devaluation succeeds in remedying a balance of payments deficit depends crucially on the elasticity of demand and supply. If the sum of the elasticities of demand for imports and exports is greater than unity (i.e. the Marshall/Lerner condition discussed in Chapter 4, section 4.6.1) then devaluation will improve the balance of payments position. This is a necessary but not a sufficient condition, because unless there are resources available (i.e. idle capacity) to meet the increased demand for exports and domestically produced import substitutes devaluation on its own will be insufficient. At full employment there is a need to combine an expenditure switching policy, such as devaluation, with an expenditure reducing policy. Even at levels of unemployment below full employment some expenditure reducing policies may be necessary if inflation is affected by demand pressure as the economy approaches capacity output.

Although we have discussed the situation in terms of fixed exchange rates the above analysis is still applicable to a system of managed floating exchange rates. In this case the exchange rate would be pushed down by market intervention rather than a statement that the parity is reduced as in the case of devaluation.

One of the problems with exchange rate changes is that they take time to have an effect. Volumes of exports and imports only respond slowly to a reduction in the relative price of British goods. In the short run the sterling value of imports rises because an increased sterling price is associated with an unchanged quantity of imports. At the same time both the sterling price and the quantity of exports remain unchanged. The initial effect of devaluation is to make the balance of payments position worse. As time passes the quantity of imports decreases following their increased sterling price and the quantity of exports increased following their reduced foreign currency price. Thus the balance of payments will ultimately be more favourable than at the time of devaluation provided the Marshall/Lerner conditions are satisfied. This initial worsening of the balance of payments before ultimate improvement is known as the *J* curve.

An interesting example of a *J* curve is provided by the aftermath of the 1967 devaluation of sterling. In November 1967 the Labour government devalued sterling by 14.3 per cent from $2.80 to $2.40. Reference to Table 10.1 reveals that following devaluation the visible

TABLE 10.1. UK balance of payments: current account, 1964–72
(£ million)

	Visible balance	Invisible balance	Current balance
1964	−543	+185	−358
1965	−260	+230	−30
1966	−108	+238	+130
1967	−599	+330	−269
1968	−712	+468	−244
1969	−209	+714	+505
1970	−34	+857	+823
1971	+190	+934	+1,124
1972	−748	+995	+247

Source: Central Statistical Office (1981), United Kingdom Balance of Payments (Pink Book), (London: HMSO), Table 1.1.

balance moved further into deficit in 1968. After a time lag the visible deficit fell sharply and the balance of payments on current account moved into a surplus between 1969 and 1972. However it should be stressed that the improvement in the balance of payments position cannot be attributed solely to the delayed effects of devaluation. Other contributory factors included expenditure reducing policies (e.g. the deflationary budget of 1968), the introduction of a temporary import deposit scheme between 1968 and 1970 and the rapid growth of world trade in manufactured exports. Finally, it is interesting to note that the competitive advantage gained from devaluation was eroded due to inflation and by 1972 the visible balance had moved back into deficit.

10.3 Import controls

Another possible instrument available to the authorities to solve a balance of payments deficit is the introduction of various restrictions or direct controls on imports. Import controls can take one or more of the following forms:

(1) a tariff or duty imposed on imported goods;
(2) a control over the quantities of goods imported i.e. quotas; and
(3) restrictions on the availability of foreign currency by the authorities.

Method (1) operates via the price mechanism raising the domestic price of imported goods by imposing an additional cost by the way of the import duty. For example, the Labour government imposed an import surcharge (initially at 15 per cent but later reduced to 10) on most manufactured and semi-manufactured goods between October 1964 and November 1966. A variation of this method is to impose a deposit (based on the value of the imported goods) which must be paid to the authorities when the goods are imported. Although the deposit is subsequently returned the importer loses the use of the funds during the time the authorities keep the deposit. The net effect is to discourage imports. For example, in 1968 the Labour government introduced a temporary import deposit scheme whereby importers of certain goods had to deposit half the value of imported goods with the government for a period of six months. The deposit was subsequently reduced and the scheme ended in 1970. Method (3) involves the authorities refusing to provide foreign currency for imports which they do not consider to be essential. Before turning to the question of applying quotas we should also like to emphasise that restrictions on imports may be implicit rather than explicit. For example, onerous quality requirements imposed by a government may make it difficult for foreign producers to export to that country.

The other main option open to the authorities is to impose physical controls on the volume of imports. This method has a superficial attraction because direct controls are quick to take effect and, subject to the major qualification regarding the possibility of retaliation discussed below, they will lead to an improvement in the current account of the balance of payments. Nevertheless the subject of import controls is highly controversial and we now consider the main arguments against using import controls to solve a balance of payments deficit.

First, import controls may not be compatible with a country's existing trade agreements. It is particularly relevant in this connection to note that discriminatory controls are against the General Agreement on Tariffs and Trade (GATT). Since its creation in 1947 GATT has sought to promote international trade by reducing trade barriers on a non-discriminatory basis. Under the 'most-favoured-nation' clause each nation agrees not to apply rates of tariff duty to a single country any less favourably to those applied on similar goods to other GATT members. Negotiated tariff cuts on foods are extended to all member countries (more than eighty countries are at present members of GATT) thereby ensuring the principle of non-preferential treatment. Furthermore import controls directed against European countries are inconsistent with membership of the European Economic Community (EEC).

Second, controls may induce foreign retaliation thereby damaging a country's export sales abroad. In the extreme case of retaliation the decline in exports may be greater than the fall in imports so that the balance of payments actually deteriorates and unemployment increases; a result quite opposite to that intended by the introduction of controls. Third, specific controls will remove competition from foreign production and may lead to inefficiency with the controls propping up inefficient domestic industries. Fourth, consumers will have to buy domestically produced goods which are either higher priced or of an inferior quality instead of the preferred imported goods. Either way domestic consumers and producers lose out. Real costs rise because of the need to use more expensive and/or inferior products with consequent inflationary effects. Fifth, quantity controls on imports obstruct the free operation of the market mechanism and result in a misallocation of resources. This last point is controversial because some economists believe the market mechanism to be an efficient method of allocating resources.

In the UK one of the most vociferous advocates of import controls has been the Cambridge Economic Policy Group (i.e. the New Cambridge School) and we now turn to a discussion of their views. The starting point of their argument is that the quantity of goods a country can import is limited by its exports to the rest of the world. This is the same as saying that the appropriate balance of payments objective of any country is a zero balance on the current account. In their view a particular problem of the UK economy is its high marginal propensity to import. Relating this to the state of the UK economy in 1983, government expansion to reduce unemployment would produce a deficit on the current account of the balance of payments due to rising imports. However this could be avoided if the rate of growth of the quantity of imports were suitably restricted by the imposition of general import controls (i.e. not directed against individual products). It is important to realise that if the rate of growth of imports were restrained no reduction in the existing quantity of imports would occur. The New Cambridge School recommend a policy of government expansion of the economy combined with the introduction of general import controls. They argue that this would restore full employment without a deficit being incurred on the current account.

Several points are worth noting about their proposals. First, they assume that the increase in production and output would come about without any increase in prices. This view is inconsistent with the Phillips curve analysis put forward in Chapter 5, section 5.3, and arises from their belief that the level of wages is determined within the wage bargaining process and is not influenced at all by the state of the labour market i.e. the demand for and supply of labour.

Second, they argue that if the rate of growth of imports were restrained countries would find such a policy more palatable than a policy of actually cutting the level of imports. The danger of retaliation would therefore be reduced. In fact as domestic employment and output increased imports would rise (without an excessive deterioration in the current account) so other countries would benefit from the scheme. Third, it is argued that because the proposed scheme of import restrictions is non-discriminatory it does not offend the rules of GATT and this again would reduce the danger of retaliation. All these arguments are controversial. Perhaps the greatest risk of such a policy is that of retaliation by other countries but the true extent of the danger is not known because no such policy has ever been introduced.

At present most goods can be imported into the UK free of control under 'open general licence'. Quotas do however exist for the importation of particular goods from certain countries. These controls take three main forms. First, the Multi-Fibre Arrangement has sought to control the rate of growth of certain textile exports from less-developed countries (e.g. Singapore, Malaysia, and Hong Kong). Second, import quotas exist for certain non-textile items (e.g. gloves, footwear and certain types of domestic electrical appliance) from State Trading Countries (e.g. Bulgaria, Czechoslovakia, the German Democratic Republic, Hungary, Poland and the USSR). Finally, less formal arrangements exist which voluntarily restrain the growth of certain exports to the UK. For example, a voluntary agreement reached between Britain's Society of Motor Manufacturers and Traders and its Japanese counterpart, JAMA, limits the level of Japanese commercial vehicle imports to an 11 per cent share of the UK market. Such agreements are of course difficult to enforce. It remains to be seen whether the authorities succumb to the mounting pressure to introduce general import controls.

10.4 Export assistance

A third potential expenditure switching policy to help remedy a balance of payments deficit is that of export assistance. A wide range of policies is available to the authorities to assist exporters. For example, subsidies can be given to exporters to change the relative price of domestic to foreign goods in favour of domestic production. Generally these offend the terms of GATT but one exception widely practised is to refund Value Added Tax on exported goods. Alternative policies consist of giving financial assistance to exporters, finance to assist trade fairs, the use of diplomatic channels to sponsor the sale of goods abroad, etc. These measures operate on the volume of exports only so that in terms of Figure 10.1 the export curve (*XX*) would shift upwards without any change in the import function.

10.5 Concluding remarks

With regard to the UK economy some economists have argued that balance of payments problems stem from the actions of trade unions who continuously push for wage increases above productivity growth and make export/import prices uncompetitive/competitive. If this sociological view of the inflationary process is correct balance of payments problems initially arise from the failure to find an appropriate policy instrument to maintain relative price stability compared to competitors abroad. In the next chapter we discuss the role of prices and incomes policy to prevent inflation.

11 Prices and Incomes Policy

11.1 Introduction

In this chapter we consider another instrument of economic policy, namely prices and incomes policy. From time to time since the Second World War this particular instrument has been used by the authorities in the UK and the other Western industrial countries to influence the rate of increase of money wages and prices. A number of justifications have been advanced in favour of implementing this policy measure (e.g. to influence the distribution of income) but the main objective has been to control or moderate the rate of inflation. One's views on the need, or otherwise, for such a policy largely depends on an assessment of the underlying cause of inflation (see Chapter 5).

In what follows we look at (a) the nature of such a policy (section 11.2), (b) the way in which it may help moderate the rate of inflation (section 11.3), (c) the difficulties involved in the implementation and administration of the policy (section 11.4), and (d) the possible side effects of a prices and incomes policy (section 11.5). In the final sections we summarise past prices and incomes policies in the UK (section 11.6) and the empirical evidence regarding the effectiveness of such policies (section 11.7).

11.2 Nature of a prices and incomes policy

The form the policy normally takes is to specify (a) a norm for the rate of increase in money wage rates and at the same time (b) rules governing increases in prices. It should be stressed that the control is of wage rates and not earnings which would be expected to move in the same direction as output due to such factors as the operation of piece rates, bonus schemes, overtime, etc. For wage increases not to be inflationary the norm would have to be set to coincide with the expected average increase in productivity (i.e. the trend rate of growth of output per worker). Even then, a general rise in prices could occur if the prices of imported goods rose. The productivity rule would be long-term aim. On the other hand during the period of transition from a relatively high to a lower rate of inflation, the norm might be set higher than the rate of growth of productivity, and then gradually be reduced to that envisaged in the long term. Conversely, on some occasions, if inflation has suddenly increased from quite low levels, the norm could be set at zero.

The essential feature of a prices and incomes policy is that it operates outside the market. It consists of a series of rules or direct controls designed to produce an outcome (with respect to price and wage increases) which differs from that produced by the market mechanism.

11.3 The transmission mechanism

We now consider how a prices and incomes policy may be used to reduce the rate of inflation, or prevent inflation in the first place. It is quite clear that the mere prohibition of price and money wage increases does nothing to introduce a cure for inflation in the long term. At best it will lead to a temporary suppression of inflation. Any cure for inflation must be directed against its root cause. Analysis of the possible transmission mechanism of a prices and incomes policy is vitally dependent on the view taken with regard to the causation of inflation. In Chapter 5 we discussed how it is possible to identify two broad approaches, namely a sociological and an economic explanation (i.e. consisting of monetarist and Keynesian sub-schools). This classification is adopted merely for ease of exposition and the reader should recall that it is perfectly possible to take an eclectic or compromise stance. Within this framework we discuss the role a prices and income policy can play and only briefly summarise the two approaches since they were discussed in detail in Chapter 5, sections 5.3 and 5.4.

11.3.1 *Transmission mechanism: sociological view of inflation*

Proponents of the sociological approach argue that wage increases are at the centre of inflation (i.e. they are the initiating force). They further claim that such wage increases can occur and continue independently of demand and supply conditions in the labour market due to a variety of social pressures. These pressures include the actions of trade union leaders, inconsistent views of a fair wage structure, and government guarantees of full employment. If money wages continually rise faster than the growth of productivity inflation will result because wages are the most important component of cost. In the absence of expansionary government policy, rises in unit costs will lead to increases in the general price level and reductions in output. Consequently unemployment will rise as real output falls. In practice because of the commitment to a target of full employment UK governments have until recently tended to expand the money supply to validate the increase in prices. According to the sociological view, inflation is either not particularly responsive to changes in excess demand or even if it is any attempt to curb inflation by not validating the price increases by monetary expansion would require levels of unemployment far too high to be politically acceptable.

Direct controls on the growth of wages seem therefore to offer an ideal escape from this dilemma. Controls would prevent or control inflation without large increases in unemployment. It is for these reasons that prices and incomes policies are advocated by those who believe inflation to be a largely sociological phenomenon. It should also be noted that a prices and incomes policy is seldom used on its own. Often it is accompanied by measures incorporating additional policies designed to alleviate social tensions which are believed (according to the sociological view) to lead to wage increases. Such changes (e.g. help for the lower paid) are often introduced in order to help gain trade union co-operation with the policy. The possible effects of such measures are considered in section 11.5 below.

Two additional points should be borne in mind. First, because wage pressure is believed to be the root cause of inflation it is envisaged that a prices and incomes policy will be used for quite long periods of time. This contrasts with the position taken by some proponents of the economic view (see section 11.3.2). Second, it is pointless using prices and incomes policy as a cover to control prices whilst simultaneously pursuing inflationary monetary and/or fiscal policies. Unless the extreme viewpoint is taken that excess demand never affects wages or prices, excess demand must lead to inflation which will lead to the breakdown of a policy constraining a lower growth of money wages.

This completes our examination of the role of a prices and incomes policy within the framework of a sociological view of inflation. The question examined in the next section is whether this policy has any role to play if inflation is caused by economic rather than sociological factors.

11.3.2 *Transmission mechanism: economic view of inflation*
The importance of sociological and political factors in the economic view of inflation lies in the way they influence the fiscal and monetary policies pursued in an economy. The starting point is expansionary fiscal and monetary policies which create an excess demand for both goods and services and factors of production, which leads to rising product and factor prices and inflationary expectations. As

expectations of further inflation become widespread in the economic system increased nominal wage claims would be made to protect real wages (i.e. the short-run Phillips curve shifts upwards over time). The reader is referred back to Chapter 5, section 5.3 for a more detailed discussion of the Phillips curve analysis. In this section we merely reproduce the basic outline necessary to clarify the distinction between Keynesians and monetarists.

Within this broad explanation it is possible to make a distinction between monetarists and Keynesians who differ as to (a) whether there exists a trade-off between inflation and unemployment in the long run i.e. whether the long-run Phillips curve is vertical and (b) the role assigned to wage increases made independently of the state of excess demand.

Within the monetarist school, the central distinguishing beliefs are that (a) inflation is always and everywhere a monetary phenomenon and (b) that there is no trade-off between unemployment and inflation in the long run. This latter belief is characterised by the expectations augmented Phillips curve which may be expressed as:

$$\dot{W} = f(U) + 1\dot{P}^e \tag{11.1}$$

Where (1) $U =$ unemployment (a proxy for excess demand for labour)
     (2) $\dot{W} =$ the rate of change of money wages rates
     (3) $\dot{P}^e =$ the rate of inflation expected to exist during the period of the wage bargain.

Clearly within this framework a permanent reduction in the rate of inflation can only be achieved by reducing the level of excess demand. In monetarist analysis this can be achieved by a reduction in the rate of monetary expansion. From equation (11.1) it can be seen that such a policy must cause unemployment to rise (given $\dot{P}^e$) in the short run before the rate of increase of money wages ($\dot{W}$) will be reduced. It is in this connection that some, but certainly not all, monetarists see a role for a prices and incomes policy. It is argued that a prices and incomes policy may assist the transition to a lower rate of inflation through influencing expectations of future rates of inflation.

Consideration of this role is dependent on the precise mechanism of the formation of expectations. If expectations of future rates of inflation are formed by extrapolating rates of inflation experienced in the past, it is possible for the rate of increase of money wages ($\dot{W}$) to increase even in the absence of excess demand. This would occur if a positive value for $\dot{P}^e$ in equation (11.1) outweighed a negative component due to a negative excess demand. In this situation the introduction of a prices and incomes policy constraining $\dot{W}$ in equation (11.1) would remove the role of expected inflation. This would enable adjustment to a lower rate of inflation to be achieved both (a) more quickly and (b) at the cost of a lower level of unemployment. On the other hand expectations may be formed rationally, i.e. according to the predictions of economic theory in the light of the best information available. Even in this situation a policy maker may have more information than the general public (e.g. his intentions regarding future rates of monetary expansion) so that a prices and incomes policy could be used as an instrument for controlling $\dot{W}$ (equation 11.1) until the additional information consistent with policy intentions became available to the general public. The policy therefore has a similar role to play as that discussed above. In general however a prices and incomes policy would serve no use if expectations are formed rationally and the public has perfect information.

To summarise the position a prices and incomes policy may be useful purely as an aid to the transition to a lower rate of inflation. It could not be used as a substitute for the appropriate monetary control (i.e. reducing the rate of monetary expansion) which monetarists argue is necessary to reduce permanently the rate of inflation. A prices and incomes policy accompanied by an expansionary monetary policy will therefore be a mere charade and accelerating inflation will quickly ensue as the policy breaks down.

In contrast to monetarist beliefs Keynesians tend to believe that there is a trade-off between inflation and unemployment in the long run and they also assign a role to wage increases made independently of the state of excess demand. In consequence some Keynesians argue that a prices and incomes policy has a long-run role to play in preventing inflation. The argument is that the trade-off could be improved by some kind of direct controls operating on wages i.e. we could achieve the same level of employment but at a lower rate of inflation, in other words the long-run Phillips curve (believed by Keynesians to be non-vertical) would shift to the left as depicted in Figure 11.1 from PC_I to PC_{II}.

Finally, Keynesian analysis of the role of a prices and incomes policy to counteract potential exogenous wage increases would be the same as that discussed within the sociological viewpoint summarised in section 11.3.1.

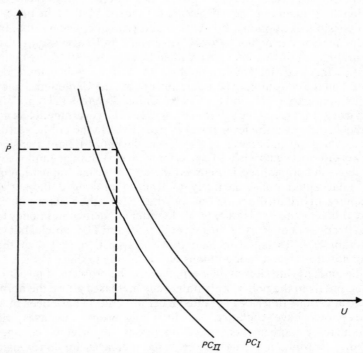

Figure 11.1. The role of a prices and incomes policy in the Keynesian view of inflation

11.4.1 *Incomes policy*

In general terms an incomes policy refers to the control of all incomes i.e. wages, dividends, profits, etc. In practice, however, because of their greater relative importance, most of the discussion centres on the implementation of a wages policy. Nevertheless wage controls are generally matched by similar controls on dividends, if only as the price of trade union co-operation. There is, however, one difference of particular importance between wage and dividend control. Dividends not paid out, given the levels of profits, merely mean an equivalent increase in retained profits thus enhancing the net worth of the company (and therefore the market value of the shares) or alternatively they may be used to increase subsequent dividend payments when controls are removed. In consequence many trade unionists argue that dividend restraint imposes less of a burden than wage restraint.

We will now discuss the main problems involved in the implementation of an incomes policy. These are (a) acceptability of the policy, (b) possible exemptions, (c) evasion and (d) supervision. First, in order for such a policy to work effectively and successfully the desirability of the incomes policy must be accepted by all the main parties involved. In Britain therefore an incomes policy must be based on the consent and co-operation of both the Confederation of British Industry (CBI) and the Trades Union Congress (TUC). This is particularly true of the private sector where the government has no direct control over the level of wages paid. Even in the public sector where the government is either (a) the employer or (b) has extensive powers to enforce its wishes (e.g. as for local government employees or those in nationalised industries) the authoritarian imposition of an unaccepted policy is likely to lead to prolonged industrial disputes. In Britain the control of both the CBI and the TUC over their individual members is rather weak. In order for an incomes policy to be effective not only is the consent of the CBI and TUC crucial but in addition it is essential to gain the widespread approval of the individual firms and trade unions which belong to these bodies.

Second, having chosen the norm there is the problem of possible exemptions to the policy. In Britain wage increases above the norm have at various times been granted if certain criteria have been met. Exceptions have included self-financing wage increases via productivity agreements, wage increases to secure changes in the distribution of manpower, wage increases for lower paid workers and increases to restore out of line pay (i.e. restore differentials or maintain comparability for similar work). If exceptions to the norm are either too broadly or vaguely defined it leaves a great deal of room for possible manoeuvre. Divisiveness may ensue if inequities appear. For example, it is extremely difficult to measure productivity in the public sector. In addition, as noted earlier, it is only in the public sector that the government has the direct power to ensure compliance with the rules of the policy. More onerous interpretations of a prices and incomes policy within the public compared to the private sector are likely to lead both to resentment, as far as the public sector is concerned, and to difficulties in recruiting adequate supplies of workers. The general impression gained from past policies is one of a relative squeeze on public sector wage rates during a prices and incomes policy followed subsequently by a faster than average increase in their wage rates when the policy is removed to restore the previous relativities. Resentment may also result among certain workers if one of the criteria of allowing wage increases above the norm is low pay. This resentment may be caused as the differentials between other more skilled workers and the lower paid are reduced. Pay differentials will also be eroded if a flat rate increase is applied. As anomalies and exceptions become more apparent it becomes increasingly difficult for the authorities to maintain the co-operation of the parties concerned.

The third major problem is that of possible evasion. While negotiated increases in basic wage rates are invariably the outcome of national bargaining, additional increases (i.e. above those nationally agreed) may result from local bargaining at the company level. If wage increases, above the norm, are desired by both sides of the negotiating table then loopholes will be sought. Basic wage rates may be supplemented by additional payments of, for example, dirt and heat money, shift premiums for unsocial hours, merit increases (i.e. promotions), long service awards, overtime payments, spurious productivity agreements, or by a range of non-wage benefits (e.g. the use of a company car, benevolent supervision of expense accounts, etc.). In consequence the gap between negotiated wage rates and actual earnings may increase as individual companies and unions attempt to evade whatever norm or guideline has been set.

Finally, there are the questions of the supervision of the operation of the policy and also what sanctions can be applied if the agreement is broken. Various arrangements are possible such as the establishment of a body to supervise the operation of the policy or the requirement that all agreements are to be notified in advance of their operation to an appropriate government department or independent body (i.e. an early warning system). The question of potential sanctions to be applied to those who break the policy is a vexed one. If the policy has the backing of law (i.e. it is a statutory policy), arraignment of unions or their members before a court raises emotive issues, which are likely to lead to widespread strikes in sympathy against such a policy. If the policy is voluntary, sanctions are difficult to impose against workers. Also few powers are available to the government to control firms. The government can reduce public sector purchases or subsidies to firms who contravene the guidelines (regulations) of the policy but this will be resented by industry as being unfair. A further alternative discussed in Chapter 13 is a tax based incomes policy where sanctions would be applied via the taxation system.

11.4.2 *Prices policy*

We have so far only discussed the main problems that arise in attempts to restrain wage increases via an incomes policy. In this section we discuss the effects of a prices policy. Goods may be divided into three broad categories as far as prices are concerned:

(i) those goods whose prices are determined in a competitive market e.g. food products;
(ii) prices for non-reproducable goods such as tenders for specific work;
(iii) prices for goods which are regularly repeated such as normal retail goods.

If controls are to be effective they are usually placed on goods of type (iii). Before raising prices, manufacturers usually have to demonstrate to either a government department or alternatively an independent commission that such increases conform to the criteria laid down. After consideration of profit margins price increases are then granted if the unit cost of production has increases as a result of an allowable cost increase. In addition legal powers are more often retained with respect to prices than wages.

Price control is also subject to potential evasion. Instead of increasing prices, firms may attempt to lower the quality or the quantity per unit of sale. If a new model of car is introduced on the market, for example, it is very difficult to distinguish between the rise in price due to an improvement in quality and that made to evade price controls. In addition, if there is excess demand, standard market demand and supply analysis would predict that the imposition of price controls would cause a black market to develop. Furthermore in an open economy, excess demand could be diverted to imported goods with adverse effects on the current account of the balance of payments. If a floating exchange rate were in operation, the exchange rate would depreciate causing imports to become more expensive. This is merely another illustration of the point that a prices and incomes policy will not control inflation if it is accompanied by other inconsistent macroeconomic policies.

11.4.3 *Concluding remarks*
The inevitable conclusion from consideration of these problems is that, in contrast to the basically simple rationale behind the policy, in practice a prices and incomes policy is not at all easy to implement successfully. This is not to imply that such problems make the implementation of an effective policy an impossibility. However above all else widespread consent is crucial because if both parties desire an agreement, but are prevented from doing so by incomes policy rules, they will attempt to find loopholes which will circumvent these rules.

11.5 Possible undesirable side effects

In addition to the problems of implementation noted above there is also a number of unfortunate side effects which may result from the operation of a prices and incomes policy. The first is that unemployment may increase for two reasons. First, the operation of the price mechanism will be impeded. The efficient operation of the market mechanism requires that wage rates in growth industries should rise relative to those in declining industries. The introduction of a norm or maximum rate of wage increase will tend to ensure that the maximum becomes the minimum to which they all think they are entitled (assuming the policy is successful). Thus it may be difficult to achieve any change in relative wage rates which are necessary to secure manpower changes (i.e. preventing labour moving from industries with a low to a high marginal product).

Second, if, as is often the case, the policy is biased in favour of low-paid labour, substitution of capital for labour may occur where the marginal product of labour is also low. Although by no means the only reason for this substitution, this possible side effect might help explain such occurrences as, for example, (a) the widespread introduction of self-service shops and petrol stations coupled with cash desk operators; (b) ticket machines at underground stations; and (c) coffee and other drink vending machines. Both possible effects noted above are likely to occur over a long-term period and could lead to an increase in the natural rate of unemployment. The effect on unemployment may also be reinforced if in order to secure agreement for the introduction of an incomes policy the bargain also allows for higher taxation on relatively high-paid workers or the erosion of differentials through flat rate increases. It may be argued that these will reduce incentives and the dynamism of society leading to lower growth rates.

The third way in which a prices and incomes policy may have deleterious effects on the economy concerns the operation of price controls. If price controls are more severe than wage controls, then the result will be falling profits. The resulting redistribution of income from profits to wages will inevitably lead to reductions in investment and hence a slower growth of productivity and output. In addition if there is an expectation that controls will prevent high profits being earned but not compensate for losses, relatively risky investment profits will be discouraged. Clearly these potential effects are the subject of considerable controversy. Economists who believe in the efficiency of the free market mechanism tend to emphasise the points discussed above. In contrast economists who believe that the market is an efficient allocator of resources tend to play down the potential of an incomes policy to raise unemployment.

11.6 Prices and incomes policies in the UK

Since the Second World War both Labour and Conservative governments have from time to time implemented a wide variety of prices and incomes policies in an attempt to influence the rate of increase of money wages and prices. These policies have differed in a number of important respects including, for example, whether they have been voluntary or statutory in nature and whether or not they have allowed exceptions to wage increases above the norm.

The first experiment in the UK at an incomes policy was introduced by the Labour Chancellor Sir Stafford Cripps in March 1948 when a zero norm for wages increases was established with the support of the TUC. For a two-year period the voluntary policy proved highly successful but the policy began to break down in mid-1950 when trade union support for it was withdrawn following rising prices due to the 1949 devaluation and the boom in raw material prices caused by the Korean War. It was not until 1961 that the next real attempt at an incomes policy was initiated. In July 1961 the Conservative Chancellor Mr Selwyn Lloyd introduced a pay pause for public sector wage increases. The pay pause was followed in February 1962 by a guiding light (norm) for pay increases set at the trend rate of growth in output per head of $2\frac{1}{2}$ per cent. The $2\frac{1}{2}$ per cent guiding light was subsequently raised to $3-3\frac{1}{2}$ per cent by the National Incomes Commission, a body established in October 1962 to review particular wage settlements referred to it by the government.

Incomes policies were also introduced by the Labour government in office between October 1964 and June 1970. Within this period it is convenient to identify three phases of policy namely: (i) October 1964-July 1966; (ii) July 1966-December 1966; and (iii) January 1967 onwards. The incoming Labour government was strongly committed to the principle of a voluntary incomes policy and persuaded employers and trade unions to sign a joint 'Declaration of Intent' to restrain price and wage increases. A $3-3\frac{1}{2}$ per cent wage norm was agreed as being central to an incomes policy which was just one component of Labour's overall strategy to achieve faster economic growth. The Labour government abolished the National Incomes Commission and established the National Board for Prices and Incomes (NBPI) to review wage and price increases in relation to the criteria laid down in the 1965 White Paper on Prices and Incomes Policy (Cmnd2639). In addition under an 'early warning system' impending wage claims were notified to and vetted by a TUC committee. The first voluntary phase of Labour's policy ended in mid-1966.

In July 1966 a sterling crisis led the government to introduce a six-month freeze (i.e. phase two) on wages, salaries, dividends and prices. Phase two was followed in January 1967 by a further six-month period of 'severe restraint' which established a zero norm for wage increases although exceptions were allowed (e.g. genuine productivity agreements). Following this period of severe restraint wage increases were allowed only where they satisfied specific criteria. The list of criteria included wage increases for low paid workers and those justified by productivity increases. Later in 1968 a ceiling of $3\frac{1}{2}$ per cent for annual wage increases was established with the exception of rises justified by the criterion of productivity increases. During the closing years of the Labour government's period of office many spurious productivity agreements were made resulting in double figure wage settlements. January 1970 marked the end of the TUC vetting committee and by the time Labour lost office in June 1970 their incomes policy was in disarray.

The Conservative government elected to power in June 1970 strongly opposed intervention in wage negotiations and there followed a period (June 1970-October 1972) when there was no official prices and incomes policy as such. The NPBI was abolished. In the private sector employers were left to resist excessive wage demands while the government adopted the so-called N-1 strategy for wage negotiations in the public sector. The N-1 strategy whereby the government attempted to ensure that each wage settlement should be 1 per cent less than the one before it met with varying degrees of success. By 1972 the Conservative government decided that there was a need for a more formal policy and after failing to reach a voluntary agreement with the TUC and CBI turned to statutory controls on wages and prices. Formal prices and incomes policy under the Conservative administration began in November 1972 and in the ensuing period three phases of policy can be identified namely: (i) November 1972-April 1973; (ii) April 1973-November 1973; and (iii) November 1973-February 1974. The first phase included a five-month statutory freeze on wages, prices, rents and dividends. Thereafter policy was administered through the newly created (i) Price Commission and (ii) Pay Board. The prices side of the policy was monitored by the Price Commission and a price code was introduced. Large firms had to give prior notice of intended price increases to the price Commission. Price increases in manufacturing were limited to cover allowable cost increases (e.g. fuel, materials and a proportion of labour costs) and firms were also subject to a maximum reference level for net profit margins. This reference level was based on the best two of the previous five years. The Pay Board was responsible for ensuring that the universal wages policy was observed. More onerous notification requirements were imposed on large firms in an attempt to restrain big wage settlements. Wage increases were specified in terms of the average amount per head paid by the firm and in an attempt to avoid evasion through spurious productivity agreements no productivity criterion was introduced. Between April 1973 and November 1973 (i.e. phase two) pay increases were restricted to £1 per week plus 4 per cent, subject to an annual maximum of £250 per person. The third and final phase of policy began in November 1973. During this phase pay increases were limited to a flat rate increase of £2.25 a week or 7 per cent whichever was the larger, with a maximum of £350 a year per person. Exceptions to these guidelines were allowed under certain criteria which included increases for low paid workers and for work considered dangerous or which involved unsocial hours. In addition a threshold agreement was introduced whereby workers received (i) a 40p a week payment if the retail price index rose above its level in October 1973 by 7 per cent and (ii) an extra 40p a week for every 1 per cent rise in the retail price index above 7 per cent.

Further changes in policy were made by the Labour government after winning the general election in February 1974. The Price Commission continued to administer price controls although these were subsequently relaxed (e.g. December 1974) as a result of company profits being severely squeezed. In contrast the Labour government abolished the Pay Board and statutory controls on wages were replaced by a voluntary incomes policy referred to as the 'social contract'. Under this joint agreement, arrived at in 1973 between the TUC and the Labour Party, the Labour government agreed to implement certain social and industrial policies favoured by the unions and in return the unions agreed to moderate their wage claims according to a set of guidelines. The main aim of these guidelines was to ensure that wage increases only matched price increases (i.e. thereby maintaining real incomes) while at the same time ensuring that pay settlements were twelve months apart. The guidelines were however too loosely defined and were easily evaded. A run on the pound in the summer of 1975 marked the end of social contract Mark I and heralded the beginning of social contract Mark II. This period of incomes policy can also be split into a number of phases. Phase one started in August 1975 when with the agreement of the TUC the government introduced a £6 a week maximum on wage increases and specified that no increases would be given to anyone earning over £8,500 a year. In addition the government announced that the whole pay increase would be disallowed for any employer who broke the pay limit when they applied to the Price Commission for a price increase. Phase two introduced in August 1976 involved in a minimum increase of £2.50 per week and a maximum of £4 per week or within these limits a guideline of 5 per cent. The TUC supported these lower limits for wage increases and in return the government granted certain income tax concessions. However by 1977 strong demands were being made by the unions for a return to free collective bargaining and the government failed to gain TUC support for the third phase of its policy in August 1977. A guideline of 10 per cent was set for wage settlements although certain exceptions were allowed (e.g. self-financing productivity deals). Pressure was placed on firms to observe the guidelines by the advice given to government departments and nationalised industries in their purchasing policy to discriminate against firms who broke the guidelines. Again TUC support was not forthcoming for the last phase of policy in August 1978 which set a limit of 5 per cent on wage increases and which was responsible for the 'winter of discontent' that followed. In a final attempt to preserve its broken incomes policy the Labour government set up the Standing Commission on Pay Comparability known as the Clegg Commission.

When the Conservatives won the general election in May 1979 they abandoned prices and incomes policy seeking to moderate the rate of inflation through tight monetary control. The Price Commission was abolished and the Clegg Commission was phased out after reporting on work outstanding which sponsored large increases in pay in the public sector. Finally, with respect to the public sector the present Conservative government has sought to moderate the pace of wage settlements by setting cash limits and expenditure ceilings (see Chapter 8, section 8.4.4).

It should be apparent from the above summary of past prices and incomes policies in the UK that policies have differed in a number of important respects. In the next section we turn to examine the effectiveness of prices and incomes policy over the post-war period.

11.7 Empirical evidence
There has been a large number of empirical studies carried out to test the effectiveness of incomes policy on the rate of inflation. Rather than discussing the statistical methods employed and results obtained from the many studies undertaken, in this final section we merely attempt to convey the general impression of the empirical work caried out in the UK for the post-1950 period.

In surveying the econometric evidence for the UK economy Parkin, Sumner and Jones (1972)[1] concluded that with the sole exception of the first experiment in incomes policy (1948-50) 'incomes policy apparently has had little effect on the average rate of wage inflation'. With regard to the effectiveness of incomes policy in other countries Blackaby (1971)[2] concluded

although it is not possible to point to a country where an incomes policy has been an obvious success over the whole post-war period, some policies have had visible success in particular countries at particular times. Most short-term wage or price freezes have been successful in stopping increases in wage rates and prices during the period in which they were in operation, though their effect in the longer term trend is more doubtful.

More recently Henry and Ormerod (1978)[3] in a study of incomes policy and wage inflation for the UK between 1961 and 1977 concluded that

whilst some incomes policies have reduced the rate of wage inflation during the period in which they operated, this reduction has been only temporary. Wage increases in the period immediately following the ending of policies were higher... and these increases match losses incurred during the operation of the incomes policy.

A summary of the thrust of the empirical evidence would, therefore, be that it has not been particularly favourable to the view that incomes policy has been effective in reducing the average rate of wage inflation especially in the long run.

11.8 Conclusion

The results of the analysis and empirical evidence presented in this chapter suggest that a prices and incomes policy on its own is no cure for inflation. It may however be useful as a component of a macro-economic strategy (incorporating, for example, appropriate monetary policies) to reduce the rate of inflation. In this case, the role of a prices and incomes policy would be as temporary and supplementary policy measure designed to assist the transition to a lower rate of inflation.

1. In Parkin, J. M. and Sumner, M. T. (eds.) (1972), *Incomes Policy and Inflation* (Manchester: Manchester University Press).
2. Blackaby, F. (1971), 'Incomes policies and inflation', *National Institute Economic Review* (November).
3. Henry, S.G.B. and Ormerod, P. A. (1978), 'Incomes Policy and Wage Inflation: Empirical Evidence for the UK 1961–1977', *National Institute Economic Review* (August).

12 Indexation

12.1 Introduction

In recent years the proposal to introduce indexation has come increasingly into vogue. Indexation involves adjusting the value of contracts denominated in money terms to bring them into line with other price changes. In this way the real value of economic variables is preserved regardless of the actual rate of inflation. Yang (1974) has noted that, 'In a completely indexed world, all of the following would be indexed: all private and public wage and loan contracts including deposits at thrift institutions, insurance, and pension contracts; social security and other transfer payments, including unemployment compensation; and of course government tax receipts.... Even money would be indexed under a completely indexed economy.'[1] In this chapter rather than discussing specific proposals for the indexation of individual economic variables we consider the nature of indexation (section 12.2) and the main advantages (section 12.3) and disadvantages (section 12.4) of introducing indexation.

12.2 Nature of indexation

One of the easiest ways to illustrate the nature of indexation is to take a familiar example concerning money wage rate increases. In Chapter 5, section 5.3.2 we emphasised that when wage rates are being negotiated what really matters to both employers and employees is the rate of real wage increase. Employers and employees, for example, may desire that real wages increase at a rate of 4 per cent (per annum), this being the rate of increase of labour productivity. Since wage bargains are struck in money terms for an advance period (e.g. one year from 1 January) the rate of inflation expected to occur through the period of the contract is particularly important to negotiators. If prices are expected to increase at 6 per

1. Yang, Y. H. (1974), 'The Case For and Against Indexation: An Attempt at Perspective', *Federal Reserve Bank of St. Louis Review* (October).

cent (per annum), money wage rate increases of 10 per cent (per annum) would have to be negotiated to achieve an increase in real wage rates of 4 per cent (per annum). As long as prices increased at the expected rate (i.e. 6 per cent) real wages would grow at the desired rate of 4 per cent (per annum). Problems arise when prices increase either more quickly or slowly than expected. If, for example, the rate of inflation turned out to be 10 per cent workers would obtain zero growth in their real wages.[1]

Now let us consider what would happen with indexation. With indexation money wage rates would be linked to an appropriate price index (e.g. the Retail Price Index discussed in Chapter 5, section 5.2). If money wage rates were indexed to the Retail Price Index workers would automatically receive on top of the agreed increase an additional 1 per cent increase in their money wages for every 1 per cent rise in the Retail Price Index. Consequently agreed increases in money wage rates would be real wage rate increases regardless of the rate of inflation. In terms of the numerical example quoted above, given a 10 per cent rate of inflation money wages would grow at a rate of 14 per cent (per annum). In other words an agreed increase of 4 per cent in real wages would be accompanied by automatic adjustments or compensation of a further 10 per cent arising from indexation. Similarly if the rate of inflation were 4 per cent (i.e. less than the expected rate of 6 per cent) the agreed increase (i.e. 4 per cent) would only be accompanied by an additional automatic compensation of 4 per cent. In this way real wages would increase at the agreed rate of 4 per cent, regardless of the rate of inflation. Wage bargaining therefore would be in terms of real wages i.e. the wage concept of prime importance to both firms and workers.

Contracts for loans of money could likewise be indexed. To take an example, assume a person borrowed £100 in year 1 and that the money had to be repaid four years later. If the price index rose from 100 to 130 during this period indexation would involve repayment of £130. In other words the borrower would pay back (and the lender receive) the same sum in real terms as he borrowed. In a similar manner indexation could be applied to a wide range of economic variables although it would be administratively impossible to compensate holders of notes and coin for the loss of purchasing power of their currency during the time in their possession. Complete indexation would mean that all contracts over time would be indexed (i.e. adjusted) so that their value was constant in real not

---

1. Note that we are ignoring the effect of taxation for ease of exposition.

money terms. As we shall discuss in section 12.3 below advocates of indexation argue that this is particularly important in easing the cost of transition to a lower rate of inflation.

12.3 Advantages of indexation

Having discussed the nature of indexation we now consider the three main advantages put forward in favour of its widespread introduction.

First, indexation has been advocated on the grounds of allocative efficiency. For example, in times of inflation assets whose value is specified in nominal terms (e.g. money, bonds) become less attractive to hold compared to real assets. This leads to a demand for assets such as gold coins because they offer a hedge against inflation. Thus scarce resources are wastefully diverted to the satisfaction of wants which occur because of inflation. Second, indexation has been justified on the grounds of distributive equity. The reader will recall from the discussion of Chapter 6, section 6.3.1 that the main costs of inflation arise from the arbitrary changes that occur in the distribution of income and wealth when inflation is imperfectly anticipated. For example, suppose creditors desire a 2 per cent real return on loans. The rate of interest on loan contracts is denominated in money terms (i.e. the nominal rate of interest). In order to establish the real rate of interest the rate of inflation must be deducted from the nominal rate of interest. With an 8 per cent nominal rate of interest and a 6 per cent expected rate of inflation, lenders would receive a 2 per cent real return on loans. Assume this is satisfactory to both lenders and borrowers then problems arise when prices don't increase at the expected rate. If the actual rate of inflation was 8 per cent compared to an expected rate of 6 per cent borrowers would gain (i.e. they would pay a zero real rate of interest) and lenders would lose (i.e. they would receive a zero real return). In contrast if the actual rate of inflation was only 4 per cent (i.e. it fell short of the anticipated rate of 6 per cent) lenders would gain (i.e. they would receive a 4 per cent real rate return) and borrowers would lose (i.e. they would pay a 4 per cent real rate of interest). With indexation the nominal rate of interest would be automatically adjusted according to the rate of change of prices thereby preserving the desired real return on loans, regardless of the actual rate of inflation. By indexing interest rates such distributional costs would be avoided when inflation is imperfectly anticipated.

Indexation of direct taxation has also been advocated on the grounds of equity. In Chapter 6, section 6.3.1 we discussed how inflation causes the real value of tax payments made by the private sector to the government to increase. For example, both income tax allowances and brackets are denominated in nominal terms. Inflation not only erodes the real value of tax allowances but, by increasing nominal incomes, also results in individuals being moved into higher income tax brackets where they must pay higher marginal rates of tax (with a progressive tax system). These distributional costs could likewise be avoided if the government linked the level of income tax allowances and brackets to an appropriate price index. Full indexation of the tax system would also require interest incomes and nominal capital gains to be linked to an appropriate price index. For example, with indexation capital gains on assets would only be taxed if the real, as opposed to the nominal, value of assets increased (i.e. the excess of nominal capital gains over the rate of inflation would only be liable for tax). Professor Milton Friedman has also argued that by reducing the tax revenue governments gain from inflation indexation would help reduce one of the incentives for governments to pursue inflationary policies in the first place.

The third main argument put forward in support of indexation is that it would lessen the social and economic costs of reducing the rate of inflation. This beneficial effect has been particularly emphasised by monetarists, notably Professor Milton Friedman. In Chapter 5, section 5.3 we discussed the monetarist view that inflation is caused by excess demand (due primarily to excessive monetary expansion) and expectations of future rates of inflation. Monetarists argue that inflation can only be reduced by slowing down the rate of growth of the money supply. Reducing the rate of monetary expansion results in an increase in the level of unemployment. As unemployment increases the rate of increase of money wages and prices is reduced. Downward pressure on the rate of wage and price inflation in turn leads people to revise downwards their expectations of future rates of inflation. Expectations of future rates of inflation take time to adjust and the speed at which the downward revision takes place is very important. The faster expectations are revised downwards the more rapidly the rate of inflation will fall and the lower will be the cost in terms of unemployment. It is in this respect that monetarists have advocated indexation as a method for reducing inflationary expectations and reducing the extent and duration of unemployment which accompanies a reduction in the rate of monetary expansion. With indexation money wage rate increases would automatically decline as the rate of inflation decreased thus avoiding the danger that employers would be committed, under existing wage contracts, to excessive money wage increases when the rate of inflation fell. Wage rate increases would be less rapid and unemployment would therefore increase by a smaller amount. In a similar manner indexation would also remove the danger of firms being locked into paying excessively high nominal rates of interst on loans as the rate of inflation declined. With indexation contracts for loans would be fixed in real terms and there would be no reason for firms to delay capital investment projects in anticipation of lower nominal rates of interest and building contract prices.

Before considering the main objections to indexation it is important to stress that monetarists advocate indexation as a supplementary measure, to monetary restraint, in controlling the rate of inflation. Monetarists assert that inflation can only be reduced by slowing down the rate of monetary expansion. Indexation would, they argue, aid the adjustment process and lessen the extent and duration of unemployment in the transition to a lower rate of inflation. At the same time it would reduce the cost of unanticipated inflation incurred through arbitrary redistribution of income and wealth and thereby help reduce social tension. This last beneficial effect may be of considerable importance if a government decides to follow a gradualist policy of reducing inflation over a long period.

12.4 Disadvantages of indexation
In spite of the benefits noted above the proposal to introduce indexation remains a highly controversial area. The main objections to indexation are threefold. First, some economists argue that indexation would cause an acceleration of inflation when the original cause of price increases was an exogenous impulse (e.g. continuous increases in the price of imported goods such as oil). Similarly if inflation is caused by rising wage costs due to the actions of trade unions (i.e. in accordance with the sociological explanation of inflation) then indexation would merely ensure that inflation proceeded at a faster rate. Nevertheless even in this case workers who were members of weaker unions would automatically receive compensation for rising prices thereby preserving social injustice. A variation of this argument depends on the partial or incomplete introduction of indexation. If fewer groups were hurt by inflation, political opposition to it would be weaker so there would be more of it, doing as much harm but more narrowly concentrated on groups which had not managed to obtain indexation of their incomes. Second, the administration of a system of indexation involves costs. This in part helps explain why discussion of indexation is more prevalent during periods of relatively high rates of inflation. In times of creeping inflation the costs probably outweigh the advantages.

Third, opponents of indexation point to a number of technical and administrative difficulties involved in introducing indexation. For example, there exists the technical problem of choosing the appropriate index of real purchasing power. In addition transitional problems could arise for those individuals and institutions who are already party to existing contracts which are not indexed.

12.5 Indexation in the UK economy

At the present time a certain amount of indexation exists in the UK economy. One of the best known examples is the issue of Index-linked National Savings Certificates commonly referred to as 'Granny Bonds'. In September 1981 all age restrictions for the purchase of Index-linked National Savings Certificates were removed and their availability was extended to include trustees and eligible non-profit making organisations in addition to personal savers. Certificates can be bought at Post Offices in £10 units up to a maximum of £10,000. The value of the Certificates is changed each month in line with the Retail Price Index, although holders who cash them within the first year of purchase receive only the face value of their Certificates. A bonus of 4 per cent of the purchase price is paid when Certificates are held for five years and all repayments of certificates are free of UK income tax and capital gains tax. The other state index-linked saving scheme at present in operation is the National Savings Save As You Earn (SAYE) scheme. The index-linked SAYE scheme is available to anyone aged 16 or over. Under the saving scheme a person agrees to make sixty regular monthly contributions of the same value (from £4 to a £50 limit) over 5 years. Each monthly contribution is linked separately to the Retail Price Index from the 1st of the month following payment to the completion of the agreement. This means that the first contribution is Index-linked for sixty months, the second for fifty-nine months, etc. Anyone failing to complete their sixty monthly contributions receives interest of 6 per cent a year on the sum saved provided repayment is made when the agreement has run for at least a year. If the contract is less than a year old the person only receives back the value of contributions made to the scheme. At the end of the five-year agreement a person may opt to leave his money invested for a further two-year period during which time no further contributions are made. Contributions remain index-linked to the seventh anniversary of the starting date of the agreement at which time a bonus of two monthly contributions is paid. Anyone requiring repayment between the fifth and seventh anniversaries of the starting date receives back what was due on the fifth anniversary of the agreement. Exceptions to these provisions are made in the case of death. Like National Savings Certificates all repayments under the SAYE scheme are free of UK income tax and capital gains tax.

Since 1972 public sector employee's pensions have been increased each year in line with the rise in the Retail Price Index. Indexation of pensions also occurs in the private sector but usually less formally. The level of pensions paid by certain firms is reviewed from time to time so that in effect they are indexed. In recent years there has also been a commitment to maintain the real value of old age pensions and other social security benefits by increasing them in line with the rise in the cost of living. Another interesting example of indexation concerns income tax personal allowances. The Rooker-Wise amendment to the 1977 Finance Act provided that income tax personal allowances should be increased each year (in the main Budget) in line with the rise in the Retail Price Index over the previous calendar year, unless the government sought and obtained the approval of Parliament to do otherwise. Since its inception this provision has been honoured. However, in the March 1981 Budget the Chancellor failed to raise the main personal allowances at all and subsequently gained the approval of Parliament of a resolution authorising the non-implementation of the Rooker-Wise provision. Finally, with respect to indexation the Chancellor Sir Geoffrey Howe in his Budget speech (10 March 1981) announced a first issue of marketable Index-linked Treasury Stock. £1 billion of the new indexed stock was offered with a maturity of fifteen years and an interest rate (coupon value) of 2 per cent (i.e. 2 per cent Index-linked Treasury Stock, 1996). In July 1981 a further issue of £1 billion of stock was offered with a maturity of twenty-five years and an interest rate of 2 per cent (i.e. 2 per cent Index-linked Treasury Stock, 2006). The interest of 2 per cent, paid half yearly, is indexed to the Retail Price Index and the value of the principal on redemption is related to the movement in the Retail Price Index over the life of the stock. Ownership of the stock is confined to eligible holders; the main eligible holders being pension funds and insurance companies and friendly societies carrying on pension business in the UK. It remains to be seen whether the gilt-edged market will eventually be opened to all dealers on an index-linked basis.[1]

1. The restriction limiting purchase of index linked gilt-edged securities to insurance companies and pension funds was removed in the 1982 Budget. These are now available to all would be purchasers.

12.6 Concluding remarks

Indexation itself is a 'second-best' solution. The best solution is to achieve price stability with no indexation since scarce resources would not be used to implement and administer indexation schemes. Proponents of indexation argue that it is particularly important to introduce widespread indexation during times of falling inflation so that the adjustment process can be achieved at a lower cost in real terms of unemployment whilst at the same time preserving social justice. However it should be stressed that indexation is no cure for inflation; it is a means of living with inflation. Such a policy finds favour with those who dislike inflation but nevertheless feel that the cost of transition to a lower rate of inflation in terms of unemployment involves high social and economic costs (see Chapter 6, section 6.2.2 for a discussion of these costs).

One way to shed some light on the relative importance of the pros and cons of indexation is to consider empirical evidence on indexation. Unfortunately as the evidence is not clear cut the proposal to introduce indexation is likely to remain controversial. In their international survey of indexation and its effects in twenty-one countries Page and Trollope (1974) concluded that: 'Indexing has not had a major identifiable effect on the economy in any of the countries studied. It does not appear to have had a significant effect on inflation either way.'[2]

2. Page, S. A. B. and Trollope, S. (1974), 'An International Survey of Indexing and Its Effects', *National Institute Economic Review* (November).

13 Supply Management Policies

13.1 Introduction

The traditional thrust of Keynesian economics is that the level of output is demand determined at least until the capacity of the economy is reached. This view is consistent with the treatment of the determination of national income contained in Chapter 1. In the simple Keynesian model changes in aggregate demand induce changes (i) only in real output until the capacity (i.e. full employment of the economy) is attained and (ii) only in the price level once capacity output is reached. Within this analytical framework wage rates are regarded as being determined exogenously through the employer/trade union bargaining procedure so that they are inelastic (unresponsive) to changes in demand.

This traditional view was undermined by the development of the Phillips curve analysis which suggested that falls in unemployment would be accompanied by rising money wage rates, i.e. an increase in demand for goods would result in rising labour costs and therefore prices as the demand for labour increased. Later, development of the augmented Phillips curve analysis (see Chapter 5, section 5.3.2) suggested that there is only a single level of unemployment (i.e. the natural rate) at which inflation is constant.

Once the idea that changes in output could be produced at constant prices began to be questioned the role of demand management as the main instrument of macroeconomic policy also became subject to questioning. Perhaps the economy could be managed by policies directed towards the supply side. Total or aggregate supply is derived from the combination of the factors of production by firms and supply side policies are policies directed towards altering the response of these factors to demand. Of course many supply side policies cost money to introduce and are therefore closely linked with demand management policies through the government budget constraint (see Chapter 3, section 3.3.1). For example, an increase in labour retraining schemes would increase both government expenditure and the PSBR given the level of taxation. Hence aggregate demand would be increased both through the increase in government expenditure and the probable monetary expansion due to the increase in the PSBR. To be a 'pure' supply side policy an offsetting increase in government revenue would be necessary so that aggregate demand remained unchanged. In theory this could be achieved by an increase in taxation. In practice of course most supply side policies are mixed demand/supply side policies but for the sake of ease of exposition we will ignore any impact on aggregate demand in the following discussion.

Finally, by way of introduction, reference to the augmented Phillips curve analysis of Chapter 5 provides a useful method of categorising supply side policies. First, certain policies are designed to assist the short-run stabilisation of the economy i.e. help maintain unemployment at the natural rate which would be consistent with any desired target rate of inflation. Second, some policies are designed to reduce the natural rate of unemployment itself and produce a once-and-for-all increase in capacity income. Third, there are long-run policies designed to produce an increase in the growth of capacity income.

Before considering supply policies it should be noted that there is little substantial experience in operating any of these three types of policy so our comments must be tentative. Furthermore in many cases discussion is illustrative only since the subject matter of some of the policies includes major issues in topics such as labour economics.

13.2 Stabilisation policies

As we have noted earlier (Chapter 6, section 6.7) one implication of the augmented Phillips curve analysis is that a reduction in the rate of inflation requires an increase in unemployment above the natural rate. This involves a cost in terms of a loss of output which may be high relative to the benefits of a lower inflation rate if it takes some time before the rate of wage increase falls i.e. before the short-run Phillips curve shifts downwards.Supply side policies may be able to operate on firms' costs so as to moderate the rate of inflation without the economy having to endure as severe a recession as would otherwise be the case.

One such possible policy would be to vary payroll taxes imposed on the employment of labour. In the UK the main candidate for alteration would be the employer's national insurance contribution. This could be lowered to reduce firms' production costs. Alternatives take the form of making supplementary payments to firms to subsidise employment e.g. job creation schemes, state assistance to firms to avoid bankruptcy, etc. Nevertheless it is also true that such policies may be used as measures to encourage employment and output without affecting inflation.

The main thrust of such policies is to lower firms' costs of production. Lower costs it is hoped will be passed on to customers by way of lower prices (or lower rates of increase of prices) thereby lowering the rate of inflation. Clearly such reductions or subsidies have a once-and-for-all effect on actual costs (unless repeated) but they might also affect future costs if a lower current inflation rate reduced expected future rates of inflation. The effectiveness however of such policies is open to question especially as payroll taxes usually form a small proportion of total wage costs. One study carried out in the USA estimated that payroll tax changes have only a small effect on inflation.[1] A variation of the policy of subsidising current costs is the holding back of increases in the price of goods/ services supplied by the nationalised industries. Recent examples include the suppression of gas and electricity prices by the UK governments.

An alternative suggestion is to vary direct taxes according to the gap between wage targets and actual settlements. Such a scheme is called a Tax Based Incomes Policy (TIP). It is closely related to the standard incomes policy discussed in Chapter 11. Norms would be set for pay increases and the penalty for contravention would be a variation in taxes paid to the central government. For reasons of administrative ease (i.e. there are fewer firms than workers) it makes greater sense to apply sanctions to firms rather than individual workers. In this case it would operate to stiffen the resolve of employers in the wage bargaining process with trade unions.

The following simple example illustrates how such a system would operate. Assume that the target rate for wage increases was 5 per cent and the standard rate of corporation tax was 40 per cent. If a firm's wage bill (corrected for changes in the level of employment) rose at a faster rate than 5 per cent the rate of corporation tax applicable to that firm would also rise with the precise rate applicable depending on the degree of overshoot e.g. 45 per cent in the case of a wage increase of 6 per cent; 50 per cent for 7 per cent, etc. Conversely the rate of tax applicable could be reduced if a firm achieved a rate of growth of wages less than the target rate of 5 per cent.

Protagonists of this type of policy make several claims in its

1. Halpern, J. and Munnell, A. (1980). 'The Inflationary Impact of Increases in the Social Security Payroll Tax', *New England Economic Review* (March/April).

favour. First, they argue that it can be used as a policy to reduce the rate of inflation without necessitating large increases in unemployment. At the same time it is not inconsistent with the view that inflation is a monetary phenomenon. Monetary contraction accompanied by a TIP could be carried out more gradually so that a given reduction in the rate of inflation would be achieved at a lower cost of unemployment. Second, it is argued that the distortion of the market mechanism would be less under a TIP than with a formal incomes policy. Firms would still be free to give wage increases above the target but would find it more costly to do so. Hence firms experiencing shortages of labour due to rising demand for their products could still increase wages to attract more labour.

Nevertheless there are problems inherent in introducing such a scheme. First, the penalty would need to be large enough to discourage excessive wage increases but not too large so as to distort too severely the market mechanism. Such a compromise would be difficult to achieve in practice. Second, there is the real danger that firms would grant wage increases above the target and raise their prices so as to recoup from customers not only the wage increase but also the penalty applied to their tax rate. Third, there are administration costs which would be significant and could be onerous. Fourth, there is the standard definitional problem applicable to all such schemes. For example, wages would have to be defined to include fringe benefits, overtime, productivity bonuses, etc. if evasion were to be avoided. Fifth, there are problems regarding fairness of treatment. If some firms were excluded from the scheme because of their small size this would raise questions of equity. Similarly how would nationalised industries be treated? Taxing their profits would make little sense. One potential source of inequity (i.e. the division between wages and profits) could be treated by applying (i) a special tax cut if wage inflation slowed more than price inflation and (ii) a special tax on corporation profits if profits rose more than usual as compared with wages.

We now turn to supply side policies directed towards reducing the natural rate of unemployment.

13.3 Policies to reduce the natural rate of unemployment

If we accept that the role of stabilisation policy is to stabilise the level of unemployment at the natural rate, there still remains the problem of what to do if the natural rate of unemployment is too high to be acceptable politically. Demand management policies are of no avail since any reduction in the level of unemployment below the natural rate will merely lead to accelerating inflation. Policies must be directed to the determinants of the natural rate itself. In Chapter 5, section 5.3.2 we noted that the natural rate of unemployment is largely a function of the structural characteristics of the labour market. Consequently the approximate policies available are those which are directed to making the labour market more efficient.

A detailed discussion of the labour market is beyond the scope of this text and we shall content ourselves with considering briefly the nature of supply policies designed to reduce the natural rate of unemployment. An efficient labour market requires (i) perfect information about employment facilities and wage rates throughout the labour market and also (ii) perfect mobility of factors of production. Clearly in the real world both these attributes are absent and it is argued that it is these imperfections which cause the natural rate of unemployment to be relatively high. Note that in this context we are identifying the natural rate of unemployment with the concepts of frictional and structural unemployment discussed in Chapter 6, section 6.2.1. With regard to informational deficiencies the obvious remedy is to provide better information on job prospects via existing official employment exchanges. Indeed the continued existence and growth of private employment exchanges suggests that there are gaps in the official system.

Restraints on labour mobility can be classified according to (i) occupational and (ii) geographical restraints. Occupational restraints are often very difficult to overcome. For example, an unemployed porter can hardly become a doctor to take an extreme example. Nevertheless greater provision of government retraining schemes could help tc alleviate this problem. Geographical mobility is retarded by such factors as family ties, suitable provision of housing, the costs of moving, educational facilities, etc. Again many of these factors are beyond the control of the government but some assistance can be given by (i) providing easier movement from council housing in one area to such housing in another area or by (ii) financial assistance to help cover the costs of moving. Note also that the natural rate of unemployment would be reduced if unemployment were more evenly spread throughout the country. This means that active and successful regional policies would also help to reduce the natural rate of unemployment.

In addition there is the question of the level of unemployment benefits. Calculations show that after allowance for benefits in kind and the cost of working, a man with a wife and two children would obtain permanently in benefits a living standard about three-quarters of what he would obtain on average earnings.[1] The higher

---

1. Minford, P. and Peel, D. A. (1981), 'Is the Government's Economic Strategy on Course?', *Lloyds Bank review* (April).

this ratio the less keen an unemployed worker will be to accept the first job offered to him. This effect will be heightened if he also values leisure. Thus one way to reduce the natural rate of unemployment would be to reduce the real level of unemployment benefits. Labour would then find unemployment more costly in terms of foregone income and would therefore reduce the time spent searching for the job, i.e. frictional unemployment would fall. Of course such a policy has serious overtones regarding the government's social policy and it may therefore be unwilling to follow this remedy. Nevertheless it must then be accepted that a rise in unemployment is inevitable if unemployment benefits are raised.

Finally there is the question of attempting to reduce unemployment by introducing tax reforms designed to alleviate the so-called poverty trap. It is argued that some unemployed (particularly the low paid) may be reluctant to seek employment because of the high marginal effective tax rate. This is due to the fairly low threshold at which individuals commence to pay income tax at the standard rate coupled with the fact that as incomes rise so individuals lose various welfare benefits. Easing of this high effective marginal tax rate would it is argued increase the attraction of work relative to leisure.

13.4 Policies to promote economic growth
As noted in Chapter 6, section 6.4.1 economic growth correctly refers to an increase in the actual productive potential of the economy i.e. its capacity. It is important to note that persistent increases in the capacity of the economy are the only method of producing sustained economic growth. Stabilisation policy can produce short bursts of increases in national income as the economy makes increasing use of existing spare capacity but sustained economic growth requires sustained growth in the productive potential of an economy. It therefore depends heavily on the supply side of the economy.

Economic growth arises from (i) an increase in the quantity of the factors of production (land, labour and capital) and/or (ii) an increase in the efficiency with which the factors are combined (i.e. the growth of technology). In discussing economic growth it is customary to concentrate on the supply of labour and capital together with the growth of technology. Some indication of the relative importance of these two factors is contained in a study by Dension of the growth of total national income of the USA over the period 1929-69.[1] The contributions of the various factors were as

1. Denison, E. (1974) *Accounting for United States Economic Growth 1929—1969,* The Brookings Institute.

shown in Table 13.1.

TABLE 13.1. Contributions to growth of national income in the USA, 1929–69

	Growth rate (percentage per annum)
Total factor input	1.82
(Labour 1.32)	
(Capital 0.50)	
Output per head	1.59
(Knowledge 0.92)	
(Resource allocation 0.30)	
(Economies of scale 0.36)	
(Other 0.01)	
Total national income	3.41

Source: E. Denison (1974) Accounting for United States Economic Growth 1929–69, The Brookings Institute.

The salient feature of Table 13.1 is the importance of the growth of technology (i.e. output per head) in which the growth of knowledge plays an important role. Resource allocation refers to the movement of labour from less productive to more productive uses (e.g. agriculture to industry). Regarding factor inputs, growth of capital stock plays a relatively small but significant role. However if we are concerned with growth of national income *per head*, growth of capital and the growth of technology are the relevant determining factors.

We now consider policies available to the government to stimulate economic growth. Any policy which stimulates the rate of growth of capital stock (i.e. investment) also assists growth. Financial assistance for investment usually takes the form of cash grants and tax relief on investment expenditure. All such measures are designed to reduce the cost of investment. The government can have a more direct influence on investment in the public sector via the capital expenditure programmes of nationalised industries and by the provision of necessary infrastructure such as road networks, electrification of railways, etc. Turning to the second source (i.e. technology), the government can assist the growth of knowledge by the provision of educational facilities, retraining schemes and assisting research expenditure. Nevertheless the role of government in promoting economic growth is the subject of controversy. Some people argue that the best action the government can take is to reduce its intervention in the economy. Cutting back government expenditure would, they argue, 'get the government off the backs of the people' and allow private enterprise to function without hindrance. Reduction of government expenditure would permit reduction of direct taxation thus increasing rewards and providing greater incentives to undertake risk. Broadly speaking these types of arguments are put forward by those on the right of the political spectrum. In their view the role of government is to create a stable economic environment in which private enterprise can act.

13.5 Concluding remarks
In section 13.2 to 13.4 above we have surveyed the potential role of supply side policies. In conclusion it is worth stressing that policies designed principally for many microeconomic purposes also effect the supply of goods and therefore aggregate supply. To take just one example the government's industrial policy (e.g. anti-monopoly legislation) is designed to stimulate efficiency and therefore increase output at a given price level. This also illustrates that in many cases the dividing line between micro and macroeconomic policy is blurred.

Part III
INTERNATIONAL MONETARY
RELATIONS

14 The International Monetary System

14.1 Introduction

Before studying this chapter, the reader should re-read Chapter 4 to ensure that he is familiar with the concepts and analysis contained within it. Especially important are section 4.6 which deals with exchange rate regimes and section 4.7.3 which examines the link between the domestic money supply and the balance of payments.

In Chapter 4 we pointed out that the balance of payments provides a record of transactions between residents of one country and those of the rest of the world. This definition brings out the central difference between domestic and international payments. Payments within a country (i.e. between domestic residents of the same country) are made in the same currency whereas those between residents of different countries involve different currencies. For example, if a resident of the UK buys a Volvo car imported from Sweden he will expect to pay for the car in pounds sterling but the Swedish exporter will require payment in Swedish kronor. As we shall see this exchange between currencies raises special problems. The supply of pounds is controlled by the Bank of England whereas that of Swedish kronor is under the ultimate control of the central bank of Sweden. In previous chapters we have discussed how the supply of any currency is determined by the central bank of the country concerned either as the target of its monetary policy or the by-product of other monetary policies adopted. Similarly these central banks can and will influence the rates at which the two currencies are exchanged. For these reasons there has taken place a development of financial institutions (and also branches of domestic financial institutions) which specialise in making international payments. We can therefore define the international monetary system as the network of institutions, rules and conventions under which international payments are made.

We now move on to consider the essential features of an international monetary system.

14.2 The essential features of international monetary systems

It is possible to distinguish four characteristics which serve as a background for the discussion of any international monetary system:

(1) the adjustment mechanism (section 14.2.1);
(2) the unit of account (section 14.2.2);
(3) management of the international monetary system (section 14.2.3); and
(4) promotion of the integration of economies (section 14.2.4).

14.2.1 *The adjustment mechanism*
In the long run purchases of goods and financial assets by residents of one country from abroad must be matched by corresponding sales of goods and financial securities to non-residents. In other words purchases from abroad are limited by what residents are able to sell abroad. In fact as we have seen in Chapter 6, section 6.5, the restraint for developed countries is more restrictive as it is sales of goods and services abroad which limit purchases from abroad. However in the short run these restraints do not apply and individual countries can incur balance of payments surpluses or deficits (either on the current account or the combined current and capital accounts). The adjustment mechanism refers to the methods by which these deficits/surpluses (i.e. imbalances) are eliminated.

The adjustment mechanism has two dimensions: (i) the actual process employed (e.g. exchange rate changes in the case of floating exchange rates) and (ii) the speed of adjustment. If adjustment does not have to be made instantaneously, a 'cushion' is provided so that countries can adapt without excessive hardship to changed relationships with the rest of the world. On the other hand if the time allowed for adjustment is excessive, it is likely that countries will try to evade the adjustment process. Therefore the ideal adjustment process would allow sufficient time to avoid undue hardship but not too much time so as to permit countries to evade the adjustment process.

14.2.2 *The unit of account*
The second major feature of an international monetary system is the nature of the asset used for measuring the value of other currencies. In practice such an asset is also often used to settle indebtedness between countries and as a means of holding international reserves. Temporary balance of payments deficits can be financed by running down reserves and it is therefore necessary for countries to hold reserves in the form of assets which are internationally acceptable as

a means of settling debts.

14.2.3 *Management of the internaional monetary system*

Another important distinction between international monetary systems is the degree to which they require management. Relationships between sovereign states require some give and take (i.e. bargaining) and such states are reluctant to cede too much power to supra-national bodies. For this reason the extremes of (i) permanently fixed and (ii) pure or freely floating, exchange rates have some attraction. They require little international co-operation to administer. On the other hand intermediate systems require management since the levels of exchange rates require agreement among countries as do methods of adjustment and assets in which reserves can be held.

14.2.4 *Promotion of integration of economies*

The case for free trade depends essentially on the hypothesis that if countries specialise in the production of goods for which they are best suited (i.e. where they have a 'comparative advantage') then world output of goods and services will be maximised given the level of resources available. The necessary supporting hypothesis to this proposition is that free trade will cause production to be carried out according to the possession of comparative advantage. Any system of international payments should provide a means of supporting the development of trade on an international basis so as to achieve the optimum allocation oof resources.

This may seem to be fairly obvious but it should be remembered that free trade is not to the advantage of all sections of the community. For example, imports of cheap Asian textiles into the UK benefit consumers but not UK producers of competing textiles. Consequently restrictions on the availability of finance for the purchase of goods and/or financial securities by residents have been adopted by countries at various times.

Having briefly examined the essential features of international financial systems, we now examine the various systems against this background.

14.3 The international gold standard

In this section we provide a description of the nature of the gold standard which prevailed during the nineteenth and early twentieth centuries. Three conditions were necessary for a country to be on the gold standard:[1]

(1) the price of gold was fixed in terms of domestic currency, i.e.

it was not allowed to fluctuate according to the demand for and supply of gold;

(2) either gold circulated as currency within a country or the quantity of domestic money was varied according to the quantity of gold held by the authorities;

(3) free import of gold into and export from a country was permitted.

The result of these three conditions was that gold was used as the international reserve asset and the ratio of the different domestic currency prices of gold fixed international exchange rates. To illustrate this point we use a simple hypothetical example. Consider a situation where a specific quantity of gold costs (i) £1 in the UK, (ii) $4 in the USA and (iii) $0.05 to transport from the UK to the USA or vice versa.

In such circumstances the central exchange rate would be £1 = $4. This is called the parity exchange rate. The cost of shipping gold between the UK and the USA provides limits to the possible fluctuations of the actual exchange rate. These limits are called 'gold specie points'. If the pound appreciated against the dollar it would not pay a resident of the USA to buy pounds at a price higher than $4.05 per £1 because he could buy a unit of gold for $4.0 in the USA, ship it to the UK for $0.05 (total cost $4.05) and purchase £1 in London for his gold. Hence $4.05 provides an upper limit to the actual exchange rate for sterling. Similarly of a trader in the UK found that he was getting less than $3.95 (i.e. the lower limit) for every pound, it would pay him to buy gold in London, ship it to the USA and change it there for dollars. This situation is illustrated in Figure 14.1.

The limitation to exchange rate fluctuations discussed above provides a vital component in the adjustment process. If a country experienced a surplus on its balance of payments, its exchange rate would appreciate and non-residents would find it cheaper to make payments to residents by buying the required currency with gold instead of their own currency; i.e. there would be a gold inflow into

---

1. In fact these conditions were rarely satisfied completely. Even in the heyday of the gold standard (i.e. 1870–1914) only three countries—Britain, USA and Germany—maintained perfectly free convertibility of their currencies into gold. Nevertheless most countries observed the so-called rules of the gold standard by which countries raised interest rates in response to a loss of reserves and lowered interest rates in response to an accretion of reserves. Because of this domestic money supplies did respond in the predicted way to balance of payments deficits/surpluses so that subsequent discussion is quite a good approximation to what actually happened.

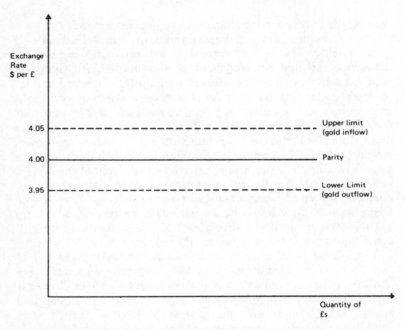

Figure 14.1. Upper and lower limits to exchange rate fluctuations.

that country. Conversely a balance of payments deficit would cause the exchange rate to depreciate towards the lower limit leading ultimately to a gold outflow. These movements in gold would lead to corresponding changes in the domestic money supply provided either the domestic money supply was linked to the quantity of gold held by the authorities or the rules of the gold standard were observed. For example balance of payments deficits would, in the last resort, lead to an outflow of gold, a reduction in the domestic money supply and consequently a reduction in economic activity. This deflationary pressure would in turn lead to a reduction in the general price level and an automatic correction of the balance of payments deficit. Conversely persistent balance of payments surpluses would lead to an inflow of gold, an increase in the domestic money supply, an expansion of economic activity and consequently a rise in the general price level. The adherence to the gold standard therefore provided an automatic correction of balance of payments surpluses/deficits through, it should be noted, a method which depended on prices and wage rates moving both upwards and downwards in response to changes in aggregate demand.

The remaining features of the gold standard can now be dealt with quite quickly. The system provided an automatic method of adjustment so that no management was needed. All that was required was that countries adhered to the rules discussed earlier. Similarly the total global quantity of reserves arose from world gold production and responded to gold discoveries. It was however far from clear that discoveries and production of gold accorded with the requirements of reserves for international monetary purposes. Finally countries adhering to the gold standard were integrated into a single economy. In equilibrium, price levels throughout the system had to be equal after allowing for exchange rates—note that we are abstracting from all transport costs for the sake of ease of exposition. Disparities in price levels in the various countries would set up balance of payments disequilibria leading to movements of gold until equality of price levels was re-established throughout the system.

The system of adjustment under the gold standard was one of asset settlement. Countries with balance of payments surpluses obtained assets (i.e. gold) whereas those with balance of payments deficits lost gold. The gold standard provides a useful backcloth against which to discuss the system of fixed exchange rates established under the Bretton Woods agreement. It is to this subject we now turn.

14.4 The Bretton Woods system

The gold standard was suspended in 1914 at the outbreak of the First World War. It was re-introduced briefly in the 1920s before finally breaking down in the early 1930s. Britain returned to the gold standard in 1926 at an over-valued pound which caused problems for the management of the UK economy leading to the adoption of deflationary policies. In 1931, Britain finally left the gold standard.

Faced with the problems of massive unemployment and depression many governments in the 1930s turned towards policies of protecting domestic industries against foreign competition. At the same time exchange rate changes were initiated to assist achievement of domestic policy aims. Against this background the governments of the victorious allies met at Bretton Woods towards the end of the Second World War to plan a new international monetary system. The resulting agreement led to the adoption of fixed (but adjustable) exchange rates and the establishment of the International Monetary Fund (IMF). It is important to realise that this was an attempt to create a 'new' order.

14.4.1 *The Bretton Woods agreement*

The agreement provided for a return to fixed exchange rates. The exchange rates of individual countries were all for practical purposes fixed in terms of the dollar as was the price of gold at $35 per fine ounce. Currencies were to be freely convertible into other currencies at least for non-residents of that country. The monetary authorities were to maintain the market exchange rate within a margin of ±1 per cent of the agreed parity in the manner discussed in Chapter 4, section 4.6.2. For example, if the value of the pound fell below the lower intervention point, the Bank of England had to buy pounds in the foreign exchange markets giving up in return foreign exchange reserves. The principal reserve envisaged in the scheme was to be gold.

Adjustment was to be achieved by internal policy adjustments but provision was made for alteration of exchange rates in the case of a country experiencing fundamental disequilibrium in its balance of payments. Permission had to be obtained from the IMF if the change in the exchange rate was greater than 10 per cent. Because of the provision for exchange rate changes the Bretton Woods system has been called an 'adjustable peg' rather than a fixed exchange rate regime.

A distinction was made between trade and capital flows. Restrictions on payments for goods were stringently discouraged but controls over capital movements were permitted. Provision was also made within the agreement for the introduction of sanctions against countries with persistent surpluses. This provision was in fact never invoked.

Finally the agreement provided for the establishment of the International Monetary Fund (IMF). The international monetary system has to cope with two different sets of problems. The first is how to finance a balance of payments deficit (or how to use a surplus) and the second is how to correct a fundamental imbalance. It is in connection with the first problem that the IMF plays an important role. The Fund provides a 'pool' from which countries with temporary balance of payments difficulties can borrow to tide them over until such time as their adjustment policies have rectified the situation. The Fund has the general task of overseeing the system. The Fund also has an influence in connection with the second problem but normally correction of fundamental imbalances in the balance of payments requires structural changes in the economy. Such changes require long-term finance which is provided by various specialist institutions including the World Bank, the International Finance Corporation (IFC), the International

Development Association (IDA) and the various development banks.

In the following sections we shall consider in greater detail the role of the IMF and the problems which arose during the operation of the Bretton Woods system.

14.4.2 *The International Monetary Fund*

The IMF was established to promote 'international monetary co-operation'. It provides a forum for discussion of international monetary matters and also a means for supervising exchange rate arrangements. Perhaps the most important function of the Fund is to provide finance to assist countries experiencing balance of payments difficulties. This was and still is regarded as an important aid to the promotion of multilateral trade as it avoids the necessity of countries restricting trade for balance of payments reasons.

Rights and obligations in the Fund are based on a system of 'quotas' which roughly reflect the importance of individual countries in international trade. Quota levels are revised every five years to reflect changes in (i) the composition of international trade and (ii) the needs of international liquidity. Quotas were originally paid 25 per cent in gold and 75 per cent in the country's own currency. More recently however gold is being phased out in the international monetary system (see section 14.6).

The highest tier in the decision making structure in the IMF is the Board of Governors consisting in the main of the Ministers of Finance or the Governors of the Central Banks of the member countries. Under this board there is an executive board consisting of members elected on a constituency basis. The managing director of the Fund is an international civil servant. It was originally envisaged that the decision making process would be divided between the Board of Governors and the Executive Board but as time passed this arrangement did not work too well in practice because the Board of Governors was too unwieldy and the Executive Board was not of a sufficiently high political status. This led to the establishment of a committee of governors whose membership reflects a constituency basis. This committee is probably the most important decision making forum in the IMF.

The functions of the IMF can be grouped into two categories: (i) supervision of the behaviour of members regarding balance of payment policies and (ii) a financial role. The supervisory role is loosely defined but it is nevertheless important. In a nutshell, members are supposed to avoid manipulating exchange rates to prevent effective balance of payments adjustment. Intervention in the foreign exchange markets should take place by individual countries to avoid disorderly conditions. At the same time intervention should not take place without considering the effect such intervention will have on other members. In pursuit of its surveillance policies, teams from the IMF regularly visit member countries and discuss policies adopted and recent changes in the economies concerned. Reports from such visits are discussed within the IMF. Naturally enough such consultations do have some impact on policy formulation but of much greater significance in this respect is the fact that the IMF will only lend to a country if it approves the programme of economic policies adopted by that country.

The Fund's financial role arises from the fact that it is an important financial institution with large subscriptions. These subscriptions are raised, as we have already noted, by the allocation of quotas to member countries and are available for lending to members to tide them over balance of payments difficulties. Borrowing from the IMF is subject to conditions regarding the borrowing country's macroeconomic policy. In practice borrowing is divided into what are called 'tranches', each representing 25 per cent of the quota of the country concerned. As each tranche is exhausted by borrowing by an individual country, the conditions of further borrowing, supervision and control by the IMF become more rigorous. Loans are, in general, provided under 'stand-by' arrangements whereby a member country receives an assurance that drawings up to specified amounts will be allowed on application. The original request is treated as a loan application and vetted according to the tranche criteria. Details of normal tranche borrowing and supplementary facilities are as follows:

Reserve tranche. The sole criterion here is balance of payments need; no control or supervision is exercised by the IMF.

First credit tranche. The IMF expects a country to adopt a programme showing that reasonable efforts are being made to overcome balance of payments difficulties. No supervision is exercised over the individual country's economy.

Higher credit tranche. For these borrowings a country must provide a programme which shows a substantial justification of the country's policy to overcome its balance of payments deficits. Drawings are often provided for by instalments, payment of which depends on the attainment of certain criteria. Normally tranche borrowing may not exceed 125 per cent of the country's quota but there are also supplementary borrowing facilities. These are listed below.

The extended facility. This scheme provides for medium-term borrowing for up to three years and is aimed at the provision of assistance to enable countries to overcome structural balance of payments difficulties. Like the higher credit tranches detailed policy intentions are required and the IMF exercises close supervision over the performance of the economy concerned. Drawing is also in instalments. There is the further restraint that combined borrowing under this facility and normal tranche borrowing may not exceed 165 per cent of a country's quota.

The compensatory financing facility. This scheme provides for assitance in the event of a temporary fall in exports which is beyond a country's control (e.g. a fall in world market prices). The shortfall in exports is calculated by the gap between current exports and a five-year average. The country is expected and required to co-operate with the Fund in finding a solution to the problem. Drawings can be up to 50 per cent of that country's quota in any one year subject to a maximum under this facility of 75 per cent of the quota. Borrowings under this facility are not restricted because of existing borrowings under the normal tranche or the extended facility.

The buffer stock financing facility. This facility was developed to assist members in their financing of contributions to a genuine[1] buffer stock scheme in times of balance of payments need.

The supplementary financing facility. This scheme was introduced in 1979 and the most important lenders are Saudi Arabia, USA and West Germany. The scheme is designed to support stand-by arrangements stretching into upper credit tranches. Supervisory arrangements and criteria for performance are normally imposed on borrowing.

In addition to these facilities, a temporary oil facility was operated in 1974 and 1975 to assist countries which suffered most from the increase in oil prices in 1973. Finance for this scheme was met entirely by the IMF's borrowing from countries with a strong balance of payments position, originally OPEC countries. Mention should also be made of the General Agreement to Borrow (1961) whereby the ten major industrial countries (plus Switzerland—later) provide

1. Defined as one set by producers and consumers (rather than unilaterally by one party) to stabilise prices.

supplementary resources to the IMF for lending to the ten countries concerned.

14.4.3 *The defects of the Bretton Woods system*
The problems experienced during the operation of the Bretton Woods system can best be analysed under three headings: (i) Liquidity (ii) Adjustment and (iii) Confidence.

Liquidity. In Chapter 4 we noted that a deficit on the balance of payments requires purchases of domestic currency to prevent the exchange rate from falling below the agreed lower limit. Conversely a balance of payments surplus requires sales of domestic currency. In both cases a medium of exchange is required to carry out the transactions. In other words in a fixed exchange rate system some internationally *acceptable* form of money is required as a means to buy and sell domestic currency. This is what is meant by the term liquidity, i.e. the existence of an adequate quantity of acceptable reserves for intervention in the foreign exchange markets. Excess liquidity means that countries are under no pressure to take measures to correct balance of payments deficits. Conversely any shortage of liquidity will necessitate countries changing their exchange rates almost immediately in response to balance of payments deficits. There is therefore a requirement for the 'right' quantity of liquidity. Under the Bretton Woods system it was envisaged that countries would hold their reserves (i.e. liquidity) in the form of gold which would be supplemented by borrowings from the IMF in times of need. Liquidity was to be controlled by review of the overall level of quotas.

In practice liquidity was a problem throughout the time the Bretton Woods system operated. During the early part of the period of the operation of the Bretton Woods agreement there were fears of inadequate liquidity. At the same time the attraction of holding reserves in the form of dollar balances became apparent. Because of their assured convertibility into gold dollars were as good as gold and at the same time they earned a return in the form of the rate of interest ruling in US money markets. The demand for dollar balances for reserves was satisfied by the USA balance of payments deficit. By the end of the period under review foreign currency holdings became the major component of countries' reserves. Within this component dollar balances was by far the major item since balances held in sterling continued to be very small relative to the total. The growth of liquidity during the approximate time the system was in operation is shown in Table 14.1 which demonstrates quite clearly the changes mentioned above. For the time being the reader can ignore 'Special Drawing Rights' since these are discussed later.

The causes of the dramatic changes revealed in Table 14.1 are quite simple. First, as we have already noted, dollar balances were, at least at the beginning of this period, attractive to hold. Second, persistent and gradual inflation accompanied by the fixed price of gold reduced the price of gold relative to that of other commodities. This caused both (i) private demand for gold to increase and (ii) the profitability of gold production to fall. The combined effect of these two factors was a reduction in the quantity of gold available for international monetary purposes. The consequences of this change were far reaching since it made the system more fragile. The growth in dollar balances necessitated persistent USA balance of payments deficits. As the cumulative value of the deficits rose so the ratio of dollar liabilities to gold holdings for the USA fell. Again this can be seen from the data contained in Table 14.1, noting that most of the growth in official holdings of foreign exchange was due to the growth in official dollar liabilities. This caused the commitment by the USA monetary authorities of free convertibility of dollars into gold to become less credible. In fact it became a 'catch 22' situation. If outstanding dollar liabilities had only risen in line with US gold

TABLE 14.1. International liquidity: official holdings of reserves, 1955–75

Asset	1955	1960	1965	1970	1975
			($ million)		
Gold	35,410	38,065	41,850	36,990	41,580
	(63)	(60)	(59)	(40)	(18)
SDRs	—	—	—	3,124	10,259
				(3)	(4)
Position in the Fund	1,880	3,570	5,376	7,697	14,778
	(3)	(6)	(7)	(8)	(7)
Foreign exchange	18,980	21,080	23,795	45,432	160,235
	(34)	(34)	(34)	(49)	(71)
Total	56,270	62,715	71,021	93,243	226,852
US official gold holdings	21,753	17,804	14,065	11,072	11,256

Source: United Nations, *Statistical Year Book* (New York), various issues.
Notes: 1. Figures refer to values at the end of the year.
    2. Figures in brackets refer to the percentage that component forms of total liquidity.
    3. Position in the Fund refers to automatic drawing rights at the IMF.
    4. The figures for gold in 1975 incorporate the effects of gold price increases.

holdings, free convertibility of the dollar into gold would have been credible but there would have been a shortage of liquidity. On the other hand if—as actually happened—dollar liabilities grew more quickly than US holdings of gold, there would be no shortage of liquidity but convertibility would become less credible and other countries would be less willing to hold dollars. Consequently, following a rush to convert dollars into gold, free convertibility of the dollar into gold was suspended in 1971.

Partly in response to the growth of these difficulties, the articles of the Bretton Woods agreement were amended in 1969 to allow for the creation of a new asset called 'Special Drawing Rights' which it was hoped would supplement the use of gold as a reserve asset. In essence Special Drawing Rights (SDRs) are a book-keeping transaction. Countries which participated in the scheme received allocations of such rights and could use them when faced with balance of payments or reserve problems. Use was subject to certain limitations. In particular the drawing country had, on average over a five-year period, to hold 30 per cent of its allocation. To the extent that its holding fell below 30 per cent, it would have to re-purchase (technically known as 'reconstitute') the excess holdings. Similarly limitations were placed on the maximum liability of individual countries to accept SDRs. Valuation of SDRs was originally in terms of gold but was subsequently changed to valuation in terms of sixteen major currencies. In January 1981, the number of currencies was reduced to five i.e. US dollar (42%), Deutsche Mark (19%), French Franc (13%), Japanese Yen (13%) and the pound sterling (13%); the figures in brackets represent the weights attached to each currency in the valuation. Additional allocations of SDRs were made during the years 1979, 1980 and 1981, i.e. well after the breakdown of the Bretton Woods system. Apart from its contribution to world liquidity, the SDR has become a major unit of account, since the IMF values its resouces in terms of SDRs. Also some countries value their currencies in relation to the SDR.

The attractiveness of the SDR as an asset lies in (i) its stability of value due to the link to a basket of currencies and (ii) the fact that interest payments are made to holders of SDRs; these are financed by charges on those countries which have made drawings.

Adjustment. We have already mentioned that adjustment under the Bretton Woods system allowed for changes in the central parity exchange rate as a cure for fundamental disequilibrium in a country's balance of payments. In the case of temporary disequilibrium, the Fund provided resources to finance a deficit while corrective measures were taken by the country concerned.

The first inherent problem arose from the identification of 'fundamental' disequilibrium. Countries were loath to alter exchange rates which, as we shall see in the next section, raised problems of confidence in the value of their currency. However adjustment of exchange rates (i.e. devaluation) became essential for deficit countries as they exhausted both their reserve holdings and the various borrowing facilities open to them in their efforts to support the value of their currency by purchases on the foreign exchange markets. On the other hand the same pressures were largely absent from surplus countries since they had only to sell their currency in return for international reserves. Such pressures as existed on surplus countries came from moral persuasion from other countries. Hence there was a bias in the adjustment mechanism in favour of countries with balance of payments surpluses and against those countries with balance of payments deficits.

A second bias or asymmetry existed in the adjustment mechanism; this was with respect to the position of the reserve country i.e. the USA. As we have noted dollar balances formed the major component of the growth in the international reserves. Continuous balance of payments deficits were essential for the growth of international liquidity. On the other hand this enabled the USA to evade any adjustment of such deficits since the resulting outflow of dollars was held by the central banks of the other countries as international reserves. Consider, for example, the purchase of a factory in Europe by a US firm. Payment would be made in dollars which would be exchanged into domestic currency by the European residents via their central bank. The central bank would then hold these assets as reserves; i.e. no asset settlement would take place between the Federal Reserve and the central bank of the country concerned. Consequently there was no pressure on the USA to alter its economic policies so as to correct balance of payments deficits. The position was further complicated by the fact that the dollar was the unit of account in which other currencies were denominated. It was therefore not possible for the USA to alter the value of dollar exchange rates without the consent of other countries. The USA therefore held a privileged position in the Bretton Woods system which was only acceptable to other countries whilst they were willing to accept additional dollar balances to augment their reserves.

Confidence. Consideration of the problem of confidence follows automatically from the other two factors i.e liquidity and adjustment. Delayed adjustment due to the reluctance to change exchange rates meant that by the time a country decided to alter the exchange rate every market participant knew in which direction the change would take place. Consequently there was considerable scope for speculative gains through capital movements. For example, in the case of an expected devaluation, speculators would sell the currency hoping to repurchase it at the lower exchange rate expected in the future. Clearly whatever else happened no appreciation was possible so that the maximum possible loss facing the speculator consisted of (i) the cost of making the transactions and (ii) any loss of interest due to interest rate differentials. These were small relative to the profits earned if devaluation actually occurred. Similar reasoning can be applied to situations when appreciation was likely though in this case speculators would purchase the currency now in the hope of selling it at a higher price in the future. For these reasons the Bretton Woods system was said to offer a 'one way option' for speculators.

The problem of confidence in the value of the various currencies became more severe the larger the volume of international funds available for speculation. These grew over time. The problem became particularly acute for the central reserve currency. If countries exercised the right to convert dollars into gold, US official liabilities and gold holdings fell by equal amounts but the ratio of the remaining outstanding liabilities to US official gold holdings deteriorated, i.e. the right of convertibility became less credible. In fact as we have already noted such conversions in the late 1960s and the early 1970s led to the suspension of the convertibility of the dollar into gold in 1971.

14.4.4 *Concluding remarks*

The defects noted above led inevitably to the collapse of the Bretton Woods system. As we shall discuss later, any fixed exchange rate system requires similar and converging rates of inflation amongst the participating members. During the 1970s inflation rates increased on average and diverged among countries. This situation was exacerbated by the way the USA financed the Vietnam War (i.e. through monetary expansion) which led both to (i) faster rates of inflation in the USA and (ii) larger US balances of payments deficits. In practice because of the monetary effects of the balance of payments surpluses corresponding to the US deficit, the USA determined monetary conditions for the rest of the world, a situation which eventually proved unacceptable to other countries.

The retreat from Bretton Woods can be briefly catalogued. In 1968 a two-tier gold price system was introduced because of the pressure on gold prices due to rising private demand. For private transactions a free market was permitted but for international monetary purposes the fixed price of $35 per ounce was maintained. Attempts were of course made to separate the two markets and, since the free market prices rose well above $35 per fine ounce, the net effect of this arrangement was to 'sterlise' the existing gold holdings. No country was willing to transfer gold at a price which was below the free market price. In 1971 the USA suspended convertibility and issued an ultimatum to the rest of the world to re-negotiate exchange rates. In December 1971 the Smithsonian Agreement was negotiated. This provided for (i) wider bands around the central parity, (ii) new central parities and (iii) a slight increase in the price of gold for international monetary purposes. This agreement was short lived; in June 1972 the £ was floated and in 1973/74 this was followed by the floating of virtually every other currency. At the same time as the breakdown of the Bretton Woods system, the first steps to European monetary co-operation were being taken (see section 14.7).

At this stage it is worth summarising the three main suggestions made for reforming the Bretton Woods system. The first concerned the role of gold. It was suggested that gold should become the main reserve asset. This raised three main objections, two economic, one political. First, an increase in the use of gold would have required an increase in the price of gold. This would not have been a once-and-for-all increase since, if inflation persisted, the relative price of gold would have continued to fall. This would have led to greater private demand and to a decrease in the profitability of gold production. Eventually speculation on further increases in the price of gold would have occurred, again disrupting the system. Second, the amount of gold available for international monetary purposes depends on the gap between total gold production and that demanded for private purposes. It is far from clear that this gap had (or has!) any sensible relationship with the requirements for liquidity by the international monetary system. Finally, with regard to the political consideration, the main beneficiaries of an increase in the price of gold would have been (i) the producers of gold and (ii) those countries who held the highest proportion of their reserves in the form of gold. The main producers of gold are South Africa and Russia neither of which country was (or is) particularly high in popularity ratings in the USA. Since the USA held a veto over changes in the official price of gold, greater use of gold in the international monetary system was not a practical proposition.

The second main suggestion made was to widen the bands around the central parity so as to allow for greater fluctuations in exchange rates. This suggestion would have done little to provide for 'trend' movements in exchange rates since, if, for example, the exchange rate was persistently at the lower limit, no flexibility would have existed in practice. This suggestion was often made in conjunction with the third proposal i.e. to allow for greater flexibility in the central parity value. This was called either a 'crawling' peg or 'gliding' parity system. The maximum change in the peg in any one period was to be predetermined. The actual parity value in the market was to be based on average market rates over the last few periods or adjusted from its previous value according to changes in a country's reserve position (appreciation in the case of rising reserves and depreciation if reserves fell). The basic idea was that the peg would have changed by small amounts in response to trends rather than by way of abrupt changes as occurred in the Bretton Woods system. It was hoped to obtain by this method the advantages of a fixed exchange rate system without experiencing destabilising speculative movements of funds. The problem with this approach was that it would have required all countries participating in the scheme to eschew all future discretionary changes in exchange rates. If this assurance had not been forthcoming or had not been credible, then speculative capital movements would still have occurred. It did not seem that such an assurance was compatible with the practical politics of the real world at that time or for that manner at any time.

14.5 Fixed versus floating exchange rates

It is convenient to summarise the main arguments for and against a system of fixed exchange rates. The reader is referred back again to Chapter 4, section 4.6 and 4.7.3 which explain the operation of the various exchange rate regimes. For the sake of ease of exposition we discuss permanently fixed exchange rates and pure or freely floating exchange rates. However in the real world the choice is less extreme, being one between varying degrees of government intervention in the foreign exchange markets.

The main advantage claimed for fixed exchange rates is in connection with international trade. Fixed exchange rates confer the same advantages on the economies of the member countries as a whole as does the adoption of money by a single economy, i.e. trade is facilitated. Pricing goods for foreign trade is as easy as it is for domestic trade. Foreign exchange market operations can be carried out at a low cost. There is no scope for speculation since the exchange rates are permanently fixed. Finally, traders are certain what foreign currency sales are worth in domestic currency since there is no chance of exchange rates changing between contract dates and the time when the resulting foreign currency is received. All these advantages facilitate the growth of foreign trade and consequently international specialisation and growth of the economies of the member states as a whole. It is worth remembering however, that these advantages are only obtained when exchange rates are permanently fixed and credibly so. Doubts as to performance or a belief that changes in rates may be imminent would provoke speculative flows similar to those which plagued the Bretton Woods system.

The second main advantage of fixed exchange rates concerns the idea of risk pooling. In Chapter 4, section 4.7.3 we discussed how a balance of payments deficit will lead to an offsetting contraction in the domestic money supply. Conversely a surplus will lead to an increase in the domestic money supply. Hence if a country makes a policy error so that, for example, it pursues an over-expansionary macroeconomic policy it will experience a balance of payments deficit and consequently a reduction in the domestic money supply. Conversely the other countries will experience corresponding balance of payments surpluses and increases in their money supplies. The net effect therefore is that some of the cost of over-expansionary policies will be passed on to other countries. Now provided individual countries' policy errors are random, they will tend to cancel each other out and each country will benefit. The problem with this argument arises when some countries err persistently in one direction so that other countries continually incur costs in the form of undesired movements in their economies. Note that this argument concerning risk pooling applies not only to policy errors but also to shocks to the economic system. In the case, for example, of an autonomous increase in saving by the residents of one country a balance of payments surplus would occur. This would lead to an increase in the money supply and hence to an expansion of economic activity whilst other countries would experience corresponding deficits and contraction in their money supplies. Again provided shocks were random they would tend to cancel each other out and all countries woud benefit.

The final argument in favour of fixed exchange rates concerns imposition of a discipline on the conduct of macroeconomic policy. Fixed exchange rates operate in the same manner as a monetary target (see Chapter 9, section 9.6). In the case of fixed exchange rates the rule is to ensure that a country's rate of inflation conforms to the world average. A higher than average rate of inflation will lead to a balance of payments deficit and necessitate corrective policy action. Conversely a lower than average rate of inflation will lead to a balance of payments surplus and an expansion of the domestic money supply. It is important to realise that the nature of this discipline is to conform to the behaviour of the rest of the world. A country is not free to choose its own rate of inflation as it is in the case of a monetary target by merely varying the target rate of growth of the money supply. Lastly, it should be noted that the imposition of a discipline over the conduct of macroeconomic policy is based on the notion that governments cannot be trusted. For electoral reasons, for example, governments tend to err in an over-expansionary direction and it is argued that some restraint needs to be placed on them to prevent mismanagement of the economy. This is certainly not a viewpoint to which all economists subscribe!

One of the major problems concerning fixed exchange rates concerns the adjustment mechanism. In principle, like the gold standard discussed earlier in this chapter, a regime of fixed exchange rates provides an automatic adjustment mechanism via the link between the balance of payments and the domestic money supply. For example, as we have already noted a balance of payments surplus leads to an increase in the domestic money supply and an increase in economic activity unless this effect is neutralised by the authorities. This adjustment process may also be assisted by discretionary policies undertaken by the authorities. However the question mark hanging over this adjustment mechanism is whether it can operate without seriously affecting the goal of full employment. If prices change quickly then the necessary adjustment can be achieved with only a minor change in the level of unemployment. In practice wages and prices tend to be relatively inflexible, especially in a downwards direction, so that adjustment may require a significant rise in unemployment to slow down the rate of inflation to a level consistent with that occurring abroad. Hence the efficiency of the adjustment mechanism will depend on two factors: (1) how responsive domestic prices are to changes in demand; and (2) how responsive foreign demand for goods is to changes in prices. If both elasticities are low large increases in unemployment will be necessary to achieve adjustment of an adverse balance of payments position.

Apart from doubts over the adjustment mechanism there is a problem over the co-ordination of macroeconomic policies among countries. In effect fixed exchange rates bind the various countries into a single economy so that divergent rates of inflation are inconsistent with a fixed exchange rate world. This can easily be seen by looking again at the definition of relative prices introduced in Chapter 4, section 4.3 i.e.:

$$\frac{e\,P_D}{P_F}$$

where (1) e = the exchange rate expressing domestic currency in terms of foreign currency

(2) P_D = the price of domestic goods in terms of domestic currency

and (3) P_F = the price of foreign goods in terms of foreign currency.

If P_D and P_F change at different speeds, then given a fixed exchange rate, relative prices will change causing balance of payments problems. Such problems can only be avoided if countries are willing to co-ordinate their policies so that on average prices in all countries participating in the fixed exchange rate regime change at the same rate. It is very debateable whether countries would be prepared to relinquish sovereignty over domestic economic policies in order to harmonise their policies with those of other countries so as to achieve uniform rates of inflation.

The case for pure floating exchange rates is largely the same as that made against fixed exchange rates. However it is convenient to elaborate on some of the points. First, because a government is not intervening in the foreign exchange markets it requires no foreign currency reserves. This is an extreme position but it is certainly true that required reserve holdings (i.e. the demand for liquidity) are reduced. Second, a government does not need to pursue policies to restore external balance since adjustment to produce a zero balance of payments (i.e. on the combined and capital accounts) is achieved by exchange rate adjustments so that the demand for and supply of that currency are equal (see Chapter 4, section 4.6.3). This does not mean that adjustment is costless or for that matter that economic activity in any country is independent of that in the rest of the world. For example, if inflation in the UK is faster than that in the rest of the world, the sterling exchange rate will depreciate causing sterling prices of imports to rise. This imposes higher living costs on the inhabitants of the UK. Closely connected with the preceding arguments is the claim that pure floating exchange rates remove the balance of payments as a policy aim or constraint in a government's overall macroeconomic strategy. By adopting pure floating exchange rates a government is freed from the necessity of considering external constraints when devising policies to achieve domestic aims (e.g. full employment) since the exchange rate will adjust to ensure balance of payments equilibrium. Nevertheless too much should not be made of this freedom. As we have seen changes in exchange rates involve some costs on the inhabitants of an economy and in reality this freedom is only the right of a country to choose its own rate of inflation. In other words the adoption of floating exchange rates is not a panacea for all economic ills.

Furthermore floating exchange rates are themselves the subject of controversy. Two questions of particular importance are (i) will the market set the right exchange rate? and (ii) will free markets lead to undesirable exchange rate fluctuations? The exchange rate which equates the demand for and the supply of a currency on a particular day may not be the one appropriate for the medium-term equilibrium for that economy. If this were so the market would provide incorrect signals to economic agents. Speculators may provide a useful function in this connection. If they believe that the exchange rate is different from the true equilibrium rate their transactions may move the exchange rate towards its long-run equilibrium rate. For example, if they believe the sterling exchange rate is too low, they will buy sterling now thus raising its current price thereby moving the rate towards the correct equilibrium exchange rate. Although there is no guarantee that this will happen the fact that speculators will lose money if they are wrong will tend to ensure that they assess markets carefully before taking action. This contrasts with the position of fixed exchange rates where decisions are taken by government officials who have little to lose if their decisions are incorrect save for their promotion prospects. Nevertheless there may be situations where government intervention is desirable; for example, to offset a lack of knowledge by the private sector regarding future government policy. A second potential problem for floating exchange rates concerns the role of speculators. In the example quoted above the actions of speculators help to stabilise the exchange rate i.e. move it towards the correct equilibrium rate. Suppose however that speculators are not so efficient and their actions destabilise the exchange rate, i.e. move it away from its true equilibrium rate. In that case their behaviour will exaggerate rather than dampen fluctuations in exchange rates causing uncertainty and reducing international trade.

One way of examining the problem of the stability of floating exchange rates is to examine the behaviour of market exchange rates since the adoption of floating exchange rates. This approach is open to objection because of the degree of government intervention in the foreign exchange markets. Thus it could be argued that the observed

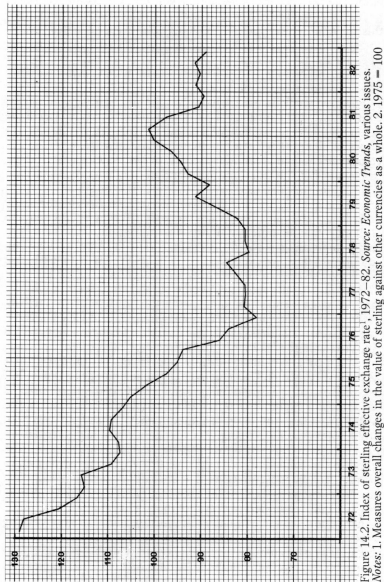

Figure 14.2. Index of sterling effective exchange rate[1], 1972–82. *Source: Economic Trends*, various issues.
Notes: 1. Measures overall changes in the value of sterling against other currencies as a whole. 2. 1975 = 100

fluctuations are due to erratic government intervention. Nevertheless it is worth looking at the behaviour of the sterling exchange rate since the adoption of floating rates in 1972. This is reproduced in Figure 14.2.

In our discussion of fixed and floating exchange rates we have examined the case for permanently fixed or pure (i.e. with no government intervention) floating exchange rates. In practice governments in recent years have opted for a situation of floating exchange rates but have retained the right (and have as we noted exercised this right) to intervene in the foreign exchange markets. The real world situation is further complicated by the fact that domestic policies influence the behaviour of the exchange rate. For example, and increase in domestic interest rates will attract capital inflows leading to an appreciation of the exchange rate. Thus a government who wished to reduce the domestic price of imports as an aid to the reduction in the rate of inflation could raise domestic rates of interest. The effect on the exchange rate would be similar to that of direct intervention in the foreign markets (i.e. through purchases of sterling). At the same time as the adoption of floating exchange rates there has been a movement towards a regional system of fixed exchange rates within Europe.

In the following section we briefly review the operation of managed exchange rates since 1972/73 and in section 14.7 the development of the European Monetary System.

14.6 Managed floating since 1973

With the breakdown of the Bretton Woods system most countries adopted floating exchange rates. However as we have noted governments intervene in the exchange markets so that the system is one of managed rather than pure floating exchange rates. The essential difference between this system and the Bretton Woods system is that governments are not compelled to intervene in foreign exchange markets. They intervene because they choose to do so. As we have already seen the level of exchange rates affects the level of domestic economic activity and not many governments choose to leave exchange rate determination purely to market forces.

The main advantage of the present system is that it is undemanding. Commitments by countries largely take the form of not doing something rather than undertaking specific tasks. Financial crises have been conspicuous by their absence as compared with their frequent occurrences under the Bretton Woods system. Nevertheless all is not gain. Exchange rate fluctuations have been quite large as reference to Figure 14.2 demonstrates. The uncertainty engendered by these fluctuations must have hindered the growth of international trade to some extent.

At the same time there has been a movement away from a gold based international monetary system. The role of gold has diminished as a result of the agreement reached by members of the IMF at Jamaica in 1976. The official price of gold was abolished. One-sixth of the gold paid into the IMF in quotas was to be returned to members, one-sixth to be auctioned by the IMF to private buyers with the proceeds being used to benefit the developing countries. The IMF was to retain the remaining two-thirds. Finally, gold was no longer to be the unit of account of the system.

14.7 The European Monetary System

In this section we trace the development of the European Monetary System (EMS). As a backcloth to this development it is desirable to discuss the rationale behind the grouping of countries into a single currency area. In the literature this is called the theory of optimum currency areas.

The discussion mirrors to some extent the discussion of fixed and floating exchange rates. The main advantages of single currency areas are the certainty of exchange rates facilitating development of international trade and the low costs of conversion of currencies. The main disadvantage is the loss of exchange rate changes as an instrument of macroeconomic policy. The theory of optimum currency areas looks at the factors which determine how large a single currency area should be; in other words it is concerned with the advantages and disadvantages of integration of monetary systems. In this context the concept of a nation state may not be relevant. The relevant concept is the one that can be applied to a group of nation states such as the members of the EEC as well as a single large country such as the USA. In the following discussion we shall concentrate on the case of a group of nations rather than that of a single large nation.

The relevant factors that need to be considered are (i) the trade potential between the countries, (ii) the share of trade in total output, (iii) the mobility of factors of production, (iv) the degree of integration of financial markets and (v) the political will to integrate economic policies. The first point is easily seen. The greater the volume (actual or potential) of trade between countries the greater the costs (and therefore loss) through the individual countries maintaining their own exchange rates. The cost of joining a single currency area is the loss of the use of exchange rate changes as an instrument of policy. The weight of this cost will depend on how easy it is to achieve adjustment of balance of payments disequilibria by other means. If foreign trade forms a large proportion of total output then only small adjustments will be necessary to correct a balance of payments deficit. Similarly if factors of production are free to move and are mobile within regions there is less need to use exchange rate changes. Again if financial markets ar highly integrated, small adjustments to interest rates will be adequate to attract the capital inflows necessary to finance a deficit until corrective measures have time to take effect. All these factors indicate a low cost of giving up exchange rate changes as a policy instrument and therefore indicate the desirability of integrating the currencies. What is perhaps even more important is the political will to harmonise economic policies. As we have seen this is an essential ingredient for the success of any fixed exchange rate system. If these requirements are absent, for example, the economies are not particularly open, financial markets are not integrated, factors of production are immobile between the countries, etc., then it remians more sensible for each country to adopt flexible exchange rates rather than combining to form a single currency area.

Currency areas can be created by the adoption of (i) a single currency e.g. the dollar in the USA of (ii) permanently fixed exchange rates between members. Both methods bind the economies of the countries or regions concerned into a single economy. In the case of fixed exchange rates this is acieved through the link between the balance of payments and the domestic money supply. There is a difference of degree however between the two methods since a country can withdraw far more easily from a system of fixed exchange rates than a system where a single currency circulates. European monetary integration has followed the pursuit of fixed exchange rates and it is to this topic we now turn.

The idea of European monetary integration dates back to the Treaty of Rome but practical attempts to achieve integration started from 1971 when certain European countries declined to adopt the wider parity bands of ±2.25 per cent which were introduced following the Smithsonian agreement. Following the general adoption of floating rates the close links (±1 per cent) between these currencies were maintained by the countries concerned. Because these currencies floated upwards or downwards together against the currencies of other countries within the prescribed margins, the arrangement became known as the 'Snake in the Tunnel' or more briefly as the 'Snake'. The 'hard-core' member countries of the snake were West Germany, the Benelux countries and Denmark. Other countries who were members at some time and non-members at other times included France, Italy, UK, Norway and Sweden.

The death-blow to the widening of the snake into a general European monetary area was the diverging rates of inflation experienced in the mid-1970s which led to countries experiencing great difficulty in maintaining relatively stable exchange rates.

The idea of monetary integration was revived in 1978 in particular by the leaders of France and West Germany against the background of, and no doubt influenced by, the weakness of the dollar. After some delay the new European Monetary System (EMS) came into being. Its membership consisted of all members of the EEC, but it should be noted that the UK has remained outside the fixed exchange rate system. We now go on to consider the institutional arrangements of the EMS.

The basic nature of the EMS is that fixed exchange rates operate between members but floating exchange rates exist between currencies of members and those of non-members. Therefore the whole block of currencies within the EMS will move up and down together against external currencies. The institutional arrangements include three central features: (i) fixed exchange rates; (ii) a new unit of account, the European Currency Unit (ECU); and (iii) the establishment of borrowing facilities for members in case of balance of payments problems. Despite the fact that the UK has remained outside the exchange rate system, sterling is one of the currencies used for the valuation of the ECU.

The scheme provides for fixed exchange rates with compulsory intervention at limits of ± 2.25 per cent around the central parity.[1] An exception to this general rule is allowed for weaker currencies in which case the countries concerned may opt for wider limits of ± 6 per cent if they so desire. Only Italy has availed herself of this facility. Technically each country values its currency in terms of the ECU and this then sets a system of bilateral central rates between the currencies of member countries, known as a parity grid. To take a simple illustrative example (based on the Bank of England, *Quarterly Bulletin,* June 1979) suppose:

$$1 \text{ ECU} = 2.5 \text{ DM} = 6 \text{ FF} = 40 \text{ BF}$$

where (1) DM = Deutsche Mark
      (2) FF = French Franc
      (3) BF = Belgian Franc

Then by simple division 1DM = 2.4FF (6/2.5) or 16BF (40/2.5). In

1. The intention is for the width of these bands to be reduced in the future.

Table 14.2 these valuations are entered in column A. Similar calculations can be made for other currencies and these are entered in columns B and C.

The rows in Table 14.2 show the price of foreign currency in terms of domestic currency. Thus Belgian residents must pay 16 BF for every DM purchased. This method of valuation is the reverse to that customary in the UK (see Chapter 4, section 4.6.1) so that depreciation of the currency is represented by an increase in this price. Commitment to a fixed exchange rate means that the central banks (i) sell foreign currency as the price of foreign currency rises against domestic currency (i.e. as domestic currency depreciates) and (ii) buy foreign currency as the price of foreign currency falls against domestic currency (i.e. domestic currency appreciates). In conjunction with the fixed margins of ±2.25 per cent it is possible to construct a matrix or grid showing for each currency (i) central parities and (ii) compulsory intervention points. This information for the example discussed above is shown in Table 14.3

To illustrate Table 14.3 consider what happens if the French Franc strengthened against the Deutsche Mark. The Banque de France would be compelled to buy DM at 2.35 FF and the Bundesbank sell FF at 0.43 DM. Such transactions would have to take place in sufficient quantities to keep the French Franc/Deutsche Mark exchange rate within the agreed limits. Note that in this example the Banque de France is gaining reserves (DM) and conversely the Bundesbank is losing foreign currency reserves. Similar transactions are undertaken by the other central banks in line with the figures contained in Table 14.3. Thus the central bank of each member country is intervening continuously in the foreign exchange markets so as to maintain the agreed rates. In addition to the compulsory intervention points, there is also a divergence indicator which is supposed to indicate when a particular currency is moving out of line and corrective action is expected to be taken by the central bank concerned when a currency crosses that threshold

TABLE 14.2. Parity grid

	Deutsche Mark A	Belgian Franc B	French Franc C
Deutsche Mark	1.00	0.063	0.42
Belgian Franc	16.00	1.0	6.67
French Franc	2.40	0.15	1.0

Source: Bank of England, *Quarterly Bulletin*, June 1979.

TABLE 14.3. Central parities and compulsory intervention points

		Deutsche Mark	Belgian Franc	French Franc
Deutsche Mark:	buying		0.062	0.41
	parity	1.0	0.063	0.42
	selling		0.064	0.43
Belgian Franc:	buying	15.64		6.52
	parity	16.00	1.0	6.67
	selling	16.36		6.82
French Franc:	buying	2.35	0.147	
	parity	2.40	0.150	1.0
	selling	2.45	0.153	

(action is only 'expected' *not* compulsory). This indicator is linked by a complex formula to the value of the ECU.

The ECU is valued in terms of a basket of currencies of which the £ content is £0.0885 with a weight of roughly 13 per cent. Similar figures for the French Franc are 1.15 FF with a weight of approximately 20 per cent. The ECU functions:

(1) as a denominator for the exchange rate mechanism;
(2) as a basis for the divergence indicator;
(3) as a means of settlement between the monetary authorities of the members of the EMS;
(4) as a denominator for operations in both the intervention and credit mechanisms.

Finally, in this respect it should be noted that the ECU does not circulate as a currency.

The agreement setting up the EMS provided for the establishment of a European Monetary Co-operation Fund (EMCF). Participating member countries deposit with the EMCF 20 per cent of their gold and dollar holdings and receive an equivalent issue of ECUs. Support arrangements are as follows:

(1) *Very short-term facility.* Virtually unlimited borrowings are available for up to ten weeks and for a further three months if necessary.
(2) *short-term monetary support.* 14 billion ECU are available for

up to nine months with member countries being allocated ceilings for drawings.

(3) *medium-term financial assistance.* 11 billion ECU are available to member countries. Credits are granted for two to five years subject to conditions regarding the conduct of economic policy imposed by the Council of Ministers of the EEC.

It should be noted that the EMS has a close resemblance to the old Bretton Woods system discussed in section 14.4. It is therefore potentially subject to the same problems as were experienced under that system. Whether the closer political interests of the members of the EMS will enable them to overcome these potential problems remains to be seen and only time will tell. As indicated before the vital requirement is that member countries should experience on average identical rates of inflation otherwise a regime of fixed exchange rates is untenable in the long run. It is also worth noting that some adjustments to parities took place in September 1979 when the Deutsche Mark was revalued by 2 per cent against most currencies in the system and again in November 1979 when the Danish Kronor was devalued by 2 per cent against all other currencies within the EMS. A further and more general re-alignment of exchange rates within the EMS took place in October 1981. Further re-alignments of exchange rates within the EMS took place in February and June 1982, and March 1983. The frequency of the changes emphasises the difficulties inherent in a regime of fixed exchange rates given differing rates of inflation experienced by member countries.

APPENDIX A

Eurocurrency Markets

A14.1 Origins

A Eurocurrency deposit is a deposit denominated in a currency other than that of the country in which the bank is located. The market originated with European banks accepting deposits of dollars, i.e. the so-called Eurodollar market. Subsequently markets for other currencies and in other centres developed so that the term Eurocurrency is applied to all transactions in currencies other than that of the bank's host country. It is therefore applicable to such transactions in centres as far apart as Singapore and the West Indies.

To emphasise the nature of a Eurocurrency deposit consider the following simple example. If a multinational corporation makes a deposit of Deutsche Marks with a bank based in London, it is a Eurocurrency transaction. In contrast if the same company places the deposit of Deutsche Marks with a bank located in Germany it is *not* a Eurocurrency transaction since the bank is accepting a deposit in the currency of the country in which it is located.

The Eurocurrency markets originated during the late 1950s with dollar deposits being made in London. Various factors contributed towards this development. First, certain East European countries wished to hold reserves in the form of dollars but preferred to hold them outside the USA as an insurance against the USA ever taking action to prevent their withdrawal. Second, restrictions were placed on the level of interest payable on deposits in the USA (regulation Q) so that holders of dollar deposits were able to earn higher rates of interest on dollars deposited in banks outside the USA. At the same time restrictions were placed on capital movements out of the USA so the growing Eurodollar market provided an alternative source of funds for US firms wishing to finance overseas investment. An additional impetus to the development of this market came from the introduction in the late 1950s of convertibility of most currencies thus making it easier to switch funds from one country to another.

A14.2 The nature of the markets

In general the markets are wholesale inter-bank markets with dealings in large transactions; normally the size of each transaction is $1 million or more. The main transactors are banks, multinational corporations and in some cases governments, with the greater part of the total volume of transactions being between banks. The initial deposit is likely to be passed on between banks several times before reaching an ultimate borrower. It is important to realise that these currencies are borrowed and lent like other currencies so that the relevant 'price' is a rate of interest not an exchange rate. At each stage of lending the bank concerned will earn a margin albeit a small one. This has three major consequences. First, the large number of participants in the markets ensures that the funds will ultimately end up with the borrower willing to pay the highest rate of interest. Second, no one bank (except the last in the lending chain) knows precisely who is the ultimate borrower. Third, statistics of total lending/deposits within the Eurocurrency markets overestimate their importance since the inter-bank lending components should be netted out in order to obtain the true picture.

Since 1971 the major central banks have agreed to refrain from participating in the Eurocurrency markets so as to avoid the creation of additional liquidity. To understand the reason for this consider the following simple example. A British firm exports goods to the USA and receives payment in dollars. These dollars are then changed into sterling via the Bank of England. If the Bank of England invests these dollars in the Eurocurrency markets they are re-activated and some borrower will then be able to use the dollars to finance expenditure. In contrast if the Bank of England holds the dollars in its portfolio of reserve assets no additional credit is created.

The market for Eurocurrency deposits is essentially a short-term market. This arises because of the use made by both the multi-national corporations and banks of these markets to manage their short-term cash flows to achieve the best possible return. A wide range of currencies and maturities of both loans and deposits is available and this assists in the attraction of deposits. However the success of the market in attracting, and subsequently finding outlets for, funds depends primarily on its ability to offer competitive rates of interest on deposits and yet charge relatively low interest rates on loans. In part this is due to the fact that dealings are in large sums so that economies of scale are obtained by the banks participating in the Eurocurrency markets. A second factor is that these banks are not subject to reserve ratio requirements similar to those imposed by governments on purely domestic operations. Such requirements invariably force banks to hold low interest bearing assets (zero interest in the case of normal deposits at the Bank of England—see Chapter 2) which act as a kind of tax on bank operations forcing them to charge higher rates of interest on lending than would otherwise be the case. Banks operating in the Eurocurrency markets are free from such restraints and, in any case, tend to match deposits with liabilities rather than look to liquidity for protection.

A14.3 Significance of the markets

Three features of the Eurocurrency markets have received considerable discussion in the literature: (i) their ability to create credit; (ii) their role in the propagation of inflation; and (iii) the supervision and control of such markets.

The first question we consider is whether the operation of the Eurocurrency markets has enabled a multiple expansion of credit. We have discussed how Eurocurrency deposits are created by the acceptance of a bank deposit denominated in a currency other than that of the country where the bank is located. This bank deposit is then passed on via other banks to an ultimate borrower. If it is re-deposited in the Eurocurrency market it is available for relending. This has provoked the question whether these banks have the ability to cause a multiple credit expansion in a manner similar to that of domestic banks. However there are two salient differences. First, there is no standard reserve ratio which can act as a fulcrum for the creation of credit. Second, there is no authority providing and controlling the supply of specific assets designated as reserve assets. If the banks wish to attract more resources they do this by bidding for deposits in the desired currency. Banks operating in the Euro-currency markets operate lending not payment facilities. They relend large deposits placed with them and are therefore more akin to non-bank financial intermediaries. As such the standard textbook credit multiplier analysis cannot be properly applied to their operations.

The second question is the degree to which the development of such markets has aided the international propagation of inflation. Eurocurrency markets have certainly provided an efficient means for the transfer of credit between different currencies. In the absence of controls on capital movements the existence of the Eurocurrency markets makes it more difficult for individual countries to operate restrictive monetary policies. Nevertheless such evasion of monetary restraint is not without cost for the economic units concerned. Extensive borrowing in the markets will tend to raise interest rates in the Eurocurrency markets relative to those elsewhere. In addition exchange rate movements will tend to make borrowing more expensive as increases in demand for a foreign currency will raise its price relative to domestic currency. Thus progressive evasion of domestic monetary controls via Eurocurrency markets will tend to raise the cost of the necessary operations.

The third point refers to supervision and control. There is no lender of last resort or overall regulator of the market. Nevertheless supervision of the banks operating in these markets does take place by the authorities according to (i) the location of the bank's head office and also (ii) the host country in which the bank operates. This division of roles must make adequate supervision more difficult to exercise and, from time to time, concern has arisen as to the nature of the control and supervision of Eurocurrency markets.

Part IV
CONCLUSION

15 Conclusion

15.1 Introduction

From the discussion of the preceding chapters it should be apparent that both the 'true' model of the economy and the conduct of macroeconomic policy are the subject of a considerable degree of controversy. Although these two issues have been central to the study of macroeconomics the nature of the controversies has changed over the years as circumstances have changed.

In the 1930s the central problem facing economists was the need to provide an explanation of, and remedy for, the severe unemployment which prevailed at the time. In his *General Theory of Employment, Interest and Money* (1936), Keynes put forward the view that unemployment reflected a state of deficient aggregate demand. A major theme interpreted from the General Theory by Keynes' disciples and policy makers alike was the importance attached to fiscal policy to prevent substantial unemployment which was regarded as the normal state of an advanced capitalist economy. Since government expenditure is an important component of aggregate demand Keynesians believed that an increase in government expenditure would have a strong and direct effect in reducing the level of unemployment. In contrast changes in the money supply were held to operate indirectly through changes in the rate of interest which would alter private investment. Since investment was not thought to be particularly sensitive to the rate of interest it was generally agreed in the period from the 1930s through to the 1950s that money did not matter very much for analysing aggregate demand and unemployment. Traditional theory developed during this period tended to regard money as having only a limited importance with respect to the determination of macroeconomic variables. Instead the importance of fiscal policy was stressed as the main tool of macroeconomic policy.

The revival of the belief in the potency of monetary policy that has occurred since the 1960s has largely been associated with the so-called monetarist counter-revolution in economic thought. This counter-revolution has emphasised (i) the importance of controlling the money supply and (ii) the need to follow a monetary rule in the conduct of monetary policy in order to avoid economic instability. During the 1950s through to the mid-1960s instability in Western capitalist economies was largely reflected in the problem of inflation, whereas in contrast many economies have experienced not only high rates of inflation but also high levels of unemployment since the end of the 1960s. Monetarists have argued that the inflation of the post-war years was stimulated by the widespread adoption of cheap-money policies and resulted from excessive money creation. More specifically they have argued that (i) the acceleration of inflation in the late 1960s was the consequence of the financing of the Vietnam War via monetary expansion by the USA and (ii) under the system of fixed exchange rates that existed up to 1972/73 the inflationary pressure initiated in America was transmitted to other Western economies through the balance of payments deficit of the USA. In their view the main source of instability has been too rapid and erratic monetary growth.

The controversy over the potency of money and the role of monetary policy has resulted in an ongoing debate in which monetarism has come to be associated with rules and guidelines and Keynesianism/fiscalism with activism and discretion. As we have already discussed the main issues involved in the monetarist/ Keynesian debate in some detail at appropriate places in this book (in particular, Chapters 3, 5, 8 and 9) we merely summarise the basic tenor of, and main differences between, monetarist and Keynesian schools of thought. It is important to emphasise that we adopt this classification purely for the sake of ease of exposition. The reader should bear in mind that not only are there differences of opinion and emphasis within each school of thought but also the dividing line between these two main schools is becoming increasingly blurred on many issues.

15.2 The monetarist view

Monetarists believe that most of the disturbances which affect the economy are monetary in origin. This belief in the predominance of monetary impulses is based on the quantity theory of money which asserts that changes in the money supply are the predominant, though not the only factor, explaining changes in nominal income. Monetarists argue that the demand for money is a stable function of a limited number of variables and that most of the observed instability in the economy is attributable to fluctuations in the money supply induced by the authorities. From this belief arises the first of two policy prescriptions central to monetarist analysis, namely that the authorities should seek to control the money supply. It is recognised that under certain circumstances the money supply will become endogenous and in order to control the money supply monetarists suggest that the authorities need to abandon policies which aim to stabilise interest rates and the exchange rate.

The second policy prescription central to monetarist analysis is that the authorities should follow a monetary rule rather than pursue discretionary policy. This policy recommendation is based, as we have seen, on a number of arguments. Some monetarists have argued from a basic political philosophy that governments can't be trusted and that monetary policy should be carried out according to some rule. Others have rested their case on the basis of one or more of the following four main arguments. First, that in the 'present' state of economic knowledge the consequences of varying the rate of monetary growth in a discretionary manner cannot be predicted with sufficient accuracy to permit successful fine-tuning. Second, those monetarists who believe in rational expectations[1] deny that discretionary monetary expansion can influence output and employment even in the short run. The third argument put forward to support a monetary rule is the view that the economies of advanced capitalist countries are inherently stable at a generally acceptable level of unemployment unless disturbed by erratic monetary growth. In the absence of discretionary intervention it is argued that the economy will tend to return fairly rapidly to equilibrium after being subjected to some disturbance. Finally, monetarists dispute that any permanent reduction in the level of unemployment can be brought about by discretionary demand-management policies and argue that accelerating inflation will occur if the authorities try to maintain unemployment below the natural rate (i.e. there is no trade-off between inflation and unemployment in the long run). Monetarists take the view that discretionary monetary policy can only be used to influence the level of unemployment in the short run and that the long-run effect of monetary changes will be mainly on prices. With regard to fiscal policy they believe that while 'pure' fiscal expansion (i.e. without accommodating monetary expansion) may influence economic activity in the short run, in the long run some components of private expenditure will be crowded-out or replaced so that fiscal policy actions will have little or no effect on real income. For these reasons monetarists suggest that discretionary demand-

1. Monetarists who believe in rational expectations and continuous market clearing are generally called the 'New Classical' school.

management policies should be replaced by a monetary rule as the main tool of economic stabilisation.

It is worth emphasising that monetarist analysis does not automatically imply a policy of non-intervention. The belief in the quantity theory, the inherent stability of the economy, the natural rate hypothesis and the analysis of crowding-out together and individually imply that counter-cyclical fiscal policy has no major role to play in stabilising the economy. In addition the prescription to follow a monetary rule in order to create a more stable economic environment eliminates the need for discretionary demand management policy. Although monetarism implies non-intervention in macroeconomic policies involving the management of aggregate demand, intervention especially on a micro basis is quite compatible with monetarist analysis of how the economy works. In monetarist analysis the natural rate of unemployment is determined by the structure of the real side of the economy and by the institutional framework of the labour market. Monetarists argue that if governments wish to reduce the natural rate (i.e. achieve higher employment levels) they should pursue microeconomic policies towards improving the structure of the labour market in order to increase (i) the efficiency of labour markets and (ii) the occupational and geographical mobility of labour.

15.3 The Keynesian view

In contrast to the monetarist views discussed above Keynesians argue that most of the disturbances which affect the economy occur from the real sector. In interpreting changes in nominal income Keynesians have traditionally emphasised the relationship between nominal income and investment or autonomous expenditure. Although mainstream Keynesians no longer claim that changes in the money stock are unimportant modern Keynesians deny that they dominate changes in nominal income. Furthermore, they contend that the economy is inherently unstable and subject to fluctuations between long periods of unemployment and stagnation and periods of rapid expansion and inflation. The erratic shocks which cause these fluctuations in the level of economic activity are attributed by Keynesians as primarily due to real disturbances (e.g. changes in the marginal efficiency of investment). Modern Keynesians argue that (i) in the case of a disturbance the economy may take too long to return to the neighbourhood of equilibrium, and (ii) consequently discretionary demand-management policies are necessary to maintain the economy at a high and stable level of employment. Not only do Keynesians stress the need for stabilisation policy but they also argue that fiscal and monetary policy can and should be used to stabilise the economy. The use of discretionary fiscal policy is advocated as the main policy instrument because the effects of fiscal policy changes are considered to be both more predictable and faster acting on economic activity than those of discretionary monetary policy.

Another important difference between Keynesian and monetarist schools of thought concerns the question of whether there is a long-run trade-off between inflation and unemployment. Contrary to monetarist beliefs Keynesians tend to believe that there is a trade-off between inflation and unemployment in the long run (i.e. the long-run Phillips curve is not vertical). The pursuit of an unemployment target via discretionary demand-management policies will, they contend, involve inflation due to the trade-off that exists between unemployment and inflation. Given this apparent conflict between the goals of full employment and relative price stability most Keynesians believe that the long-run Phillips curve can in fact be shifted downwards (i.e. thereby achieving the same level of employment but at a lower rate of inflation) by the adoption of a prices and incomes policy. Also contrary to monetarist beliefs many Keynesians assign a role to wage increases made independently of the state of the excess demand and in consequence advocate that a prices and incomes poilicy has a long-run role to play in preventing inflation. In contrast, while some monetarists believe that a prices and incomes policy has a role to play in assisting the transition to a lower rate of inflation monetarists argue that this is only a temporary role and one which would easily be frustrated if the government followed expansionary policies which created excess demand and were incompatible with price stability. Finally, Keynesians believe that balance of payments disequilibria can be corrected by changing the exchange rate (e.g. by devaluation in the case of a deficit) and argue that the exchange rate is an important policy instrument in achieving equilibrium in the balance of payments.

15.4 Macroeconomic models of the UK economy

In view of the wide publicity given in the news media to the forecasts of the various UK macroeconomic models we have decided to include a brief description[1] of the main models of the UK economy. The models selected for discussion are those which have in the past received and continue to receive fairly wide publicity, that is those

1. For a more detailed discussion of these models the interested reader is referred to 'Modelling the UK Economy: An Introduction' by Holden, Peel and Thompson (Martin Robertson 1982).

developed by the Treasury (HMT), the National Institute of Economic and Social Research (NI), the London Business School (LBS), the Cambridge Economic Policy Group (CEPG) and the Liverpool Project on the International Transmission of Inflation. A word of caution is necessary at the outset. A model is not neutral concerning the controversies discussed earlier in the text but rather reflects the views of the model builders. In the context of the monetarist/Keynesian controversy the HMT and NI models are generally regarded as Keynesian and the LBS model as monetarist though none of them take an extreme position. This contrasts with the position of the other two models which are regarded as being more radical though with different viewpoints. The CEPG model takes a strong Keynesian stance whereas the Liverpool model adopts a strong monetarist view.

Before discussing the nature of these models it is as well to describe what a macroeconomic model actually is. In our examination of economic theory in Chapters 1 to 5 we employed a diagrammatic or geometric approach. In contrast a macroeconomic model describes economic theory by way of a set of simultaneous mathematical equations. These equations can then be solved using computer programmes to provide economic forecasts or predictions of the results of policy changes—remembering of course that these forecasts/predictions reflect the underlying philosophy adopted by the model builders. The size of the model will also vary. For example, the HMT model is a large model consisting of some 700 equations and identities whereas in contrast the Liverpool model comprises only some 20 or so equations. The other models mentioned above fall within this range.

Apart from the Liverpool model the other four models broadly follow the income/expenditure approach discussed in Chapter 1 of the text. The HMT and NI models also contain fairly sophisticated monetary sectors. However monetary factors play a more important role in the HMT model particularly via their influence on the exchange rate. A further difference between the HMT and NI models occurs with respect to the Phillips curve analysis adopted in both models. In the HMT model the long-run Phillips curve is vertical. In contrast in the NI model the long-run Phillips curve, whilst steeper than the short-run curve is not vertical thus providing a long-run trade off between inflation and unemployment.

In contrast the CEPG model contains little direct links between unemployment and the rate of increase of money wage rates, i.e. no Phillips curve analysis. This permits the prediction that expansionary policies will mainly go into real output rather than inflation. Similarly there is only an almost derisory monetary sector so that monetary changes have little impact on inflation. In terms of Chapter 5 their explanation of inflation follows the sociological view.

The LBS model adopts an international monetarist perspective of inflation. Again no Phillips curve analysis appears in the model but inflation is linked to monetary forces via the exchange rate mechanism. Monetary expansion in the UK relative to that in the rest of the world leads to a depreciation of the sterling exchange rate and consequently more inflation.

The Liverpool model does not follow the traditional income/expenditure approach but lays great stress on stocks of wealth as determinants of private sector expenditure. A second difference lies in the adoption of the rational expectations hypothesis discussed in Chapter 7, section 7.6. In practice this implies that, within the model, expectations are consistent with the model forecasts. It also means that the model predicts fast adjustment of the economy to disturbances. For example, a monetary change leads to changes in the expected rate of inflation. Actual rates of inflation respond quickly to these changes in expectations with a consequent fast effect on private expenditure because of the consequential changes in real wealth. It can be seen therefore that the Liverpool model takes a stance approaching that adopted by the so-called 'New Classical' school.

Finally we would like to stress that each of the above models is continually being improved in the light of the performance of the model and also new theoretical advances. Consequently we are only able to describe how the models looked in the recent past. Nevertheless our discussion should provide a satisfactory insight into the structure of these models.

15.5 Concluding remarks

From this brief summary of monetarist and Keynesian views it should be apparent that while there is still a number of important analytical differences between the two schools (e.g. concerning the source of the main disturbances that affect the economy) the major issue dividing monetarists and Keynesians today concerns the role of macroeconomic stabilisation policy. Keynesians tend to emphasise the inherent instability of the economy and the potential role for stabilisation policy whereas monetarists argue that the economy is inherently stable (unless disturbed by erratic monetary growth) and that policy should be carried out according to rules. Whatever convergence may have taken place over recent years on the 'true' model of the economy it is clear that the controversy over the conduct of policy is likely to remain the central issue debated in connection with macroeconomics in the foreseeable future.

Recommended for Further Reading

Bain, A. D. (1980), *The Control of the Money Supply* (Harmondsworth: Penguin).

Beckerman, W. (ed.) (1972), *The Labour Government's Economic Record 1964-1970* (London: Duckworth).

Beckerman, W. (1976), *An Introduction to National Income Analysis* (London: Weidenfeld and Nicolson).

Black, J. (1982), *The Economics of Modern Britain: An Introduction to Macroeconomics* (Oxford: Martin Robertson).

Blackaby, F. T. (ed.) (1979), *British Economic Policy 1960-1974: Demand Management* (Cambridge: University Press).

Cairncross, Sir Alex (ed.) (1970), *Britain's Economic Prospects Reconsidered* (London: Allen and Unwin).

Caves, R. E. and Associates (1968), *Britain's Economic Prospects* (London: Allen and Unwin).

Chrystal, K. A. (1983), *Controversies in British Macroeconomics* (Oxford: Philip Allan).

Crockett, A. D. (1977), *International Money: Issues and Analysis* (Walton-on-Thames: Nelson).

Crockett, A. D. (1979), *Money: Theory, Policy and Institutions* (Walton-on-Thames: Nelson).

Dow, J. C. R. (1964), *The Management of the British Economy 1945-1960* (Cambridge: University Press).

Flemming, J. S. (1976), *Inflation* (Oxford: University Press).

Friedman, M. (1970), *The Counter-Revolution in Monetary Theory,* IEA Occasional Paper No. 33 (London: Institute of Economic Affairs).

Friedman, M. (1974), *Monetary Correction,* IEA Occasional Paper No. 41 (London: Institute of Economic Affairs).

Friedman, M. (1975), *Unemployment versus Inflation? An Evaluation of the Phillips Curve,* IEA Occasional paper, No. 44 (London: Institute of Economic Affairs).

Harbury, C. D. and Lipsey, R. G. (1983), *An Introduction to the UK Economy* (London: Pitman).

Johnson, H. G. and Nobay, A. R. (eds.) (1971), *The Current Inflation* (London: Macmillan).

Kay, J. A. and King, M. A. (1980), *The British Tax System* (Oxford: University Press).

Maunder, P. (ed.) (1980), *The British Economy in the 1970's* (London: Heinemann).

Mishan, E. J. (1967), *The Costs of Economiic Growth* (London: Staples Press).

Modigliani, F. (1977), 'The Monetarist Controversy or, Should We Foresake Stabilization Policies?' *American Economic Review,* Vol. 67 (March).

Morris, D. (ed.) (1979), *The Economic System in the U.K.* (Oxford: University Press).

Peston, M. H. (1982), *The British Economy: An Elementary Macroeconomic Perspective* (Oxford: Philip Allan).

Posner, M. (ed.) (1978). *Demand Management* (London: Heinemann).

Prest, A. R. and Coppock, D. J. (eds.) (1982), *The U.K. Economy: A Manual of Applied Economics* (London: Weidenfeld and Nicolson).

Revell, J. (1973), *The British Financial System* (London: Macmillan).

Shaw, G. K. (1978), *An Introduction to the Theory of Macroeconomic Policy* (London: Martin Robertson).

Trevithick, J. A. (1980), *Inflation: A Guide to the Crisis in Economics* (Harmondsworth: Penguin).

Vane, H. R. and Thompson, J. L. (1979), *Monetarism: Theory, Evidence and Policy* (Oxford: Martin Robertson).

Official publications:

Bank of England, *Bank of England Quarterly Bulletin.*

Central Statistical Office (London: HMSO)

    (i) *Economic Trends* (monthly and annual supplement)

    (ii) *Financial Statistics* (monthly)

    (iii) *National Income and Expenditure* (Blue Book: annual)

    (iv) *United Kingdom Balance of Payments* (Pink Book: annual)

    (v) Treasury, *Economic Progress Report* (monthly) (London: HMSO)

Index